Black and White Women
of the Old South

The Peculiar Sisterhood
in American Literature

Black and White
WOMEN
of the Old South

The Peculiar Sisterhood
in American Literature

MINROSE C. GWIN

THE UNIVERSITY OF TENNESSEE PRESS

KNOXVILLE

Library of Congress Cataloging in Publication Data

Gwin, Minrose.
Black and white women of the Old South.

Bibliography: p.
Includes index.
1. American literature—Southern States—History and
criticism.   2. Women in literature.   3. Afro-American
women in literature.   4. Race relations in literature.
5. Southern States in literature.   6. Women—Southern
States—History.   7. Afro-American women—Southern
States—History.   8. Race relations—Southern States.
I. Title.
PS261.G85   1985   810'.9'975   85-3238
ISBN 0-87049-469-4 (alk. paper)

ACKNOWLEDGMENTS

In producing this study I have incurred many debts—scholarly, pedagogical, and personal—which I am happy to acknowledge. I have been fortunate to explore a field rich with insightful historical and literary scholarship. I am grateful to those who produced that wealth and to those who encouraged me to pursue my interest in it, particularly my professors at the University of Tennessee, the late Richard Beale Davis and the late Herman Spivey, who, in vastly different ways, introduced me to the complexities of regional experience as literary theme.

I am greatly indebted to members of my dissertation committee—professors William H. Shurr, director; Marjorie Pryse; R. Baxter Miller; and Susan Becker—for their continued willingness to think of the manuscript in terms of a book and to offer thoughtful, specific suggestions for its expansion to a publishable work. I have also received some excellent suggestions for strengthening the manuscript from professors Thadious Davis, Benita Howell, and Anne Goodwyn Jones. Of course, all errors and shortcomings are mine alone.

For her continuing belief in the validity of this study, I owe a great debt to Carol Orr, director of the University of Tennessee Press. I am grateful as well for the John C. Hodges Dissertation Fellowship, given me by the University of Tennessee Department of English, and for the released time from teaching at Virginia Polytechnic Institute and State University, both of which were crucial to my completion of this project.

Several faculty members at both institutions have been helpful and supportive. I wish to thank professors Marilyn Kallet, Michael Lofaro, Joseph B. Trahern, Jr., and Bain T. Stewart at the University of Tennessee; and Susan Blalock, Arthur H. Eastman, Virginia Fowler, Peter Graham, and Ruth Salvaggio at the V.P.I. & S.U. Professor Salvaggio made several valuable suggestions about the manuscript, and Professor Fowler offered the best of all support, the services of her student computer operator, Beth Simmons, whose excellent and tireless efforts enabled me to meet my deadlines. I am grateful also to Marilyn Caponetti and Evelyn Early Raines for their careful and cheerful efforts in preparing this manuscript, and to Hilde L. Robinson, who copyedited this work with care, creativity, and insight.

For support and encouragement, I am also deeply grateful to Linda Jane Barnette, Doug Barnette, Rebecca Caldwell, Delores Karter, Bobbie Lemontt, Susan Mayberry, Erin Clayton Pitner, Billiee Parker, Sammy Parker, Alice Templeton, Martha Jane White, and Les White.

I wish to thank the following publishers:

Alfred A. Knopf, for permission to quote from *Sapphira and the Slave Girl* by Willa Cather, copyright 1940.

Houghton Mifflin, for permission to quote from *Jubilee* by Margaret Walker, copyright 1966.

W.W. Norton, for permission to quote from *On Lies, Secrets, and Silence: Selected Prose 1966-1978* by Adrienne Rich, copyright 1979.

Random House, for permission to quote from *Absalom, Absalom!* by William Faulkner, copyright 1936.

Yale University Press, for permission to quote from *Mary Chesnut's Civil War* edited by C. Vann Woodward, copyright 1981.

Parts of Chapters 2 and 5 have appeared as essays respectively entitled "Green-Eyed Monsters of the Slavocracy: Jealous Mistresses in Two Slave Narratives" and "*Jubilee*: The Black Woman's Celebration of Human Community" in *Conjuring: Black Women, Fiction, and Literary Tradition*, edited by Marjorie Pryse and Hortense Spillers, published by Indiana University Press, 1985. I am grateful for permission to republish these sections.

Acknowledgments

I owe the most to members of my immediate family. My daughter, Erin Carol Gwin, has been remarkably patient and helpful. My husband, Louis M. Gwin, Jr., never faltered in his support. Despite a demanding job of his own, he offered essential ideas and suggestions, and supported my work in every way possible. It is to both of them that I dedicate this book, for it has been their commitment as well as my own.

CONTENTS

Black and White Women of the Old South

The Peculiar Sisterhood in American Literature

The mutual history of black and white women in this country is a realm so painful, resonant, and forbidden that it has barely been touched by writers either of political "science" or of imaginative literature. Yet until that history is known, that silence broken, we will all go on struggling in a state of deprivation and ignorance.

As I thrust my hand deeper into the swirl of this stream—history, nightmare, accountability—I feel the current angrier and more multiform than the surface shows: There is fury here, and terror, but there is also power, power not to be had without the terror and the fury. We need to go beyond rhetoric or evasion into that place in ourselves, to feel the force of all we have been trying—without success—to skim across.

ADRIENNE RICH

INTRODUCTION

I cried "And you too?
And you too, sister, sister?"
ROSA COLDFIELD

In William Faulkner's *Absalom, Absalom!* an old and anguished Rosa Coldfield describes to Quentin Compson her explosive confrontation with Clytemnestra, Thomas Sutpen's daughter by a slave woman. The confrontation occurred decades ago and resulted only from Clytie's refusal to allow Rosa, then nineteen, to climb a flight of stairs leading to the room where Judith Sutpen mourned over the corpse of her husband-to-be and brother Charles Bon. Years after, Clytie's *"black arresting and untimorous hand"* upon her *"white woman's flesh"* continues to haunt Rosa Coldfield. In her obsessive imagination Rosa reshapes from memory that moment between her and the black woman whose touch stopped her *"dead"* at the foot of those stairs so many years ago. She recalls that as she hurled herself *"into that inscrutable coffee-colored face,"* she saw in it for the first time the Sutpen features and realized to her utter horror that Clytie was Sutpen's daughter and Judith and Henry's sister. In her anguished response to that knowledge voiced in the cry *"And you too? And you too, sister, sister?"*[1] young Rosa recognized not only Clytie's paternity but the dark terror of cross-racial relationships engendered by slavery. Clytie's touch upon her arm becomes in Rosa's memory an encounter of the flesh which, paradoxically, both intensifies and abrogates the differentiations of color. In Rosa's white consciousness these

3

two women are bound as sisters in one electrifying moment of interconnection and rejection, in a tension which defies resolution but which binds them both, finally and irrevocably, to a despairing heritage of human connection dissolved by racial antipathy.

Clytie's touch, frozen in Rosa's consciousness and in our own, seals black woman to white in one epiphanic gesture. It is this touch—this volatile, often violent *connection* between black and white women of the Old South—which I seek to explore in American fiction and autobiography. Clytie and Rosa's moment of pulsating immobility, of black female will pitting itself against white female racism, reverberates beyond Faulkner's fictional world into the American cultural and literary consciousness. Likewise, in its paradox and conflict, in its connective tissues of race, gender, and power, the relationship between black and white women in the nineteenth-century South may be seen as paradigmatic of the central ambiguity of southern racial experience: its antipathy, bitterness, and guilt on the one hand, its very real bonding through common suffering on the other. As literary signifiers of that experience, Clytie's touch and Rosa's cry evoke not only dark truths about the Old South and its women, but the immense complexity of human conduct, the mysteries of racism and sexism, and their engagement in the human rage for order and power.

Women, as Quentin Compson said of Clytie, "own the terror" in much of southern history. In the Old South, the Afro-American woman's survival from the shackles of institutionalized rape, backbreaking labor, yearly breeding, and personal degradation is a study in endurance, strength, and incredible will. Just as black women were forced to be strong, white southern women often were compelled to appear weak. Although they usually were not—Anne Firor Scott and Catherine Clinton show just how strong they actually were[2]—the patriarchy of the Old South seems to have firmly assisted its ladies up onto the pedestal, that emblem of chastity and powerlessness, just as surely as it forced black women into the dark corners of the Big House to be used as vessels of sexual pleasure or to breed new property.[3] The virgin/whore dichotomy which was imposed upon white and black southern

4

women must have deeply affected their images of themselves and of each other. Since white women were victims of adulation rather than violence, they often internalized stereotypical forms and attempted in great earnestness to become what they were expected to be—faithful standard-bearers of the patriarchy and its racial constructs.

In exploring this regional female experience as a powerful metaphor for the paradox of human pain and human connection in racial encounter, this study examines cross-racial relationships in two nineteenth-century novels—one abolitionist, one proslavery—in dozens of autobiographies by nineteenth-century black and white women, and in three modern novels. My inquiries are limited to American literary reflections of the antebellum period, the Civil War, and Reconstruction in the South on the supposition that cross-racial female relationships during this time and in this place embody psychological and social bases for modern biracial female experience and its literary reflections. I have set these historical parameters in the hope that this study will break some ground, treacherous and unsure though it be, for further studies of such relationships in American life and literature,[4] and toward a critical awareness of biracial female experience as a literary paradigm for understanding the tension implicit in racial experience of the Old South and, by implication, in human racial experience.

In all of these works, by blacks or whites, males or females, nineteenth- or twentieth-century writers, there is one constant. White women—fictional or actual, writers or subjects—rarely perceive or acknowledge, except in Rosa Coldfield's brief and violent epiphany and in the rare day-to-day cross-racial closeness of a few earlier writers, the humanity of their black sisters. Most of these white women in life and literature see black women as a color, as servants, as children, as adjuncts, as sexual competition, as dark sides of their own sexual selves—as black Other. They beat black women, nurture them, sentimentalize them, despise them—but they seldom see them as individuals with selves commensurate to their own. In these writings, real and fictional black women respond to their white sisters' myopic vision of them in a number of ways. They run from it, they are enraged by it, they forgive it, they re-create it into more palatable forms. Strangely and sadly, those writers of fiction who try to create the closest bonds of friendship between black and white women characters often do so out of stereotypical characterizations or expectations based, as James Baldwin might instruct us, on simplifications of human nature and an unwillingness to look with unblinking eye on the real terror of life.[5] In this context those bonds seem less than real, often creating false reconciliations based on simplified perceptions of human behavior. Interestingly, of all the writers considered here, it is a southern white male who evokes, in *Absalom*, a most complex and intense rendering of the terror and mystery of racism; and a southern black woman, Margaret Walker, whose black female character offers reconciliation of racial hatred through forgiveness of her dead mistress for a childhood of terror and cruelty.

My method being selective rather than comprehensive, I have chosen works from the nineteenth and twentieth centuries that deal extensively and in some depth with the relationship of black and white women during a particularly difficult period in southern history, from about 1840 to 1875, and have attempted to justify my selections where there were many works to choose from, as among the proslavery novels, slave narratives, and journals. Harriet Beecher Stowe's *Uncle Tom's Cabin* (1851), Faulkner's *Absalom, Absalom!* (1936), Willa Cather's *Sapphira and the Slave Girl* (1940), and Margaret Walker's *Jubilee* (1966) are obvious choices for this study. Mary H. Eastman's *Aunt Phillis's Cabin* (1852), the first fictional proslavery response to Stowe by a southern woman, provides fertile material for the study of cross-racial female relationships in a proslavery novel that outsold all others and focused upon a black woman character in a plantation setting. Many of these writings have defined and clarified American and southern perceptions about race and gender. Although many—actually most—of the women of mixed blood discussed are as white as they are Afro-American, I refer to them as black women because, in the eyes of the Old South, they were exactly that. Charles Bon's octoroon is as black in her fictional world as Vyry Ware, the daughter of her master, is in hers—or as

Harriet Jacobs, daughter of two mulattoes, is in her brutally real world of bondage. While I have tried to include a variety of American writers and literary works to make those perceptions as broad and illuminating as possible, I have concentrated my attention solely upon fiction and autobiography about the nineteenth-century South on the supposition that these women's connections are indeed tied to region, to the totality of southern experience, and provide valuable commentary upon its profound ambiguity and its lingering imprint upon American thought.

This is not to say that northern women writers did not depict such relationships as conflicted and bitter. In Harriet Wilson's autobiographical novel *Our Nig*, the heroine Frado serves a "harsh indenture" of terrible beatings and tortures from an evil mother and daughter who almost kill her before her service expires at age eighteen. Likewise, Sylvia Dubois relates that her New Jersey "Missy" treated her with great cruelty. In both cases, the black women rebel actively. Dubois proudly relates that she knocked her mistress down and "blamd ner kild her."[6] The climax of *Our Nig* comes when Frado, who throughout her indenture has been beaten with rawhide whips, has had knives thrown at her, and has been tortured unmercifully, shouts at her sadistic mistress, "Stop! . . . strike me, and I'll never work a mite more for you."[7] Obviously, neither of these acts of defiance was a realistic option for mistreated black women of the southern slave society.

Free black women writers of religious autobiographies such as Ziltha Elaw, Julia Foote, Jarena Lee, and Nancy Prince do not seem to have had such horrific experiences and tend to depict white women as insignificant personages in their lives and travels.[8] Prince writes of ill treatment at one place of employment and kind treatment at another, while Lee relates that she counseled a white woman with a call to preach. Elaw, whose parents died when she was young, lived with a Quaker master and mistress in Pennsylvania until she married. She writes that her mistress scolded her on occasion, but also that she comforted her when she, a highly emotional and imaginative adolescent, had nightmares of "the awful terrors of the day of judgment." Foote recalls that a white woman taught her the Lord's Prayer when she was growing up in the state of New York. Although the woman for whom she worked as a child tried to beat her for a theft she did not commit, she refused to return to work until her mistress promised to desist. For the most part, though, these autobiographies are filled with tales of religious travels and experiences. Unlike the southern women writers of slave narratives, these devout northern black women focus upon issues of religious, not racial import.

I have limited my study further to book-length autobiography and fiction on grounds that, in the case of the journals and slave narratives, the longer manuscript, actually written by its author, provides a sustained, often a more conscious literary endeavor and thereby affords more substantial analytical opportunities. For that reason, collections containing black women's oral narratives, letters, and essays, such as those gathered by the Federal Writers' Project or compiled by George Rawick and John Blassingame, have been omitted,[9] as have longer published slave narratives, such as *Horrors of the Virginian Slave Trade* and *The Narrative of Bethany Veney*, which were dictated to amanuenses rather than actually written by literate southern black women.[10] The act of writing itself is in many ways for these women, black and white, a shaping or assertion of female self in a male-controlled world. For the freed woman, the written word, her own *sign*, becomes at once a vehicle toward individuation through the reordering in language of past experience, and the creation of order and freedom from the chaos of a dominated slave self. My focus upon longer, more sustained writings about cross-racial female relationships of the Old South, with its mixture of genre and period, should suggest new contexts which may lead to further studies of racial connections in these shorter, often orally transmitted works. As conscious, extended re-creations of the southern past, these longer autobiographical and fictional writings become powerful, often problematic commentaries upon "the peculiar institution" as an immense, irrevocable burden upon southern cultural consciousness past and present, white and black, male and female.[11]

Seymour Gross writes that literary criticism "can bring to the surface what otherwise might lie buried in the culture's subconscious."[12] This is surely a fundamental function of criticism—to disclose what lies hidden both in the literature and in the culture which produces that literature. What lies hidden in the past, and this is particularly true of the southern past, lives within many of us whether we know it or not, whether we wish it or not. Just as we can learn about the psychodynamics of that past through its own literature, we can also come to know modern literature differently and more fully by examining its relationship with the past and the texts and subtexts that relationship may produce. I seek to create a critical intersection at which black and white, male and female, southern and northern writers and their literary responses to southern racial experience, particularly female experience, may be considered together for the first time. Yet my focus upon literary reflections of a particular time in southern history and a particular relationship is not meant to have a leveling effect upon these works or the individuals whose unique imaginations created them. My spectrum of such disparate works is designed instead to create new critical contexts that neither detract from such monumental literary achievements as *Absalom, Absalom!* nor elevate polemic fiction like *Aunt Phillis's Cabin*—contexts which periodization and fixation upon the traditional canon have not produced.

New contexts are always syntheses of the old. Yet their value becomes more than the sum of their parts. They teach us about the literature we already know. They expand our sense of what literature is. They teach us about ourselves. They point to new directions for critical inquiry. My purpose is not so much to answer questions as to ask them—to suggest areas of inquiry into cross-racial female relationships, what those relationships become in American fiction and autobiography, and why they become what they do. The reality of the past, which is both of the factual and beyond it ("Was," as Faulkner would call it) is an amalgam of the experience, values, perceptions, myths, and societal expectations that mold human conduct. Literary reconstruction of that amalgam of "Was," in its variousness of genre, period, and creator, may become a way of knowing the past more intensely and more pervasively. "The peculiar sisterhood" of biracial female experience in the Old South serves as an entry into American literature which is both exegetic and epiphanic. Our consideration of such experience enables us not only to interpret the reality of the southern past—to discover meaning—but also to experience that meaning more intensely in literary reconstruction. In this sense literature about the Old South and its women may become, in Rosa Coldfield's words, *"more true than truth"* because so many of these ingredients in the amalgam shape the reconstruction and can be deciphered and experienced therein. The simultaneous study of this variety of American literature also creates new critical relationships between works of the traditional canon and those outside of it, and reflects the sheer metaphorical weight of southern slavery in the American literary consciousness.

I have found various critical methods helpful, particularly many of the recent feminist approaches, with their dual emphases on women's relationships in the texts of male and female writers and on the artistic consciousness which creates such relationships. Jungian theory and terminology have been helpful in explicating the peculiar and often terrifying duality of cross-racial nurturance in which southern women engaged, willingly or unwillingly, during the mid-nineteenth century. My methodology is essentially circular and holistic. I seek to explore culture through close readings of its literary reflections, past and present; yet at the same time to discover new meanings in texts and subtexts through an exploration of the tensions between that culture and the writer's responses to it. At the base of my concern are literary explorations of the institution of slavery and its moral and psychological reverberations within the American literary consciousness, as that consciousness is expressed by male and female, black and white American writers, and as it is created in women characters.

Although Harriet Beecher Stowe's judgment about the morality of slavery is diametrically opposed to that of Mary H. Eastman, author of the proslavery *Aunt Phillis's Cabin*, both women discussed in Chapter 1, the southerner as well as the northerner, create in their fictional worlds cross-racial female bonds which generate power and strength in response to the male sphere.[13] Stowe particularly associates slavery with the male marketplace and creates female bonds that are empowered with moral values and that dilute the strength of the materialistic male world. Likewise, in *Aunt Phillis's Cabin,* women are the voices of morality and practicality that often make white and black men seem callous or ridiculous. Though the novels are opposite in their polemic intents, Stowe's and Eastman's creations of cross-racial female nurturance and female power through that nurturance create ironically similar subtexts. In both of these fictions of the Old South, black and white women together form an active, ongoing challenge to the patriarchy. It is an even greater irony that Stowe and Eastman manipulate these female bonds with such apparent ease to support both abolitionist and proslavery polemics. Yet this second irony is in itself a commentary upon the nature of these novels. Both present fictional sisterhoods in a fictional South based upon stereotypical characterizations founded in racial myth and clouded by sentimental visions of female bonding which had little correlation with the real, often brutal world of slavery.

That real world comes to life in the autobiographical writings of southern women, whose cross-racial relationships were built upon a shared sense of societal demands which placed them in opposite but mutually dependent roles. These women were both drawn to and repelled by their racial female Other; and their writings, considered in Chapter 2, betray above all the intensity of their feelings for one another. Real southern women of both races, bound by their dichotomous images in the popular mind and, in the case of black women, by actual enslavement, often viewed one another as missing pieces of a female identity denied them by the patriarchal culture. Female narrators of the slave narratives reveal their yearning for the chaste respectability of their white sisters, while the diaries and memoirs of the white women show their intense jealousy of the stereotypical sexuality of the slave woman. Each is only one half of a self. What is so terribly ironic is that the missing piece of self so fervently desired by one race of women seems to have caused so much suffering for the other.

As reflected in their writings, many white women "love" their female slaves or servants only when the black women assume a demeanor of inferiority and powerlessness. When

11

black women express affection for their mistresses, they seem to find in them the natural nurturance that circumstance has denied them in their real mothers. The kind mistress emerges in the writings of both races; the cruel and jealous mistress only in the writings of black women. There, as a literary reconstruction created by her former slave, she becomes a vindictive monster who blames forced miscegenation not on her licentious husband but his hapless victim. From both white and black female perspectives emerge moments of real closeness in the face of common suffering. But for the most part racism blinded white women to the reality of that suffering in their black sisters and built in Afro-American women impenetrable layers of hatred and resentment toward the fair ladies who refused to see them or the immensity of their pain. The autobiographical mirror of self is therefore often dim and warped—by blindness, and by anger or denial engendered by that blindness.

In their writings, women of both races remake their realities in language. Although there was no one South and no central experience for women of either race, white women tend to evoke effusive sentimentality or petty anger to mask their fear of the black Other; black women use language to gain control of their cruel mistresses, or negate their own servitude by rendering their mistresses as kindly, maternal forces in their lives. While the white retrospective autobiographies often become re-creations of a diminished culture and a fractured self, black women seem to evoke the autobiographical process as an avenue toward individuation, understanding, and order. The most anguished of these writings comes not only from the black woman who must come to know herself as a freed, individuated self, but from the rare white woman who, like Kate Stone of Louisiana, clearly sees what slavery has done to black women and men and who must ask the chilling, reverberating question: ". . . what would be our measure of responsibility?"[14]

The question of moral accountability is, of course, central to *Absalom, Absalom!* In Rosa's blindness to Clytie's humanity, Faulkner powerfully connects the regional blindness of a country which sends the young Thomas Sutpen to the back door without hearing what he has to say to the universal mystery of racism and its terrible power in the human psyche. As discussed in Chapter 3, the force and resonance of *Absalom* are created out of that mystery and terror, and out of Faulkner's as well as Quentin's response to it. Both Quentin and his creator are heirs of the patriarchy, and both seem to feel that inheritance as a destructive force. Although we do not know the extent of Faulkner's acquaintance with white and black women's autobiographies of the Old South, Rosa Coldfield and Clytie Sutpen are powerfully connected to these real women and their writings in the sense that, as fictional representations, together they become a metaphor for the brutalizing and destructive power of a racist society and the lingering impingements of that power in American culture. As Faulkner re-creates the female autobiographical process in Rosa's own remaking of the past and as she, like many actual white women of the Old South, tells of her relationship with the black Other, we become, like Quentin, drawn into a web of mutual terror and pain. We too become mired in the past; to free ourselves we too must deconstruct, analyze. Rosa and Clytie's sisterhood of yearning, antipathy, and despair becomes "*the fell darkness*" both of and beyond the southern racial experience. It is a darkness glimpsed only fleetingly in the autobiographical writings and polemic fiction, yet in a significant way, *Absalom* both re-creates and interprets the texts which come before it. In the context of this literature, Clytie and Rosa's tragic sisterhood becomes a mutual epiphany of the human need and human perversity which pervade the autobiographies and polemic fiction; the novel itself becomes an exegesis of earlier reconstructions of racial encounter in the Old South. Forever frozen in a quivering tension of connection and rejection, Clytemnestra Sutpen and Rosa Coldfield make us feel the mystery and know the power of racism which is so interwoven into the fabric of these earlier works.

Cather's vision of the slave South is more problematic than epiphanic. *Sapphira and the Slave Girl*, published four years after *Absalom*, probes the complexity of human motivation that produces the evil act and presents a more equivocal view of slavery and the relative merits of "the peculiar institution," which provided, above all, an ordering of society and a powerful force for stability.[15] As discussed in Chapter 4, the problematic nature of southern experience is epitomized in Cather's ambivalent depiction of Sapphira, the crippled southern aristocrat who imagines that her miller husband is enamoured of one of her young slave women, Nancy Till. Throughout two-thirds of the novel Sapphira is the embodiment of white female rage who mistreats the slave girl shamefully; yet in a later section of the book Sapphira is depicted by Nancy's mother as a quiet heroine at the end of her life, a woman who deserves to be forgiven for earlier iniquities.

In the context of the black and white female autobiographical writings of the nineteenth-century South, Sapphira thereby becomes, at once, the black woman's nightmare of the jealous cruel mistress and the mistress's view of herself as a woman of good will but trapped in a system which denies her sexuality and humanity. Furthermore, because of Sapphira's cruelties, Nancy escapes to Canada and becomes the Everywoman of the slave narratives who has asserted her own identity in a free land, who has become an individuated self in reaction to the racist evil of her white mistress. The troubling aspect of *Sapphira* is that as it suggests the mixed nature of human motivation and conduct through its cross-racial female relationships, it also implies that human evil can be without serious consequence, that the black woman of the slave South could indeed escape North from a cruel mistress with no serious emotional scars, that slavery usually had no grave and irrevocable psychological effects upon the enslaved. In Cather's fictional Southland, the jealous mistress can repent; the beleaguered slave woman can escape; all can work for the good; all can be forgiven.

The female autobiographical mode suddenly evoked at the end of the novel, although disconcerting, does enlarge our perception of the complexities of southern racial experience and the enduring qualities of cross-racial female relationships. It also suggests implicitly the problematic nature of that experience, which cannot be conveyed through stereotypical modes and single points of view such as those employed polemically by Stowe and Eastman. Like *Absalom, Sapphira and the Slave Girl* filters the ambiguity of southern racial experience through an alembic of many voices and many listeners, and in the metaphor of the cross-racial relationships of southern women. In both narratives the multilayered and complex process of revelation serves as the vessel which refines, clarifies, and intensifies the ambiguity of that experience. Yet, unlike Faulkner, Cather seems to accept that ambiguity quietly, unquestioningly. Hers is a world where evil does not hurt, and like the nostalgic worlds of the white female memoirs, it is less than believable and ultimately impenetrable.

Walker's fictional creation of the Old South, subject of my final chapter, is the world of the slave narrative, of the black perspective. In *Jubilee* evil hurts badly and is invariably linked to whiteness. Yet despite its emphasis upon acutely depicted deeds of white cruelty and scenes of black suffering, the novel evolves out of violence and pain into a fiction of vision and reconciliation.[16] Walker's vision of southern experience, rendered from the viewpoint of the black woman, is ultimately optimistic and humanistic. She chooses not to explore the dark web of racism in cross-racial female relationships as Faulkner has done, or to find in these relationships the mysterious mixture of human nature that we see in *Sapphira and the Slave Girl*. Yet, like Faulkner and Cather, Walker presents the volatile relationships of black and white women as inextricable from the complex whole of southern racial experience.

Walker's heroine Vyry Ware, whose story is modeled upon the life of the author's great-grandmother, epitomizes grace and forgiveness on the part of the black woman when she says that despite her mistress's many cruelties to her, she "still closed her eyes in death." It is this image of the black woman's forgiving gesture which provides in and of itself a conclusion to this study. In Vyry and in that gesture are manifested Walker's humanistic vision of reconciliation and its regenerative response to the darkness of the southern past. Though such a vision may seem to light a darkness that can never be illuminated, or to silence the clanking of the chains too abruptly, there is no denying its power as it emerges simultaneously from a black woman of the fictional world of the Civil War South and from her creator, the black woman artist, a twentieth-century southerner whose real world was molded by the southern past and the suffering of her people past and present. In this sense *Jubilee* culminates more than one hundred years of American literary struggle with the paradoxical South and its women, fictional and real, white and black. At the same time, it celebrates the power of what its creator calls "black humanism" in a book which is part history and part fiction—a synthesis of life and literature.

All of these works show women's blindness and women's pain. Several show women's mutual nurturance. In re-creating white blindness and black pain and in rare instances cross-racial sisterhood in fiction and autobiography about the Old South, these writers—knowingly or unknowingly—impart profound insight about racism and the cultural and literary responses to it. Often by negative example we learn not merely about nineteenth-century southern women and the psychodynamics of their cross-racial relationships; we also learn something essential about true mutuality in such relationships, simply by seeing what it is not—in fiction and in fact. This critical intersection of race, gender, and region suggests too that issues of racism, perhaps of sexism as well, are so complexly interconnected to place that it is difficult and perhaps even impossible to examine them outside of a regional perspective. At the same time they are, even in their regionality, universal issues which touch us all.

In a profound sense the white South has known literal and moral defeat because of its failure to acknowledge the black South. More than anything else, the relationships studied here reflect that white failure and the volatile, moving, powerful responses of the black self to it. These black and white women, fictional and real, mirror the paradox of the South. Their bonds are often deep and strong. Yet they are those of victim and oppressor, and they are cemented by suffering. These fictional women teach us, as Rosa and Clytie taught Quentin, that the southern racial experience is ultimately ambiguous. They teach us further that their creators were profoundly affected by the ambiguity—whether, like Faulkner and Cather, they re-create and intensify it in their fiction; or, like

16

Stowe, Eastman, and Walker, simplify or resolve it. Those who attempt to reconcile racial oppositions in female relationships often fail to make such resolutions psychologically dynamic. Yet we learn also from their failures to recognize the depth and complexity of these oppositions. We learn not to underestimate them.

The dark web of female racial reality becomes most powerfully realized in Clytie's touch and Rosa's slap—and in their impact upon Quentin's southern male consciousness. As Quentin hears and tells Rosa and Clytie's story, he and we recognize it as a parable of the Old South. Clytie's touch is both female and black. It asks for human connection, for human community. Rosa's slap both recognizes that touch and rejects it. It is, at once, acknowledgment and denial of black humanity. Rosa's slap seals Clytie's black Otherness to the white South just as Clytie's touch becomes an unforgettable metaphor for what Walker would call "black humanism," which seeks human dignity in a racist world.

Whether these writers create fictional female lives or re-create their own in autobiographical writings, they remake the world of the nineteenth-century South. And, in so doing, they teach us the enormous complexity of that world and its electrifying connections between race, gender, and region. "The peculiar sisterhood" which they create between their black and white fictional women or re-create from their own experiences serves us well in that it provides a new entry into literary explorations of that darkness of the southern past that continues to live in the American cultural consciousness. At the same time it creates critical relationships among and within these enormously diverse renderings of that mysterious, twisted, volatile past. Not insignificantly, it also allows us to see human experience through biracial female experience and therein offers a powerful lens through which we may envision new critical relationships, new illuminations.

CHAPTER I

"A Lie More Palatable Than the Truth"

FICTIONAL SISTERHOOD IN A FICTIONAL SOUTH

> . . . literature and sociology are not one and the same; it is impossible to discuss them as if they were.
>
> JAMES BALDWIN
> "Everybody's Protest Novel"

> Because writers of fiction and poetry tend to grope for meanings rather than superimpose them—Yeats called this process the "public dream"—literary criticism can bring to the surface what otherwise might lie buried in the culture's subconscious.
>
> SEYMOUR L. GROSS
> *Images of the Negro in American Literature*

It is in the very fabric of the polemic novel to impose a rigid frame upon reality. In such fiction rarely is there obvious groping for new meanings and new ways of viewing the world. The method is deductive rather than inductive; the world and its problems are presented *a priori*. Such novels become primarily means to specific ends, not movements toward the unknown, the new, the unreckoned. No one can accuse America's nineteenth-century abolitionist and proslavery fiction of attempting many artistic or epistemological leaps into the void, certainly not the two novels most widely read on both sides of the slavery controversy. Moral outrage rather than artistic impulse set Harriet Beecher Stowe's pen in

19

motion on *Uncle Tom's Cabin*, first published in the abolitionist *National Era* in 1851 and later selling millions of copies in dozens of countries after its publication in book form in 1852. In *Aunt Phillis's Cabin*, also published in 1852, Mary H. Eastman produced a proslavery response which—it is generally agreed—slightly outsold the flood of seventeen vituperative "feeble tractarian novels" attempting to prove Stowe wrong.[1] Both novels are guilty to a degree of James Baldwin's biting castigation of protest fiction in general and Stowe's book in particular—that such writing reduces the complexity of life to simplistic formulas and wrenches flesh-and-blood human beings into stereotypical straightjackets. Novels like these, writes Baldwin, become "mirrors of our own confusion": by creating false worlds and implying false solutions, they do more harm than good. Their sole and dubious achievement is not the expression of a new cultural truth, Yeats's "public dream," but simply the creation of what Baldwin calls "a lie more palatable than the truth."[2]

These are harsh words which evoked passionate critical rebuttal,[3] and yet they may serve as cautionary to this study. It would be foolhardy to seek in these two novels the historical *reality* of what white and black southern women meant to one another.[4] Stowe and Eastman wrote with certain purposes in mind, and those purposes determined what kind of novels their books became and what kind of characters inhabited their pages. Their southern women characters, black and white, have meaning primarily as mouthpieces of the authors' political and moral views concerning what Stowe called "the truth" of chattel slavery in the antebellum South.[5] The relationships among their southern women characters are often fictional constructs in which the characters may function most effectively in their roles as propagandists.

What is more significant, and deeply ironic, is that the women characters in these two novels, which purport to represent opposite sides of the slavery controversy, are actually cut from a common mold and imprinted with a common assumption of white superiority and black inferiority. Like the male characters in both novels, these women are recognizable as stock southern characters, types that were well ingrained by

1850 in an American cultural and literary consciousness already familiar with the plantation legend and the southern cult of chivalry and its patriarchal power structure.[6] In their depictions of white women as well as black, Stowe and Eastman serve as *prima facie* evidence of David Levy's thesis that "those who attacked slavery in fiction portrayed the races in precisely the same terms as those who defended it."[7]

Whether we look in the slave cabins or in the Big House of these two novels, we find the familiar silhouettes of the female stereotypes of southern plantation fiction: the mammy, the belle, the plantation mistress. Like many fictional slave women of the nineteenth and twentieth centuries, Mammy and Chloe of *Uncle Tom's Cabin* are Aunt Phillis's sisters in their maternal qualities of endurance, loyalty, and kindness. All three slave women embody the mother image of the black mammy, and their sisterhood as fictional mammies provides a striking illustration of how the referential weight of that image may be manipulated with ease in one propagandistic direction or the other.[8] The lovely Alice Weston in Eastman's novel is an older version of little Eva, who, had she lived through her disease as Alice manages to do, would surely have grown up to become a chaste beautiful generous southern belle too. Mrs. Shelby of *Uncle Tom's Cabin* is the sister of Eastman's Mrs. Weston, the kindly plantation mistress who cares for the moral education and physical health of the servants (slaves are seldom called slaves in *Aunt Phillis's Cabin*). Both women conform to the ideal of the planter's wife, portrayed in novels of the 1820s and 1830s as what William Taylor calls "the heart and soul" of the plantation system, whose "benevolent rule extended over the whole household."[9] Likewise, many of the black female characters in both novels are delineated within the literary tradition described by Catherine Starke, in which contented slaves are "accommodative chattels" supported by "the myth of white superiority."[10] Even runaways like Stowe's Eliza and Eastman's Susan maintain fond relationships with their white mistresses.

White women of the two novels are depicted not only in the plantation ideal of benevolence and beauty (with the notable exception of Marie St. Clare); but are also pressed into the mold of the nineteenth-century Victorian cult of domesticity, "the cult of True Womanhood" which insisted upon the "four cardinal virtues—piety, purity, submissiveness, and domesticity."[11] The southern white woman, in life and often in the literature of the period, was fully obligated to uphold moral virtue in the domestic sphere—a sphere enlarged in southern society to include the plantation. The female characters in both of these novels, as in other antebellum fiction about the South, reflect therefore a set of cultural assumptions not only of what slave women and their mistresses were, but also of what white women should be. Whether they are proslavery or abolitionist mouthpieces, these fictional women and their relationships to one another cannot avoid stereotypical delineations based upon identical assumptions about racial and sexual roles in the Old South.

And yet both novels resonate deeply and peculiarly with the relationships between these white and black female characters, stereotypical though they may be. Critics of *Uncle Tom's Cabin* have long noticed both its distinctly female ambience and the odd way Stowe's characters have of making us feel their humanity.[12] It is perhaps in the relationships between black and white women that we can find a clue to the paradoxical power of *Uncle Tom's Cabin*. It is a novel which is in a very real sense the distortion of reality Baldwin says it is. But in another sense, it is much more, more even than Stowe may have consciously designed it to be or thought it was.

Generally, scholars have pointed to characterization as pivotal point of the emotional power of *Uncle Tom's Cabin* and have remarked at the paradox of "conventional literary characters and sociological stereotypes or roles express[ing] genuinely human qualities,"[13] or put another way, of characters who "act partly as mouthpieces for their creator and at the same time are genuine individuals."[14] Certainly Stowe's characters are what we remember about her book. It is, as Charles Foster suggests, "the book's working at the deep places of the human personality that makes the reader feel that slavery is a personal tragedy."[15]

Although *Aunt Phillis's Cabin* is by any standards a less effective work, it does emit, almost as if by accident, an undercurrent of something beyond its obvious proslavery argument. That something which hovers around the outer corners of the book's contrived plots and sentimental outpourings has, like *Uncle Tom's Cabin*, the strong flavor of a feminist subtext (perhaps in the case of Eastman surprisingly strong). Though both writers use their black and white southern women characters as mouthpieces of the proslavery or abolitionist factions, paradoxically those same women develop similarly strong interracial attachments. Significantly, these attachments often are developed in response to a male-initiated crisis. Often too these women gain strength from their cross-racial relationships and, more often than not, overcome or circumvent problems together. In these novels, pairs of white and black women also face another common enemy: death. They nurse each other, mother each other, and initiate each other into the mysteries of death. Their bond is their common womanhood. Their sphere is the family. Their enemy is anything that seeks to degrade or destroy either.

The implications of these fictional women's close cross-racial relationships and their bonding against common threats remain rather shapeless currents submerged under the smooth polemic surface of both novels, despite Stowe's clear opposition of the female spheres of maternity and domesticity to the male mercenary interests of slavery.[16] Like much of the sentimental woman's fiction of the nineteenth century, *Uncle Tom's Cabin*, though it does not fall into that category, suggests that women's values are moral values and that the ideal nation should be "organized on the principle of familial love": the woman's sphere is associated with basic human values; the mercenary male sphere barters in human lives and destroys familial ties.[17]

In *Uncle Tom's Cabin*, where slavery is linked to the male sphere, the bonds between white and black women not only provide succor but can generate enormous power against that sphere. The bonds between Mrs. Shelby and two of her female slaves, Eliza and Aunt Chloe, provide a literal and metaphorical frame for the novel. All three women characters are stereotypes. Stowe herself acknowledged Mrs. Shelby as "a fair type of the very best class of Southern women"—and the

Shelbys' Kentucky farm as "the fairest side of slave-life, where easy indulgence and good-natured forbearance are tempered by just discipline and religious instruction, skilfully and judiciously imparted."[18] Eliza is, of course, the beleaguered mulatta; and Chloe, like Eastman's Phillis, the mammy with the strength to move mountains.

Yet again the real wonder of the novel is that Stowe can bring these women characters to life. Where they operate most dramatically and most believably is in their relationships with one another. This is true even in relationships between women of the same race; one of the most moving relationships in the book is between Cassy, who is looking for a child, and young Emmeline, who needs the protection of a mother. Although many of the interracial female relationships also are based on the maternal impulse, others are developed in an acknowledgment of common womanhood and common humanistic values. The importance of these female bonds cannot be overstated. More than anything else, they show the generative power of love and devastatingly delineate by contrast the rapacity of a system that tallies human life in profit and loss columns.

The opposition of female and male values becomes immediately apparent in the opening scene of *Uncle Tom's Cabin*. Mr. Shelby's willingness to sell Uncle Tom, his valued faithful slave, is contrasted with his acknowledgment to the trader of Mrs. Shelby's ties with Eliza. The fact that Mrs. Shelby cannot believe that her husband would ever agree to sell Eliza's child ("I would as soon have one of my own children sold," she tells Eliza)[19] reflects not only her attachment to the beautiful quadroon whom she has herself nurtured but the vast gulf between the female and male views of responsibility to valued chattels. Unlike her husband, Mrs. Shelby has committed herself to a parental role which she cannot dismiss merely because there are money troubles.

Even though such a role as conceived by Stowe is surely based on racist presumptions, the bond between the Kentucky mistress and Eliza is described in warm maternal terms. Mrs. Shelby has protected the young beautiful girl from sexual abuse, acted as matchmaker "to unite her handsome favorite with one of her own class who seemed in every way suited to her," adorned Eliza's hair with flowers on her wedding day, and arranged to have her married in her own parlor (p. 17). In the past she tried to comfort Eliza upon the loss of two infants and "directed her naturally passionate feelings within the bounds of reason and religion" (p. 17). Obviously Stowe couches her description of the mistress-slave relationship in the premise of white superiority; still, there is stark and chilling contrast between Mrs. Shelby's loyalty to Eliza, reflected in her horror at having to sell little Harry—"If I could only at least save Eliza's child, I would sacrifice anything I have," she mourns—and Mr. Shelby's matter-of-fact attitude about selling Tom and Harry: ". . . the price of these two was needed to make up the balance, and I had to give them up" (pp. 38-39).

Mrs. Shelby's loyalty to Eliza actually supersedes her loyalty to her own husband. She is glad when Eliza runs away. To prevent the slave woman's capture, Mrs. Shelby joins the slaves in league against her husband and Haley the trader. She directs Sam and Andy to "lose" the horses; she and Chloe conspire to make dinner late. Once the meal is on the table, she detains the trader "by every female artifice" (p. 61). Her bond with Eliza makes her "feel too much," as her husband says— "an awful feeling of guilt" for having pushed the desperate slave woman to the extreme of risking her life and that of her child on the treacherous ice floes of the frigid Ohio River. Her reaction to the news that Eliza made it to the other side of the river is in ironic contrast to her husband's response. "Are we not both responsible to God for this poor girl? My God! lay not this sin to our charge," she says, to which Mr. Shelby responds, "What sin, Emily? You see yourself that we have only done what we were obliged to" (p. 76). Likewise, her outraged response to the sale of Eliza's Harry and her willingness to take responsibility for what she considers to be an immoral act against the slave woman contrast sharply with Shelby's lack of emotion and his refusal to take moral responsibility for the selling of Tom. Shelby, never one to accept guilt, absents himself from the farm on the day his loyal slave is to be taken so "that he might not witness the unpleasant scenes of the consummation" of his own act of separating Tom from his family.

Stowe herself maintained that "the worst abuse" of slavery

was "its outrage on the family";[20] and generally she saw women, white and black, as the keepers of moral virtues and domestic values. It is *because* of this ideal of woman as upholder of right action that Marie St. Clare becomes, by contrast, such a despicable character and that Ophelia's racism is so shocking. It is also this maternal, familial ideal that makes Cassy's protectiveness of Emmeline believable and moving. Similarly Chloe's passionate refusal to forgive Mr. Shelby and her wish to send all slave-traders to hell is not so much a black rejection of Christian principles, as David Levin has suggested,[21] as a female rejection of the male sphere, which buys and sells human beings for profit and callously disregards familial ties. In *Uncle Tom's Cabin*, then, the bonding of white and black women against the dehumanizing greed of a male marketplace has enormous thematic force.

The plot reverberates with that force. Mr. Shelby's decision to sell Tom and little Harry breaks up two families. Stowe's purpose was, of course, to muster sympathy for black families who lived under the specter of slavery; and her story shows women, black and white, reacting in dismay and rage at the destruction of these families. Eliza, with Aunt Chloe's and Mrs. Shelby's help, flees to safety after her treacherous journey across the ice. The slave woman, who responds with active rebellion to her son's imminent sale, is happily reunited with her husband George in Canada. Meanwhile, Tom's misfortune increases after being separated from his family, going from the relatively easy existence he finds on the Louisiana plantation of the humane Augustine St. Clare to actual torment at the hands of Simon Legree. Although Stowe seems to praise Tom's long-suffering Christianity, his downward plunge in fortune to eventual death shows, interestingly, that his passivity gets him nowhere. He dies, the victim of his own goodness. His relationships with little angelic Eva St. Clare and Legree's mistress Cassy are full of love and tenderness; yet in the end he is, in many ways, beaten by the institution of slavery and the cruelty and inhumanity of its perpetrators Marie St. Clare and Simon Legree. His willingness to suffer and to die contrasts sharply to the active efforts of his wife Chloe to save him by earning money to buy him back. In their denial of passivity, the cross-racial female relationships in the book reflect the implication of plot in *Uncle Tom's Cabin*—that those who do not fight a rapacious system ultimately lose themselves to it.

Stowe's development of women's cross-racial bonds here (and later in *Dred*) has obvious implications for the abolitionist cause: if mistresses and their female slaves can be friends and work toward the same goals, then they may be seen to share a common humanity and a common morality. This relationship also implies a connection in Stowe's mind between feminism and abolitionism. Certainly in the popular mind of the period there resided a strong connection between such "similar repressions" and the submissive virtues of women and blacks.[22] John R. Adams and others have suggested that Stowe's sympathy with slaves might be traced to her own experiences with the servitude of domesticity.[23] She was the mother of seven children, one of whom died in infancy. Her professor husband, Calvin, was absent for long periods, and the family often was pinched for money.[24]

As to her feminist views, or lack of them, Stowe has most recently been placed somewhere between what feminist critics and historians call the "domestic feminism" of her older sister Catharine Beecher, who wrote books and articles on the stabilizing influence of women upon society, and the radical feminism of her youngest sister, Isabella Beecher Hooker, who became an avid follower of Victoria Woodhull and who was convinced that the world was soon to become a matriarchy and that she, Isabella, would rule as Christ's vice-regent.[25] Perhaps the single most visceral connection in Stowe's mind between feminism and abolitionism was her intense admiration for Sojourner Truth, the powerful black spokeswoman for human rights during the fifties. Truth, a freed slave who traveled through America in behalf of women's rights and abolition, visited the Stowes in 1853 and won whole-hearted admiration from the whole family. "There was both power and sweetness in that great warm soul and that vigorous frame," Stowe later wrote of "The Libyan Sibyl."[26]

Stowe's moderation in such issues as women's suffrage—she supported but did not actively campaign for the vote—may be due partly to the fact that she was perhaps more concerned about extending the realm of the domestic sphere with its humanistic values into the world around it than moving women out of that sphere into the world of male materialism. Yet, Severn Duvall points to the immense threat that *Uncle Tom's Cabin* and Stowe posed to the southern patriarchy. Like the slave, the white woman had her proper place "on the scale of Nature" and thus in the antebellum familial hierarchy. White southerners were horrified at a woman "unsexing herself" enough to write a novel on slavery, perhaps because for the first time masculine dominance of the southern social order was being challenged publicly.[27]

The antislavery movement, like moral reform and temperance, was at its core in a very deep sense a woman's issue.[28] Northern women were urged to "rise up in the moral power of womanhood; and give utterance to the voice of outraged mercy" and to hear "the sighs, the groans, the death-like struggles of scourged sisters at the South."[29] Theodore Weld's *American Slavery As It Is*, which Stowe claimed to have kept under her pillow during the writing of *Uncle Tom's Cabin*, listed incident after incident of the sexual degradation and physical abuse of slave women. During the 1830s and 1840s thousands of northern and western women formed antislavery societies, and their activism carried them into state and national politics, making them "subjects of intense controversy."[30] The bonding of white and black women in an abolitionist novel and the feminist implications of these fictional cross-racial relationships should not be suprising, then.

It is the relationship between Mrs. Shelby and Chloe which provides the most insight into Stowe's emphasis on the strength of female values and female bonds. Uncle Tom is the submissive Christian; his wife is the Christian warrior. He accepts inhumanity; she rejects it. Together Chloe and Mrs. Shelby become a Christian chorus of remonstration and reproof. The beginning of the book shows them brilliantly playing the womanly roles expected of them in order to save Eliza: Mrs. Shelby is the gracious southern lady making witty conversation at the dinner table to detain the slave trader Haley from taking up the chase; Chloe is the energetic mammy laboring to prepare what *must* be the quintessence of dinners for the white gentleman at that table. Theirs is a concerted effort to save another woman and her child—an effort which probably would have failed had it not *been* concerted. This is perhaps one of the few places in the novel where race becomes unimportant. An invisible, powerful, yet unspoken thread runs from kitchen to table and back; both women work desperately within their own spheres to buy Eliza time, yet their efforts blend and merge into a wonderful, peculiarly female mire of food and talk which engulfs Haley's efforts to take up the chase.

Behind this humorous account of Chloe's bad gravy and Mrs. Shelby's chatter are an intense urgency and an electrifying three-way connection between the two black women and their mistress. There are two integral dramas played out in Eliza's behalf as she frantically races against the clock in her movements across the countryside: Chloe slows time, dragging it out with methodical preparations of "watching and stirring with dogged precision"; and Mrs. Shelby's pleasant cultured voice chats and drones, compartmentalizing the moments, making them fly lightly, imperceptibly. Linked by their manipulations of the same unit of time, the three women challenge male attitudes and actions: Mrs. Shelby circumvents her husband's decision to sell Harry; Chloe rejects Tom's passivity; Eliza rebels against a white, male-controlled system that counts slave children as so many cattle. Stowe shows the strength of this three-way female bond and its humanistic challenge to a dehumanizing system as the epitome of courageous, active love, a balance for Tom's passive Christian response to Legree's evil.

These active women in *Uncle Tom's Cabin* may in fact provide a strong counterargument to the moral and critical dissatisfaction which has given the term *Uncle Tom* its pejorative sense. In depicting Eliza's escape, Stowe has pitted three women, two of them black, against the white male world—and she has allowed them to win. Nor is it any accident that it is often women—the hostess of the public house, the Quakers, Mrs. Bird—who respond to Eliza's desperation and who actively assist her. While Tom's willingness to endure cruelty and tragedy is in some sense a grand defiance, these women respond against slavery practically and actively. Like Chloe, they decry the system and they cripple it by helping others escape its clutches. It is interesting generally that Stowe chose to make so many of her female characters so active, perhaps with the exceptions of Eva and Marie St. Clare, and so many of her white and black males—Mr. Shelby, Tom, St. Clare—so passive. Only the young men, George Shelby and George Harris, seem to have much force to their personalities.

Throughout the novel, Chloe and Mrs. Shelby continue to cooperate in an actively ongoing effort to return Tom to his home. Mrs. Shelby, who has sworn to repurchase Tom, soon finds that she cannot count on her husband to make any effort to save money toward that end. Possessor of "a clear, energetic, practical mind, and a force of character every way superior to that of her husband" (p. 259), she rejoices in Chloe's proposition that the black cook hire herself out. Together they figure how long Chloe will have to work at the bakery for four dollars a week to save enough to buy Tom back and Mrs. Shelby promises to save what she can to add to Chloe's earnings. Significantly, the scene in which Chloe and her mistress make these arrangements is preceded by one in which Mrs. Shelby begs her husband to straighten out his financial matters by selling some of his horses or farms. When he refuses (we are given the distinct feeling that Mr. Shelby could have sold something besides Uncle Tom to even up his debts) and she suggests that she herself earn money by giving music lessons, he reacts with indignation: "You wouldn't degrade yourself that way, Emily? I never could consent to it" (p. 260). We are reminded of his horrified response to Eliza's escape after he has promised Harry to the slave trader: "It touches my honor!" (p. 45). Mr. Shelby's concern with his "honor" seems to supersede all moral obligations. His negative response to his wife's pleadings is thus a strong contrast to her own affirmative response to Chloe's request, which will leave the Shelby household without a cook.

Actually Mrs. Shelby and Chloe seem closer emotionally and ideologically than either woman does to her own husband. Though both are fond of their husbands—Chloe is certainly heartbroken over the sale of Tom—they refuse to share their husbands' attitudes toward slavery. Just as Mrs. Shelby cannot accept her husband's idea of slaves as convenient means of settling debts, so Chloe rejects Tom's Christian acceptance of his fate. ". . . de Lord lets drefful things happen, sometimes," she says. "I don't seem to get no comfort dat way" (p. 98). Despite Tom's protests, she places blame where it is due—directly upon Mr. Shelby. "Mas'r never ought ter left it so that ye *could* be took for his debts. . . . Them as sells heart's love and heart's blood, to get out thar scrapes, de Lord'll be up to 'em!" (p. 99). Unlike their husbands, both women hold individuals morally accountable for their actions.

The tie that binds Chloe and Mrs. Shelby is further strengthened by their joint role as a chorus of lamentation at what Stowe felt to be the central evil of slavery—the disruption of family ties. Twice Mrs. Shelby shares Chloe's grief, first when Tom is sold away and finally at the end of the book, when George comes home without Tom. Unrealistic as these scenes are, there is a sense in both of shared female outrage. Interestingly, in each scene Chloe is presented as first rejecting Mrs. Shelby's displays of mutual sorrow, and then accepting the white woman as fellow mourner. Stowe was aware, seemingly, that the black woman may resent a white woman's intrusion into her own peculiar realm of despair. When, as she is preparing Tom's belongings for his journey, Chloe receives word that "Missis" is coming, she immediately retorts, "She can't do no good; what's she coming for?" (p. 101). When Mrs. Shelby enters her cabin, Chloe sets a chair for her "in a manner decidedly gruff and crusty" (p. 101). It is only when Mrs. Shelby sits down and begins to sob that Chloe ceases to associate her mistress with Mr. Shelby's devastating decision to sell Tom, accepts her common grief, and finally weeps with her.

Likewise, when Chloe is told of her husband's death, she deals Mrs. Shelby a gesture of rejection by giving her the money she had earned for Tom's freedom: " 'Thar,' said she, gathering it up, and holding it, with a trembling hand, to her mistress, 'don't never want to see nor hear on 't again. Jist as I knew 't would be,—sold, and murdered on dem ar' old plantations!'" (p. 450). But when Mrs. Shelby responds only with sympathy and grief—"My poor, good Chloe!"—the black woman accepts her as a fellow mourner and again all weep together and lament Tom's death and the system that caused it. This mutuality of grief, though limited always by the fact that Mrs. Shelby and Chloe are stereotypes based on racial myth, is nonetheless moving. We are reminded of archetypal scenes of women throughout history weeping for their lost men and lamenting the loss of peace and harmony among men. To have black and white women join in this timeless chorus of grief extends the dimensions of the novel from the polemic to the mythic.

These dynamic female bonds also define the concept of motherhood in *Uncle Tom's Cabin*. Since what it means to be a mother is so closely tied in the novel to what it means to be a true Christian and a caring human being, the process of defining a good mother becomes a basic pattern that knits the novel together. Weaving in and out of the relationships between black and white women, the maternal impulse, or lack of it, becomes a criterion upon which to judge their humanity. Mrs. Shelby teaches Eliza how to be a good mother. Mammy mothers Eva when the child's own mother, Marie St. Clare, shows no maternal interest in her daughter. Eva mothers Topsy when Ophelia's racism precludes such nurture. The depravity of Prue's mistress is felt so intensely because she interferes with Prue's maternal impulses; she refuses to give the black woman milk to feed her starving infant. As Elizabeth Ammons points out, the cruel separations between mothers and children in *Uncle Tom's Cabin* dramatize "the root evil of slavery: the displacement of life-giving maternal values by a profit-hungry masculine ethic; . . . mothers and motherless children show the human cost of the system."[31] Stowe herself says that she wrote *Uncle Tom's Cabin* because of her own empathy with slave mothers. After the death of her infant son, she writes, "at his grave . . . I learned what a poor slave mother may feel when her child is torn away from her."[32]

The discrepancy between Marie's selfishness and indifference to maternal obligation and Mammy's loving maternal nurture is meant to be particularly acute. Marie's relationships both to her own daughter and to her black servant illuminate the white mother's egocentric corruption and illustrate Stowe's thesis that total power breeds evil. Unlike Mrs. Shelby, who is described by the author as "a fair type of the very best class of Southern women,"[33] Marie St. Clare is "the type of a class of women not peculiar to any latitude, nor any condition of society." In the North, Stowe writes, such a woman has "no end to her troubles" in retaining servants, whom she invariably overworks and underpays. But with the absolute control which slavery permits her, the southern Marie becomes an unleashed fury who can do as she wills to whom she likes and inflict "the most disgraceful and violent punishments."[34] More subtle torture she measures out upon Mammy, keeping the black woman at her beck and call every night and then complaining at Mammy's "selfishness" in sleeping so soundly. Like Prue's mistress, Marie shows her inhumanity by denying Mammy her own children. Marie is characterized as less than a whole woman, having "no heart," thoroughly selfish (p. 160). Her relationship with black women—her inhumane treatment of Mammy and later sending Rosa to be whipped—serves as an index of her total corruption, as does her marked lack of interest in her own daughter.

In contrast, Mammy's love for Eva and her nurture of the white child show the black woman's humanity and unselfishness. The scene in which Eva returns home with her father and Ophelia reveals the vast difference between Marie's and Mammy's responses to the child. Stowe draws the distinction heavy-handedly. When Eva kisses her mother, Marie's response is half-hearted: "'That'll do,—take care, child,—don't you make my head ache,' said the mother, after she had languidly kissed her" (p. 170). But as Eva kisses Mammy, Stowe writes, "this woman did not tell her that she made her head ache, but on the contrary, she hugged her, and laughed, and cried, till her sanity was a thing to be doubted of . . ." (p. 170). While Marie takes no notice of the child's declining health and strength, Mammy is acutely aware of Eva's oncoming death. More than that, Mammy, like Tom, intuitively knows Eva for who she is—a rare and mysterious good spirit whose time on earth is limited. Like Tom, who sees "the

33

Lord's mark in her forehead," Mammy knows Eva "wasn't never like a child that's to live—there was allers something deep in her eyes" (p. 281).

Marie is obviously jealous of Mammy and Eva's closeness. One of her most despicable acts is to keep the black woman away from Eva's deathbed with her own incessant demands, "so that stolen interviews and momentary glimpses" of Eva are all Mammy can obtain (pp. 298-99). The relationship between Marie and Mammy is characterized by the white woman's constraints upon the black woman's maternal feelings. Marie denies Mammy her own children and later her surrogate child. Though these denials are only one facet of Marie's egocentricity, they are telling ones. Marie is not only a bad mother herself; she forces Mammy to be one as well. Stowe shows in this relationship the institution of slavery at its worst. It is the system which permits Marie to control Mammy's maternal impulses—surely a power no woman should have over another.

Just as Marie will not fulfill her maternal obligations, Ophelia's antipathy for blacks makes her unwilling to provide much-needed nurture for Topsy. Interestingly, Eva, who is denied the same nurturance by her own mother but given it freely by Mammy, steps into that role with Topsy, who has internalized much of the racial hatred directed toward her during her short life. In a most significant way, Eva becomes the force which moves Topsy from self-hate and forces Ophelia to see the psychological destructiveness of her own racism. While Mammy provides the positive maternal force in the Marie-Mammy-Eva relationship, Eva is the sustainer of true motherhood in the Ophelia-Eva-Topsy triangle. With a childish mother herself, Eva takes on the cloak of motherhood that saves Topsy. Although the scene is overdone, Eva's "burst of feeling" and her pronouncement of love are moving in that they seem to engender in Topsy, for the first time in her life, a sense of self-worth and a realization that she was wrong in thinking "there can't nobody love niggers, and niggers can't do nothin'!" (p. 288). Though as children they are mirror images, Eva saves Topsy by mothering her. The vitality and all-encompassing nature of this motherlove give the black girl peace and wholeness. It also shows Ophelia the psychological destruction caused by racism and helps her overcome her aversion to Topsy so that she can learn to be a true mother to the child.

True motherhood is often denied the slave women of the novel. Nowhere is this denial felt more deeply than in Prue's story. Simon Legree's cruelty seems mild compared to that of Prue's mistress, who refuses to buy milk for the slave mother to feed her starving infant. When the child "cried, and cried, and cried, day and night," the white woman forces Prue to put the infant away in a garret where it starves to death, wailing continuously (p. 223). Prue's misery at the child's murder makes her wish for her own death, which—grotesque though it is—puts her at last out of imaginary earshot of her dying infant's crying. The white woman's denial of food for the child is worsened by the fact that Prue's own milk dried up as the result of a fever contracted by nursing her mistress.

In the shadowy character of this villainous mistress surely Stowe, whose own children were so important to her, was sketching the worst that could be said of slavery. When white women embrace the materialistic dehumanization of slavery, depicted as a male attitude in this novel, they seem to become so warped and twisted by absolute power that they deny the maternal bonds that link them to all women (those that Mrs. Shelby, Eliza, and Chloe feel so deeply), and become asexual monsters who destroy human lives and psyches more out of pique and carelessness than conscious cruelty. In this fiction, slavery generates such female monsters, and they are best shown through their relationships with those over whom they exert the most power, yet with whom they should feel the most common bond—black women.

Yet these relationships in *Uncle Tom's Cabin* most often show white and black women in a peculiarly female and often powerful opposition to the materialism of slavery; as such, these bonds reveal the vast gulf between humanistic values and materialistic assessments of human life. What it means to be human in the profoundest sense is often connected to what it means to be truly maternal—to nurture others, as Eva does Topsy, and so to encourage generative growth in lives other than one's own. Motherhood and Christian nurture are closely associated. In a sense, then, Marie St. Clare and Prue's mistress become in their relationships with their black women slaves more evil than Legree himself. They deny their own maternal impulses as well as those of their slaves; they are thus doubly evil. Yet they demand maternal nurture for themselves from those same women. In their relationships with black women, they become children and evil ones at that, whose behavior shows above all the sinful nature of all human beings, and the horrifying consequences of allowing that sinful nature full rein.

As is to be expected, Mary H. Eastman paints a rosier picture of human nature in general and woman's nature in particular in *Aunt Phillis's Cabin; or, Southern Life As It Is*. As a southern white woman, Eastman was the most likely respondent to put the heretical Yankee Stowe in her place. In the popular mind the southern lady was keeper of the hearth, human link between master and slave, and moral voice of the slave South. As Duvall points out, many southern white women, Chesnut among them, opposed slavery because of the opportunities it provided for miscegenation.[35] Of the seventeen novels which sought to refute the assertions of *Uncle Tom's Cabin* in the years 1852-1854, five were written by women who were born in the South. I have selected *Aunt Phillis's Cabin* from the seventeen fictional replies to Stowe for the following reasons: It is one of those written by a southern white woman and thus is interesting to compare to the work of the northern white woman, particularly since the focus of my study is upon relationships between women, fictional or real. Eastman's novel is generally agreed to have outsold all other proslavery novels of the period (about 18,000 copies in a few weeks) and thus may be assumed to have been at least among the most influential. Unlike several books of this type, the novel has most of its action on the plantation, therefore providing a fictional backdrop for cross-racial relationships between southern women. Its focus, as Jeannette Tandy points out, is unusual in that it gives particular attention to the attitude of a slave woman toward slavery, and therefore toward masters and mistresses. And finally, *Aunt Phillis's Cabin*, written in 1852, was the only immediate fictional response to *Uncle Tom's Cabin* by a southern woman.[36]

Southern white women would be expected to defend not only the South's "peculiar institution" but the place of white and black women in the social and familial order. Yet, in this best seller of all the proslavery novels, Eastman, a Virginian by birth, who traveled extensively in the West with her Army officer husband, also questions the place of woman in the family hierarchy. Her diatribe about the relationship of slavery and matrimony follows obvious approval of Phillis's ability to get the best of Bacchus, her childlike husband. Beginning with Stowe's own words, Eastman moves almost imperceptibly in this passage from a sarcastic, antiabolitionist tone to a scorching analysis of husband-wife relationships, and finally to a reevaluation of Phillis's actions in asserting her will upon Bacchus by cutting the ruffles off his shirt. In this passage Eastman thus turns Stowe's abolitionist statements about generic man into feminist diatribe about real men:

"To you, generous and noble-minded men and women of the South, I appeal, (I quote the words of a late writer on Abolitionism, when I say,) Is *man* ever a creature to be trusted with wholly irresponsible power? Can anybody fail to make the inference, what the practical result will be?"* Although she is here speaking of slavery *politically*, can you not apply it to matrimony in this miserable country of ours? Can we not remodel our husbands, place them under our thumbs, and shut up the escape valves of their grumbling forever? To be sure, St. Paul exhorts "wives to be obedient to their own husbands" and "servants to be obedient to their own masters," but St. Paul was not an Abolitionist. He did not take into consideration the necessities of the free-soil party, and woman's *rights*. This is the era of mental and bodily emancipation. Take advantage of it, wives and negroes! But, alas for the former! there is no society formed for *their* benefit; their day of deliverance has not yet dawned, and until its first gleamings arise in the *east*, they must wear their chains. Except when some strong-minded female steps forth from the degraded ranks, and asserts her position, whether by giving loose to that unruly member the tongue, or by a piece of management which will give "an old fool a lesson that will last him all the days of his life."

Uncle Tom's Cabin[37]

37

This passage is odd in that Eastman seems to begin with the intention of criticizing feminists and then ends up, in spite of herself, admiring Phillis's mastery over her husband. Although again, the interracial relationships among women in *Aunt Phillis's Cabin* are designed to show first of all how happy and contented slaves are in the South, the bonding between these women has much more in common with the feminist suggestions of *Uncle Tom's Cabin* than we might expect. In *Aunt Phillis's Cabin* the ties between slave women and their mistresses are powerful and often are formed, as in Stowe's novel, in response to some external threat. The strength of these female ties, and the humanistic values they imply, are what we remember about both books.

Eastman's narrative, polemical as it is, opens predictably with a biblical justification for slavery as a necessary evil "authorized by God, permitted by Jesus Christ" (p. 24). The story revolves around the Weston family members who live on Exeter plantation in Virginia. Mr. Weston is a "true Southern gentleman" who lives with a household of women: Mrs. Weston, his dead brother's wife; Alice, her daughter; and Cousin Janet, "a dependant [*sic*] and distant relation; a friend faithful and unfailing; a bright example of all that is holy and good in the Christian character" (p. 28). Cousin Janet assists Mrs. Weston in "the many cares that devolved on the mistress of a plantation, especially in instructing the young female servants in knitting and sewing, and in such household duties as would make them useful in that state of life in which it had pleased God to place them" (p. 28).

Such as it is, the plot is episodic. Eastman presents a series of *exempla* to show just how carefree slave life is for "the servants," and how devoted they are to their white folks. Much of the action comes second-hand from tales told on the front porch of the Exeter Big House. The action, real and related, skips erratically from Big House to slave quarters and even includes incidents that happen up North. The love interest in the novel involves a triangle of Alice, the Byronic Walter, who is not suitable marriage material, and the plodding Arthur, who is. Though Alice loves Walter, she comes to her senses and marries the rather stuffy Arthur. Her mother instructs her on the responsibilities of the plantation mistress, the role she will assume as Arthur's wife, and she declares herself ready to take up the twin mantles of responsibility and hard work to fulfill her destiny in that role. Phillis has a short life. She does not appear until the midpoint of the book, and she dies before the end—but not before she asks Mr. Weston's forgiveness for sometimes wishing she weren't a slave (he does forgive her) and rejects his half-hearted offer to free her children (they both agree that the children are better off as they are).

In such a context it is surprising to find anything remotely resembling a feminist subtext. And surely much of what is there would surprise Eastman as much as it does us. Still, the author does not appear to have been a typical nineteenth-century woman or to have had a typical nineteenth-century marriage. Though a native Virginian, Eastman had traveled widely with her husband Seth, an artist as well as an Army officer. The two apparently worked closely together, she writing books—some about Indian tribes and their customs—and he illustrating them. Together they produced several successful works and apparently had a close professional relationship. The streak of feminism that threads its way through the undersurface of the novel may not be completely anomalous to Eastman's experiences.

Loving bonds formed between white and black women in *Aunt Phillis's Cabin* create female community and female power. In much proslavery fiction, the mistress becomes "elevated and spiritualized."[38] What is surprising in this novel is that the black woman is elevated as well, and that cross-racial female bonding often develops in response to male evil or male silliness. Bacchus is stereotypically a rather stupid, silly, and weak-willed black—in contrast to his wife, who is intelligent and imposing, "a tall, dignified, bright mulatto woman" (p. 102). Phillis's mental stature is also stereotypical; Eastman makes it clear that Bacchus's wife is smarter than Bacchus because the "blood of freeman and slave" mix in her veins but not in his, yet this distinction between her character and his comes after at least three other men, all white, are shown to be either silly or evil creatures in their dealings with the women— white and black—associated with them. In these incidents, which appear early in the novel, white women and their female slaves develop close personal relationships that exclude men or react against them.

The story of Ellen Haywood and her faithful slave Lucy, related by Cousin Janet, involves such a triangle. Ellen's Mr. Lee, divorced from his first wife and therefore unmarriageable in polite society, secretly marries, impregnates, and deserts the eighteen-year-old Ellen. With only Lucy and Janet to assist her, Ellen dies in childbirth, a fallen woman. It is Lucy, not the phantomlike Mr. Lee, who begs the dying woman to live; and it is Lucy, recalls Janet, who "wept unceasingly by Ellen's side, and it was impossible to arouse her to a care for her own health, or to an interest in what was passing around" (p. 40). It is also Lucy to whom Ellen entrusts the task of placing her hidden wedding band upon her finger after her death. The closeness and trust between the older black slave and the young white woman become a reproach to the illusive Mr. Lee.

Likewise, as Lucy's miserable history unfolds in Cousin Janet's account, Ellen's father, Mr. Haywood, is seen as an even worse villain—also against a backdrop of a close interracial women's relationship. It is interesting too that Lucy's story about Haywood's cruelty is first related to Cousin Janet, who in turn is telling it to other white women. The result is a layering of points of view from black woman to white woman, a kind of artistic integration of two racial consciousnesses into one female perception of the evil perpetrated by a white southern male upon a black woman slave and her children (one of whom was probably his). As Janet relates it, Lucy's story is that Mr. Haywood, a drunkard and poor money manager, sells her seven children after sending her to accompany her mistress, Ellen's mother, to the country. The white woman's reaction is a sharp reproach to her husband's actions. Mrs. Haywood, Lucy recalls, "cried day and night, and called him cruel, and she would say, 'Lucy, I'd have died before I would have done it.' I couldn't murder him . . . 'twas my mistress held me back" (p. 43). Although this incident is obviously related so that the Westons can click their tongues at Mr. Haywood's action and explain to the reader that such things seldom occur in the South, it is nonetheless interesting that, like the Mrs. Shelby-Chloe relationship in *Uncle Tom's Cabin*, these incidents set the humanistic combination of white and black women against the callousness of white men.

Even in the far-fetched *exemplum* in which the unfaithful slave Susan deserts her mistress, indirectly causing the death of the white woman's baby, and becoming the mistreated victim of avaricious abolitionists, it is the mistress, Mrs. Casey, who is willing to take the slave woman back. Mr. Casey refuses to forgive Susan and will not allow her to return from her unhappy state as a free woman in the North to the joys of slavery in the South. Yet Mrs. Casey, in her compassion, sends Susan ten dollars to help her along in her new and frightening life. The slave woman, who abused her maternal role by abandoning her charge, is thus forgiven and nurtured by the mother of the child she deserted.

More realistic is the bond between Mrs. Moore, a transplanted southerner (probably an autobiographical figure), and her servant Polly, a freed slave who has stayed with her mistress out of loyalty. They have pitted themselves in a humorous household battle with Mrs. Moore's teetotaling husband, an Army captain, who has demanded that she keep spirits out of the house and consequently out of the cooking. Polly solves the problem by taking charge of the liquor and placing the bottles in her "old chist" on the practical assumption that out of sight is out of mind. Even though the relationship of Mrs. Moore and Polly is not set up in moral opposition to Captain Moore, they do outsmart him. The message behind the story is that men are silly, unreasonable creatures who must be fooled every now and then. As Polly puts it, "men's mighty onreasonable, the best of 'em, but when a woman is married she ought to do all she can for the sake of peace" (p. 55). Furthermore, women have their own spheres of influence which should not be invaded by men: "I dont see what a man has got to do interferin with the cookin, no how; a woman oughter 'tend to these matters" (pp. 55-56). In this case the combination of white and black women repels the captain's intrusion into that one sphere where the nineteenth-century woman reigned—the kitchen.

As a black woman, Phillis herself is Eastman's lofty example of all the good that comes of slavery. Physiologically Phillis is more white than black (she is even described as flushing), and she identifies more with whites than she does with blacks. She is the mother of twelve children, all but one of whom (his father's namesake) have inherited her energy and liking for white company and instruction. Phillis doesn't like "ordinary servants." She has a lovely house with a parlor superior to her owners' drawing room. She wet-nurses white children. She forgets her own children when Alice Weston falls ill. She is what Langston Hughes would call a "white folks' nigger."

Yet, stereotypical and one-sided though Phillis is, the bonds of mutual nurture that she forms with the white women characters suggest Eastman's belief in a common ground between women of both races and a peculiarly female strength to be generated from such bonds. This novel is full of death; and the bonds between Phillis and her mistresses Alice, Cousin Janet, and Mrs. Weston are strengthened in the face of death. During Alice's serious illness, the sheer force of Phillis's will linked to that of Cousin Janet and Mrs. Weston seems to snatch the young woman from the brink of the grave. Keeping their watch around Alice's sickbed, the three women nurse her untiringly through the crisis of her illness. This is perhaps the most memorable scene in the book. All through the night the three women kindle and rekindle the dying spark. Together they defeat death, and in so doing become archetypal maternal figures whose common nurture sustains Alice and returns her to life.

Other black women in the novel initiate white girls into the knowledge of death or comfort young white women in their grief. The narrator of the story recalls an incident in her girlhood in which two children of her acquaintance died and an old slave woman showed her their graves, "two little mounds, covered over with the dark-green myrtle and its purple flowers" (p. 100). She recalls this incident in connection with the death of her own child, and the realization that those little mounds hide "silence and pallor, desolation and destruction" (p. 101). After the drowning death of her brother William, Ellen Graham has no one to turn to but the black woman who reared brother and sister: "Ah! Ellen was an orphan now—father, mother, and friend had he been to her, the lost one. Often did she lay her head on the kind breast of their nurse, and pray for death" (p. 185).

Despite the obvious artificiality and sentimentality of scenes like this one, the oppositions in *Aunt Phillis's Cabin* pit black women and their white mistresses against men and against death. In the sexual battle, women are the voices of morality and practicality that make white men such as Mr. Lee, Mr. Haywood, and Mr. Casey appear callous or, in the case of Captain Moore, downright silly. Although white southern men are upholders of "the peculiar institution" which Eastman is supposed to be defending, her creation of these sexual oppositions is not counterproductive to her proslavery argument. In these female bonds she shows simply the closeness of slave woman to mistress and the mutuality of regard in that relationship. Yet, though the antiabolitionist message of the book is everywhere apparent, Eastman may have been more like Stowe than she consciously knew.

Though the novels are polemic opposites, ironically they contain an almost identical subtext: the power of cross-racial female bonds in opposition to the male sphere. Whether black and white women are hiding liquor from men or making the slave hunter wait for his dinner, they challenge the patriarchy and suggest an active, energetic contrast to black male acceptance of it. It is an even greater irony that these fictional women and their relationships can be put to such diverse polemic purposes. These female bonds reflect, either directly or by implication, the institution of slavery as familial and antifamilial, kind and cruel, moral and immoral. Yet this second irony is a comment also upon the nature of these two novels. Both sentimentalize and simplify the real world of human bondage and its snares of sexual jealousy, fury, and distrust that engulfed and entrapped southern women black and white. "The swirl of this stream—history, nightmare, accountability" was surely a "current angrier and more multiform than the surface shows,"[39] or than Stowe or Eastman would have us see.

CHAPTER II

Through the Autobiographical Glass Dimly

MISTRESS AND SLAVE WOMAN
AS OBVERSE IMAGES

It is part of the irony of slavery that historians studying
the institution for almost a century have failed to provide
all the answers; indeed, perhaps they have not yet asked
all the right questions.

> HARRY P. OWENS
> *Perspectives and Irony in*
> *American Slavery*

The genre of autobiography lives in the two worlds of
history and literature, objective fact and subjective
awareness. It is a dialectic between what you wish to
become and what society has determined you are.

> STEPHEN BUTTERFIELD
> *Black Autobiography in America*

. . . if autobiography is the least complicated of writing
performances, it is also the most elusive of literary documents.

> JAMES OLNEY
> *Autobiography: Essays*
> *Theoretical and Critical*

It is not the smallest irony of slavery that the nineteenth-
century southern *mythos* demanded moral superiority from
white women and sexual availability from black, and yet

simultaneously expected mistress and slave woman to live and work in intimate physical proximity. As obverse images in the popular mind, the chaste belle and the lustful female slave evolved into rigid stereotypes emerging out of the institution of slavery and its chivalric codes of conduct. As actual individuals of flesh and blood, black and white women often shared kitchen, boudoir, and Big House. Plantation mistress or slave, southern womanhood served the patriarchal master. Although many male slaveholders eschewed philanderings in the quarters for reasons of morality, religion, or husbandly devotion, perceptive historians of the southern experience have observed volatile psychological and sociological connections between the white man's sexual exploitation of the slave woman and the evolution of the lady's pedestal.[1] As Katherine Fishburn suggests, neither the southern lady nor the woman slave had a right to her own body: "whereas the lady was deprived of her sexuality, the black woman was identified with hers." White women were characterized by their "delicate constitutions, sexual purity, and moral superiority to men" while southern mythology cast black women into roles of "subhuman creatures who, by nature, were strong and sexual."[2]

Yet one of the most obvious but seldom asked questions about slavery and the southern racial experience—and certainly one of the least satisfactorily answered—concerns the explosive psychological realities of the relationships between black and white southern women of the mid-nineteenth century.[3] Placed as they were in an opposing but a similarly confining mythology, how did black and white women relate to one another? How much did their assigned roles in a culture based upon racial and sexual inequality affect their relationships with one another? How humanely or inhumanely did the white woman use her power? How did the slave woman vent her anger at her own powerlessness? These are questions which can never be answered fully, but they are important to raise. For in them lies compelling insight into both the southern racial experience and modern relationships between white and black women in literature and in life. The deeply ambivalent responses of these women to the institution of slavery and to one another may in fact constitute a paradigm for clarifying the enigma of southern history and the lingering impingements of its "peculiar institution" upon our cultural and literary consciousness.

Although truth about history is as hard to find in autobiography as it is anywhere else, autobiographical writings of mistress and slave obviously are potential sources of answers to these questions. "The decisive achievement of the art of autobiography," as Roy Pascal points out, is to give us an intuitive knowledge of "the feel of life, the feel of living" as well as an account of "events that are symbolic of the personality as an entity unfolding . . . in response to the world it lives in."[4] If Harriet Beecher Stowe's Mrs. Shelby and Mary Eastman's Aunt Phillis seem one-dimensional as fictional representations of southern myth, the female slave narratives and the white women's diaries and reminiscences of the period suggest another avenue of approach to flesh-and-blood women of both races who lived day by day with opposing but viscerally connected societal expectations which often relegated them to a mutually dehumanizing status.

These women remake in language their own selves and their own realities of the Old South. In their retrospective renderings or spur-of-the-moment jottings, they, like other literary artists, create new realities that mirror their own needs and imaginations and reflect what they perceive to be true about the Old South and their cross-racial female relationships as part of the fabric of their culture. As they write, they shape themselves as women in a male-controlled world built upon the paradoxical twin premises of racial separation and racial connection. Their literary attempts to confront that real world and the women of the other race within its bounds transform life as it was into what Willa Cather would later call life as "felt experience." It is the exegesis of this felt experience which is the critical challenge of autobiography.

In a significant sense, women's writings about other women are expositions of the female self—the writers' as much as the objects of their writing. The freed woman who writes about her cruel former mistress often tells us more about her own need to define and assert herself than about the object of her vilification. Likewise, the white woman who decries what she perceives as the uncontrolled sexuality of female slaves may be revealing resentment at her own sexual restrictions rather than making an accurate observation about the demeanor of black women. The cross-racial female relationships in these autobiographies thus become prisms that refract and ultimately transform traditional concepts of the southern experience. What the writer, black or white, says about these volatile connections with women of the other race extends our sense of southern female consciousness as multifaceted, complex, biracial, and profoundly interconnected.

Psychologically or physically manipulated into the roles expected of them, mid-nineteenth-century southern black and white women might be expected to view one another with deeply felt ambivalence. Within the patriarchal system, they were thrust into diametrically opposed but mutually dependent roles. Without the labor of the slave woman, the plantation mistress would have found it impossible to maintain what little ease she had in antebellum life, as she so painfully discovered during the Civil War and Reconstruction years. Although Anne Firor Scott and others have shown that the culturally defined image of the white southern woman was actually in conflict with her many arduous tasks,[5] still the female slave saved the mistress from difficult and unpleasant duties, moan as she would in concert with Marie St. Clare that she was the hardest-working slave on the plantation. Immured in nineteenth-century prudery and concepts of woman as a virtuous innocent, the southern lady may have felt a certain amount of relief at *not* having to be a sexual creature, at avoiding that real passion which conflicted so deeply with the Victorian ideals of a chivalric South. From a practical point of view, she may have also feared the dangers of childbirth. As W.J. Cash points out, she was

> the South's Palladium, this Southern woman—the shield-bearing Athena gleaming whitely in the clouds, the standard for its rallying, the mystic symbol of its nationality in face of the foe. She was the lily-pure maid of Astolat and the hunting goddess of the Boeotian hill. And—she was the pitiful Mother of God. Merely to mention her was to send strong men into tears—or shouts. There was hardly a sermon that did not begin and end

48

with tributes in her honor, hardly a brave speech that did not open and close with the clashing of shields and the flourishing of swords for her glory. At the last, I verily believe, the ranks of the Confederacy went rolling into battle in the misty conviction that it was wholly for her that they fought.[6]

Such "downright gynecolatry," as Cash terms it, seems to have left scant room for sexuality in the psyche of the southern white woman, who became as Cash points out, the region's "focal center" of "proto-Dorian pride."[7] Scott asserts that this image was at odds with the reality of the working lives of white women in the antebellum South,[8] yet it was also an image in direct opposition to any realistic assumptions of female sexuality, and one which many southern women may have felt compelled to uphold.

The opposite side of the coin, of course, was the beleaguered slave woman who, often considered more "savage" than civilized, was expected to be lustful and willing. Scott's statement that black women were "not much affected by role expectations" is somewhat misleading, at least to the extent that the slave woman was expected to become the obverse of the chaste southern lady and to fill in obvious gaps created by the rigidity of that image.[9] In the popular mind, Missy was frail and delicate, while the stereotypical Mammy was strong and dependable. If Missy entered that glorious and hallowed realm of motherhood, Mammy was a breeder. Where Missy was approached reverently and seldom by her husband, Mammy was often the victim of what Angela Davis calls "an institutionalized pattern of rape."[10] These polarities in the concepts of women surely affected black women, chattels with few choices, more strongly than they did white women, who were comparatively free. How then did the white southern woman view her black sister? Surely not as a sister, but perhaps as the darker side of a repressed self, her own id; or as Carl Jung might have seen it, the dark side of the Great Mother, who threatens even as she beckons.[11]

In their blindness to the harsh realities of chattel slavery, many white women felt that female slaves were "freer" than they themselves, bound by strict social mores, ever would be. In cases of miscegenation, a white wife might be expected to react with terrible vengeance and intense sexual jealousy toward a coerced slave woman, seeing in her, perhaps, something of a female sexuality which she herself had been denied. In the mistress-slave relationship the white woman exerted ultimate power and that power, as evidenced in the slave narratives, could transform sexual jealousy into perverse cruelty. The abolitionists' belief, voiced by Stowe and others, that complete power corrupts is perhaps nowhere more true than in the relationship between these southern women, whose common bonds of suffering and dehumanization might have bound them in mutual compassion. Steven Butterfield points out that black autobiography is often "a mirror of white deeds";[12] and it is in the slave narratives, not the white women's journals and reminiscences, that the jealous mistress is portrayed in all her perversity and furious cruelty. Yet the white women's writings also reveal under the surface an intense jealousy, often masked by expressions of disgust and vituperation, of the sexual "freedom" of black women.

Likewise the black women write of their resentment against their mistresses, but not as scathingly as one would think. As Frances Foster points out, writers of the slave narratives, both men and women, were writing to a white audience.[13] In the antebellum and war periods, the slave narratives were designed first of all to convince a white northern audience that slavery was wrong—not just for the slave but for everyone. Wronged mistresses were often depicted as cruel and vindictive, but they were also construed as victims themselves of an institution which allowed sexual degradation of the black women and forced an acceptance of the double standard for white women. As Harriet Jacobs writes of her perversely vindictive mistress, Mrs. Flint, ". . . I, whom she detested so bitterly, had far more pity for her than [her husband] had, whose duty it was to make her life happy."[14] When the subject matter of the narratives changed during and after Reconstruction, deemphasizing the horrors of slavery and concentrating on the contributions of blacks,[15] freed women such as Kate Drumgoold in 1898 and Annie Burton in 1909 wrote of their mistresses with affection, emphasizing a sense of female nurturance in the mistress–slave relationship.

The autobiographical writings of these women reflect their relationships to one another in ways limited by the diverse purposes of the writings, by the contingencies of their genres and, particularly in the case of the white women, by a vision limited by time and wishful thinking. Yet there is no doubt that there was a powerful connection between black and white southern women, a connection built upon a shared sense of societal demands that placed them in opposite but deeply interdependent roles. In terms of a wholeness of female identity, each had only half. Their struggles, often subconscious, to obtain the missing piece of self as it is displayed in the Other make their lives and their writings about their relationships studies in the female struggle to attain wholeness and the terrible price to be paid in that struggle.

Though it has been said that the slave narratives provide an avenue for assertion of self-definition and realization, the female narrators of these tales often express a deeply felt yearning for the "white" respectability of their mistresses. And likewise the diaries and reminiscences of white women—in all their fairy-tale romance and yearning for a lost Camelot of the Old South—reveal under placid surfaces the need for a whole sexuality embodied in part by the stereotypical sexuality of their black sisters. It is profoundly ironic that in both situations the woman's part so fervently desired by one race has been so painful for the other. W.E.B. DuBois's statement about the black psyche surely applies to both races of southern women: "It is a peculiar sensation, this double-consciousness, this sense of always looking at one's self through the eyes of others, of measuring one's soul by the tape of a world that looks on in amused contempt and pity. One ever feels [a] two-ness."[16]

It is this sense of "two-ness," coupled with the complete power of the white woman over the black, which imbues the writings of these women with a tension, a straining *toward* the Other, and an underlying violence born of repression, frustration, and fear. Faulkner would later encapsulate this tension in the confrontation between Rosa and Clytie on the stairs of Sutpen's Hundred. In these women's writings we receive only hints of it, often obscured by the trivial or the nostalgic. Yet racial tension is undeniably a part of these autobiographies, and it becomes particularly significant in the issue of control. In the Old South both black and white women were often denied self-determination. Yet, while white women were on the whole unable to exert control over their own lives, they were given the power to control the lives of their female slaves. The slave narratives often reveal the cruelty to which that total control of another coupled with a lack of self-determination could lead, as well as the battle of the black female self to reject white woman's dominance.

White women, on the other hand, tell of their dilemma: the societal directive to control the black female house slaves in their purview and their difficulty in accomplishing this task because of their conflicting emotions toward these women as racial antipathy collided with stirrings of sympathy for those of their own sex. In all but a few cases, the issue that emerges in these autobiographies is that of the black woman's need for human recognition and the white woman's inability or un-willingness to acknowledge either the need or the person behind it. This refusal to recognize the humanity of others is, at once, the flaw of the Old South and the mystery of racism. In this sense these autobiographical writings and the American fiction which evolved out of the slavery experience allow us double insight into the deeply puzzling enigmas of both south-ern history and human racial experience.

However these women perceive their cross-racial relation-ships, their autobiographies betray, above all, the powerful intensity of their feelings for one another. Yet there are im-mense difficulties in extracting these feelings from both black and white female writings of the period and in assessing the differences between what is written and what lies under the surface. As Roy Pascal suggests, the truth of autobiography begins with its purpose,[17] but those purposes vary exceed-ingly in these writings, which range in publication from 1851 to the early twentieth century. The facts that generally the autobiographers have unconscious as well as conscious motives in writing and that women are often powered by a double need, as Estelle Jelinek suggests, "to sift through their lives for explanation and understanding" and "to convince readers of self-worth, to clarify, to affirm, and to authenticate their self-image,"[18] cloud the issues further. Also, it may be expected that female autobiography often echoes societal expectations instead of revealing true identity and that autobiographies written by blacks and whites would be viscerally dissimilar in form, content, and purpose. Any perceptive assessment of *what* slave and free women have to say about their relationships must take into account, then, the impact of race, chronology, and textual problems upon content as well as the requirements of genre.

Both races of women whose writings are considered here recount the events of their lives in the South from about 1830 through about 1875–80. The white women write mainly about the Civil War period. Black and white women differed enormously in their experiences, levels of education, and perceptions of southern society, yet at the bottom of this divergence was the equation between blackness and innate inferiority and the systematic dehumanization of slaves, male and female, in all areas of life, theoretical and practical.

As a genre, the slave narrative became a means of asserting black humanity and identity in the face of that systematic dehumanization. The narratives were, as Foster puts it, "retrospective endeavors which helped the narrators define, even create, their own identities."[19] This should be particularly true for the black woman writer, yet out of thousands of slave narratives, written and orally transmitted by blacks,[20] we know of fewer than thirty women's slave narratives which were published as books during the authors' or subjects' lifetimes.[21]

These women's slave narratives published both before and after the Civil War may be divided into three basic categories: oral accounts which were transcribed or completely altered by amanuenses, fictionalized accounts which were often presented as fact, and autobiographical narratives actually written by literate freedwomen.[22] Narratives which were transcribed or completely written by a second party include *Aunt Sally; or, The Cross the Way to Freedom*, 1859; *The Story of Dinah, as Related to John Hawkins Simpson*, 1863; *Silvia Dubois (Now 116*

Yers Old.) A Biografy of the Slav who Whipt her Mistres and Gand her Fredom, 1883; *The Octoroon: A Tale of Southern Life*, 1861; *Narrative of Sojourner Truth*, 1853; *Scenes in the Life of Harriet Tubman*, 1869; and *The Narrative of Bethany Veney, a Slave Woman*, 1890. Mattie Griffith's *Autobiography of a Female Slave*, 1857, and Emily Pierson's *Jamie Parker*, 1851, which is about a man rather than a woman, are fictional accounts; and scholars have questioned the authenticity of *Aunt Sally* as well. Besides being written by someone other than slave women themselves, several of these narratives, such as those of Jarena Lee, Julia Foote, Ziltha Elaw, Nancy Prince, and Sojourner Truth, as well as Elleanor Eldridge's *Memoirs*, 1843, and Harriet Wilson's *Our Nig*, 1859, are autobiographical, biographical, or fictional accounts of the lives of free black women of the North.

The parameters of this study do not extend to these first two categories of writings by or about black women of the eighteenth and nineteenth centuries, or to autobiographies actually written by northern black women. Yet it should be pointed out that cross-racial female relationships are often significant parts of these narratives. In North Carolina, Aunt Sally's mistress, Mrs. Cone, frequently under the influence of alcohol, uses her whip upon Sally and then cannot understand why the slave woman is overjoyed to have her freedom purchased.[23] The Virginian slave Dinah, called "Di," whose bloody story of torture and rape is told by John Hawkins Simpson, has two mistresses, the wife and daughter of a planter whom Simpson calls Henry Hope, who is both Di's father and the father of several of her children. Mrs. Hope is ineffectual at preventing her husband's many physical cruelties to Di and ignores Di's reports of Hope's repeated sexual assaults. Yet Hope's white daughter Annie is more active in her half-sister's behalf and defends her with a pistol from being taken by the slavetraders to whom she is sold.[24] In New Jersey, Silvia Dubois endures cruelty from her "Missy" until she can stand no more from "the old devil." She is reported to have knocked her mistress down and "blamd ner kild her."[25] Young Harriet Tubman's mistress whips her for improper dusting and even beats the slave girl when she falls asleep at night.[26] The unnamed amanuensis who transcribes Bethany Veney's life story relates that Veney's Virginia mistress, "Miss Lucy," was sympathetic but ineffectual in preventing her husband from beating the slave woman. Finally, since Veney belonged to her mistress, "Miss Lucy" sells her in a last effort to make her life more bearable.[27]

Connections between black and white women are shown as both positive and negative forces in books by northern black women. In Harriet Wilson's autobiographical novel, the life of the heroine Frado, an indentured servant, is a terrible and constant battle against the cruel tortures of her mistress and her mistress's equally evil daughter. Mrs. Bellmont uses a rawhide whip on the girl and places wooden plates in her mouth to prevent her from screaming. Mary, the white daughter, actually tries to stab Frado. This severe treatment by white women becomes the focal point of the novel as Wilson recreates in horrific detail the events which her editor believes to be from her own life. Few such tensions or cruelties occur in the experiences of Ziltha Elaw, Jarena Lee, or Julia Foote. Elaw, whose early expressiveness and visions (she sees Christ while she is milking a cow) seem to have surprised her Quaker mistress, complains that her mistress charged her "with sullenness and mopishness" and that she often missed her dead mother. Yet she also relates that her mistress comforted her when her nightmares of hell made her cry out in the night, and years later she seems to have generally positive feelings toward her mistress. Several times Lee makes the point that her religion dissolved racial barriers, and Foote's childhood troubles with a stern mistress are resolved. "I visited both colored and white," Lee writes, "and many were concerned about sanctification." Lee even recalls counseling a white woman with a strong calling to preach yet whose Deist husband and whose own church were opposed to her religious activities.[28]

Although scholars have raised questions about the extent of editorial involvement in many of these volumes, at least six are thought to be the actual writings of literate black women of the South and border states and therefore may be approached as sustained literary endeavors, each a deliberate personal rendering of a southern female slave experience. In these extended written accounts of slave life, literate freedwomen remake historical reality and through their conscious artistry in writing about themselves as slaves create themselves anew as freed selves. This conscious re-creation of the past and, through that re-creation, the creation of wholeness and selfhood occur as sustained literary acts in the written narratives in a way that they do not in the oral accounts.[29] All of these six books were written by women who had escaped or been manumitted.

Therein lies one reason for their scarcity. Only those who went North, whether as fugitives or freedwomen, could find resources to produce such books. With such notable exceptions as Harriet Tubman, Harriet Jacobs, and Ellen Craft, most slave women were so tied to their children that they found the harrowing journey North impossible. Though theories that slaves lived essentially in a matriarchal society have been disproven in recent years,[30] the black mother did have enormous responsibility for child care, simply because her children were owned by her master and were usually kept with her in their early years. From the 1830s through the war years, the antislavery press and the northern public turned avidly to the adventurous slave narratives as testimonials of the evils of slavery and simply as exciting, sensational, even titillating reading. When black women did write or tell of their experiences, they were meant to be and often were particularly vivid testimonials of sexual exploitation and disruption of family ties, the two greatest evils of slavery in the American Victorian mind. These emphases in the women's narratives set them apart, not because they gave more accounts of sexual coercion and family disruption than the men's narratives did, but because they rendered these accounts from the female viewpoint of the rape victim, the bereft mother, the grieving wife.

This point of view was not without conflicts and problems. Although, as Marion Starling suggests, "the helplessness of the slave woman depicted in the slave narrative might serve as a galvanizing agent, spurring lukewarm sympathies into active antislavery ferment,"[31] the black woman wrote in a tradition of sentimental literature to which her experiences and life situations were anomalous. In a number of ways the slave narrative does represent, as Sidonie Smith suggests, "a spiritual transcendence over the brutalizing experience of slavery."[32] Often, however, the black woman found herself in the difficult position of attempting to explain to Victorian audiences how and why she felt it necessary to succumb to the repeated sexual blandishments of white men rather than, in the tradition of the sentimental heroine, remaining chaste though refusal might mean severe abuse, rape, death, or a combination thereof.

Foster shows that the period from 1831 to 1865, which saw the height of popularity and literary achievement of the slave narrative, was characterized by sentimental literature that "emphasized the cultivation of sensibility, the glorification of virtue, the preservation of family life, the revival of religion, and the achievement of a utopian society."[33] The ideals of sensibility and virtue were incompatible with the slave woman's experience. The black woman was indeed measured by the standards of the nineteenth-century cult of True Womanhood, as Erlene Stetson suggests,[34] but her situation of enslavement prevented her from being able to live up to the Victorian ideal of chastity. Many of her comments about sex in the narratives seem attempts to explain why her experiences did not lend themselves to Victorian behavior and how, as Bell Hooks puts it, "passive submission" to the white man's sexual demands should not be viewed as complicity.[35]

If the black woman had any choices at all, often they were merely the lesser of evils. At fifteen Harriet Jacobs became the mistress of a white man quite simply to escape the clutches of her lecherous master. Nonetheless, in writing her *Incidents in the Life of a Slave Girl,* she remains apologetic about the affair and attempts to defend her decision to give up her chastity: "But, O, ye happy women, whose purity has been sheltered from childhood, who have been free to choose the objects of your affection, whose homes are protected by law, do not judge the poor desolate slave girl too severely!" (p. 54). After explaining the hardships of slave girls that made them "prematurely knowing, concerning the evil ways of the world," Jacobs acknowledges that her decision to submit was motivated by the fact that "it seems less degrading to give one's self, than to submit to compulsion. There is something akin to freedom in having a lover who has no control over you, except that which he gains by kindness and attachment" (pp. 54–55). The black woman might be expected to view the southern white female as someone who had choices she did not have and as the embodiment of a respectability made possible by that freedom of choice.

Writing within this tradition of the sentimental novel, the black woman also adhered to the demands of the period and the genre in which she told her story. A detailed analysis of the slave narrative would not be to the point,[36] yet depictions of cross-racial female relationships were surely colored by the distinctive structures and purposes of the genre which changed drastically from the abolitionist impulse to the inspirational tracts for continued black progress in the late nineteenth and early twentieth centuries.[37] Jacobs's portrait of the horrific Mrs. Flint, who exudes evil from every pore, is obviously tied to the intense antislavery sentiment of the 1850s, just as Drumgoold's love of her "white mother" in *A Slave Girl's Story* of 1898 stresses Christian endurance and cross-racial female nurture.

In all types of slave narrative the primary purpose was, as Charles Nichols points out, quite simply to show what it feels to be a slave.[38] Such autobiographical writings tend to lend themselves to an episodic structure and a focus on external details. A peculiar tension arises out of the conflict between purpose of the narrative and psychological motivation of the narrator, who may write out of a need to assert an individual identity, to exert her own ordering power over the chaos which has been her life. Yet in this process of self-definition she must also accept the demands of the genre that she become the Everywoman of the slave experience. This tension between communal and individual self is apparent in all slave narratives.[39] It is perhaps most acute in the autobiography of the former slave woman, who was subjected to all the labor and punishments of the male slaves but was in addition sometimes subjected to denial of autonomy in sexual matters. Jacobs's gesture of taking a white lover is, in this sense, a grand show of choice, as she herself emphasizes. In a literary remaking of her life as a slave, the black woman sees herself dually as an individual with a burgeoning sense of self and as a symbol of former powerlessness. Both as black self and as black symbol, she ponders the relationship with the white female Other and either accepts or rejects the ideal of mutual female nurturance. In situations in which a mistress seems to have been particularly cruel and controlling, the black woman's narrative of her slave experience becomes an avenue toward rejection of white female dominance and an assertion of self-determination in response to the slave past.

Contiguous also to the study of women's autobiographies about the slavery experience is the issue of authenticity and the meaning of the term *autobiography*. Roy Pascal separates autobiography from memoirs, diaries, and reminiscences by its emphasis on self-examination.[40] By this definition few if any of the women's slave narratives may be considered true autobiography. The issue is clouded further by the fact that, as Starling notes, the autobiographer sometimes needed editorial assistance[41] and the extent of that assistance is often a matter of conjecture. One can only accept, as does Nichols,[42] Lydia Maria Child's assertion that her editorial changes of Jacobs's manuscript were made "mainly for purposes of condensation and orderly arrangement," and that, "with trifling exceptions, both the ideas and the language are her own."[43] But it has been speculated that abolitionist editors such as Child and the unnamed editor of *Aunt Sally* may have had essential shaping influences upon the narratives. In both early and later years of the narratives, evangelical northern ministers like G. W. Offley molded women's accounts of slave life as *exempla* of Christian endurance and triumph over great suffering.[44]

Despite the many textual questions concerning the autobiographies of black southern women published directly before, during, and well after the Civil War, four book-length reminiscences are purported to have been written by literate freed women of the South and relate in first-person accounts these former slaves' experiences with white women in a southern setting. These autobiographies, which draw sharply focused portraits of southern white women and render articulate moral and emotional assessments of those women, are Jacobs's *Incidents* (1861), Elizabeth Keckley's *Behind the Scenes;*

or, Thirty Years a Slave, and Four Years in the White House (1868), Kate Drumgoold's *A Slave Girl's Story* (1898), and Annie Burton's *Memories of Childhood's Slavery Days* (1909). Another book-length narrative written by a literate southern black woman of the period, *Reminiscences of My Life in Camp with the 33rd United States Colored Troops* by Susie King Taylor, does not discuss cross-racial female relationships. The first two narratives were prepared with editorial assistance. Child edited *Incidents* and James Redpath is believed to have helped Keckley prepare her book. As mentioned, Child writes that her impact was minimal. There is no such statement by Redpath.[45] We may reasonably assume that these are renderings of the experiences of literate black women who remake their own pasts and affirm their own identities by the self-assertive act of putting pen to paper.

The thirty-plus years between these two pairs of narratives, perhaps the most difficult in American history, decisively divide the Jacobs-Keckley autobiographies from those of Drumgoold and Burton, as does a vast difference in the women's ages. Jacobs and Keckley were born in 1818, almost two generations before Burton and Drumgoold, who were young children when the Civil War began. With the South under siege during the years of their enslavement which they can recall, the latter two had a much easier time of it. Most of the southern men were home only periodically, and discipline in the slave quarters was often lax. In Burton's first chapter, entitled "Recollections of a Happy Life," she calls to life "the memory of my happy, care-free childhood days on the plantation, with my little white and black companions. . . . Neither master nor mistress nor neighbors had time to bestow a thought upon us, for the great Civil War was raging."[46] Expectations and purposes of the slave narratives of the sixties were also quite different from those of the nineties and after. Jacobs's narrative was closely tied to the abolitionist movement through the involvement of Child, who edited the *National Anti-Slavery Standard,* a weekly published in New York, and who wrote *Appeal in Favor of that Class of Americans called Africans* which won many to the antislavery cause.[47] Although Keckley's *Behind the Scenes* was published after the war and written mainly to relate her association with the Lincolns, the early chapters about her lurid experiences as a slave woman show the influence of antebellum antislavery writings such as Theodore Weld's *American Slavery As It Is* and the essays, travel books, and journals of Fanny Kemble, the Grimké sisters, and Harriet Martineau. On the whole, the writings of both Burton and Drumgoold fall instead into sentimental depictions of plantation life which reached their heights in the nineties in the works of Thomas Nelson Page. Life in "the great Sunny South" of Burton's depiction is peopled in Drumgoold's description by "noble whites" who "all loved" the little slave girl who would "preach" to entertain them. When whippings are mentioned in Burton's accounts, they are minimized by a scant mention in the passive voice. Drumgoold, in fact, finds "no subject . . . a more delightful study than the story of a slave girl,"[48] an assertion which would have astounded abolitionists forty and fifty years earlier.

The vast gulf between these pairs of narratives is understandably reflected in the women's accounts of their relationships with their mistresses and female employers. Jacobs's monstrous mistress, Mrs. Flint, and Keckley's devious Mrs. Burwell, who arranges terrible beatings for the slave woman, have little in common with Burton's "Mis' Mary," who teaches her to read and write, or Drumgoold's "white mother." In the first two autobiographies the white women's sexual jealousy becomes perverse cruelty, and the black women are victimized again and again by their mistresses' displaced rage at their husbands' lechery. In describing these white women as enraged monsters, these two early women writers seem to perceive in their mistresses aptly terrifying and repulsive portraits of what human slavery really is. In their jealous depravity, these white women become specters of slavery itself. Far from adhering to the code of the cult of True Womanhood, which demanded piety and morality, these white women, as depicted by their female slaves, become evil creatures, nurtured by the institution that allows them and their husbands absolute power over other human beings. In Keckley's and Jacobs's autobiographies the white southern woman is morally defiled by her own acts of cruelty to the hapless black woman, whose stereotypical association with sexuality marks her as double victim of lustful master and jealous mistress.

Harriet Jacobs's Mrs. Flint is particularly vile, and Jacobs's depiction of her evil mistress deeply ironic. Yet this demonic portrait is drawn against a backdrop of the slave girl's early happiness with a mistress who taught her to read and write and who was "so kind . . . that I was always glad to do her bidding" (p. 5). Actually, though, even this kind mistress fails her: at the white woman's death when Jacobs is twelve, the slave girl is bequeathed to the five-year-old daughter of her former mistress's sister, the ogress Mrs. Flint. Jacobs had hoped to be freed by her kind mistress and feels the provisions of her will as a direct personal betrayal. She writes bitterly:

> My mistress had taught me the precepts of God's Word: "Thou shalt love thy neighbor as thyself." "Whatsoever ye would that men should do unto you, do ye even so unto them." But I was her slave, and I suppose she did not recognize me as her neighbor. I would give much to blot out from my memory that one great wrong. As a child, I loved my mistress; and, looking back on the happy days I spent with her, I try to think with less bitterness of this act of injustice. (p. 6)

This same "kind" mistress also reneged on a promise to young Jacobs's grandmother that upon her death the old slave woman should be freed. Instead, when the estate is settled, Dr. Flint, the old mistress's brother-in-law, dispatches "Aunt Marthy" to the auction block where, luckily, a family member buys her for fifty dollars and sets her free.

It is small wonder that Jacobs has a difficult time forgiving her former mistress's "one great wrong." From the time she is sent to the Flints, her young life becomes a nightmare punctuated by Dr. Flint's lechery and his wife's jealousy. To maintain some control over her life, young "Linda," then fifteen, takes a white lover and has two children, who Mrs. Flint immediately assumes are her husband's own offspring. When the Flints decide to "break in" her children on the plantation, Jacobs, realizing that they are being punished because of her, runs away, hides in the home of a sympathetic white woman, and then is concealed in a casketlike space of a shed attached to the roof of her grandmother's house, through which she bores a hole in order to watch her children as they play. After seven years of this living death, Jacobs manages to escape to Philadelphia—physically and emotionally debilitated by her experience.

Motivated as she was by abolitionist supporters and by her own outrage, Jacobs's discourse is scathingly ironic, particularly as it applies to Mrs. Flint. In the actions of her mistress toward her and toward other black women, Jacobs sees not only the cruelty perpetuated by the system but also the hypocrisy of the slave society. Jacobs has a strong sense of the moral responsibilities of woman in an immoral society, and her vivid depictions of Mrs. Flint's immorality are designed to shock those who believed that the plantation mistress was, as Catherine Clinton puts it, "the conscience of the slave South."[49] She describes Mrs. Flint as "totally deficient in energy" but with "nerves so strong, that she could sit in her easy chair and see a woman whipped, till the blood trickled from every stroke of the lash" (p. 10). The white woman's Christianity is a sham: with biting irony Jacobs writes that Mrs. Flint

> was a member of the church; but partaking of the Lord's supper did not seem to put her in a Christian frame of mind. If dinner was not served at the exact time on that particular Sunday, she would station herself in the kitchen, and wait till it was dished, and then spit in all the kettles and pans that had been used for cooking. She did this to prevent the cook and her children from eking out their meagre fare with the remains of the gravy and other scrapings. (pp. 10–11)

Mrs. Flint's sins are catalogued in horrendous detail throughout *Incidents*. Like Prue's fictional mistress in *Uncle Tom's Cabin,* she locks the cook away from a nursing baby for a whole day and night. Jacobs relates an incident in which her mistress makes her walk barefoot on a long errand through the snow. Later in the narrative, she gives an account of Mrs. Flint's treatment of her aunt, who, although she had many miscarriages, is forced to lie at her mistress's door each night to listen for the white woman's needs. When Aunt Nancy dies, a victim of mistreatment all of her life, Jacobs writes with scathing irony, "Mrs. Flint took to her bed, quite overcome by the shock." The mistress now becomes "very sentimental" and demands that the body of the black woman, whose health she has wrecked "by years of incessant, unrequited toil, and broken rest," be buried "at her feet" in the white family plot. Though dissuaded from that wish by a minister who reminds her that the black family might wish to have some say in the matter, "the tender-hearted Mrs. Flint" makes a pretty picture at Aunt Nancy's funeral "with handkerchief at her eyes," providing, writes Jacobs, "a touching proof of the attachment between slaveholders and their servants" (pp. 148–50).

Mrs. Flint's most memorable characteristic, though, is her jealous rage, which she directs toward young Harriet, the hapless victim of Dr. Flint's lust. Her mistress's behavior bears brutal testimony to Jacobs's plaint: "I would rather drudge out my life on a cotton plantation, till the grave opened to give me rest, than to live with an unprincipled master and a jealous mistress" (p. 29). Jacobs paints Mrs. Flint's jealousy as a kind of madness brought on by the institution of slavery, and sees herself the beleaguered slave girl and the scorned white woman as its mutual victims. She feels a kinship for her mistress: "I never wronged her, or wished to wrong her; and one word of kindness from her would have brought me to her feet" (p. 31). Yet in Jacobs's depiction, that feeling of kinship is not reciprocated. Like many southern white women whose husbands were guilty of philandering with slave women, Mrs. Flint is characterized as being totally blind to the plight of the female slave. "I was an object of her jealousy, and consequently, of her hatred," Jacobs writes. "She pitied herself as a martyr, but she was incapable of feeling for the condition of shame and misery in which her unfortunate, helpless slave was placed." Mrs. Flint "would gladly have had me flogged . . . but the doctor never allowed anyone to whip me" (pp. 32–33).

When Jacobs's first child is conceived, Mrs. Flint, thinking it is her husband's offspring, vows to kill the young woman. The jealous Dr. Flint, whose injunction against violence does not extend to his own, throws Harriet down a flight of stairs, shears her hair, and beats her. In her account of Mrs. Flint, Jacobs stresses also the woman's desire to dominate. When she is sent away to the plantation of Dr. Flint's son and has worked there for five years, she must wait on the table at which the visiting Mrs. Flint is served. "Nothing could please her better than to see me humbled and trampled upon," the black woman writes. "I was just where she would have me—in the power of a hard, unprincipled master. She did not speak to me when she took her seat at table; but her satisfied, triumphant smile, when I handed her plate, was more eloquent than words" (p. 95). When Jacobs runs away, the enraged Mrs. Flint is reported to exclaim, "The good-for-nothing hussy! When she is caught, she shall stay in jail, in irons, for one six months, and then be sold to a sugar plantation. I shall see her broke in yet" (p. 105). Throughout Jacobs's account Mrs. Flint is depicted as struggling for control of young Harriet, and later of her children. The white woman equates these blacks to animals to be conquered and tamed. As Jacobs depicts her, Mrs. Flint is at the same time horribly vindictive and pitifully weak. She longs to control her husband's sexual appetites, but cannot. Instead she transfers her rage to Jacobs and her children and attempts, also unsuccessfully, to control them as symbols of the lust which her husband embodies.

Jacobs writes so bitterly and so thoroughly about Mrs. Flint that she seems at times to transform *Incidents* into a vehicle of rage directed toward her former mistress. If the slave narrative is indeed a means of controlling past experiences and asserting personal order upon social indignity, then *Incidents* is surely the artifact created by Jacobs's impulse to control and dominate, through language, those who controlled and dominated her. In so doing, she herself becomes like the old slave woman with a dead, once cruel mistress about whom she relates an anecdote. When the mistress dies, Jacobs writes, the old slave woman, who has borne the brunt of her many beatings and cruelties, steals into the room where the dead woman lies: "She gazed a while on her, then raised her hand and dealt two blows on the face, saying, as she did so, 'The devil is got you now!' " (p. 48). Like the old slave, Jacobs flogs her powerless former mistress over and over throughout her narrative. At long last the slave woman controls the plantation mistress, and the vehicle of that domination, language, becomes infinitely more powerful and more resonant than the lash or the chain could ever be.

Unlike Jacobs, Elizabeth Keckley dispenses with her years

65

of bondage in the early part of her autobiography. Yet her focus, like Jacobs's, is upon the brutality of a southern mistress with a "cold jealous heart." Keckley is more reticent than Jacobs about her master's sexual coercion, which resulted in the birth of her only child. But it is easy to read between the lines. Like Jacobs, young Keckley was sent to a new master and mistress when she was in early puberty. When she was eighteen and had grown into "strong, healthy womanhood," her master, Mr. Burwell, a Presbyterian minister, and his "helpless" ill-tempered wife moved from Virginia to Hillsboro, North Carolina, taking Keckley, their only slave, with them.

It is at this point that Keckley's tortures begin. Her mistress, Keckley writes, "seemed to be desirous to wreak vengeance on me for something," and "Mr. Bingham, a hard, cruel man, the village schoolmaster" became Mrs. Burwell's "ready tool" (p. 32). At her mistress's behest, Keckley undergoes a series of savage beatings at the hands of the sadistic schoolmaster, who ties her up, tears her clothes from her back, and lashes her unmercifully. These beatings alternate with violent abuse in the Burwell home, in which Keckley has a chair broken over her head. When even the perversely cruel Bingham refuses to whip the black woman again, Mrs. Burwell urges her husband to "punish" her. Mr. Burwell, Keckley writes with grim irony, "who preached the love of Heaven, who glorified the precepts and examples of Christ, who expounded the Holy Scriptures Sabbath after Sabbath from the pulpit," cuts a heavy handle from an oak broom and beats her so brutally that her bloodied condition, she writes, touches even the "cold, jealous heart" of her mistress (p. 37). Mrs. Burwell's "pity" more likely was motivated by the prospect of losing her only maid, a valuable piece of property.

Until this point in Keckley's narrative the Burwells' sadism appears motiveless. Keckley writes only that the beatings were to "subdue [her] pride" (p. 38). But their motives, particularly Mrs. Burwell's, crystallize as the black woman admits that the savage actions of her owners "were not the only things that brought me suffering and deep mortification" (p. 38). In her half-apologetic account of her own sexual coercion Keckley chooses her words carefully. Her hesitant, tentative story shows above all a continuing psychological enslavement to the white man and to a cardinal rule that the black woman must never reveal the name of the father of her mulatto child. It also appears to reveal Burwell to be even more of a perverse monster—a minister who not only forces sex upon the slave woman but beats her savagely even after his cruel wife begs him to desist. If Keckley's implications are true, Burwell is a prime example of Davis's and Hooks's theory that sexual domination of female slaves was an avenue to power for the white male and that rape became in the slave South a symbol of white man's total dominance over blacks and over women.[50] Burwell dominates Keckley through violence and seemingly through sex as well; and although the hesitancy in her account of sexual coercion may be partly ascribed to nineteenth-century reticence on such topics, it is also testimony to a black woman's prevailing fear of patriarchal power:

> I was regarded as fair-looking for one of my race, and for four years a white man—I spare the world his name—had base designs upon me. I do not care to dwell upon this subject, for it is one that is fraught with pain. Suffice it to say, that he persecuted me for four years, and I—I—became a mother. The child of which he was the father was the only child that I ever brought into the world. If my poor boy ever suffered any humiliating pangs on account of birth, he could not blame his mother, for God knows that she did not wish to give him life; he must blame the edicts of that society which deemed it no crime to undermine the virtue of girls in my then position.
>
> Among the old letters preserved by my mother I find the following, written by myself while at Hillsboro'. In this connection I desire to state that Rev. Robert Burwell is now living at Charlotte, North Carolina . . . . (pp. 38–39)

In this account and in the letter which follows it, Keckley mentions "griefs and misfortunes" which result in family disapproval. From her specific mention of Burwell, we may infer that he was the father of her child. Keckley's account of Burwell's sexual aberrations restores, by contrast, a more sympathetic view of her mistress. Though her cruelties to Keckley are reprehensible, they are at least understandable. It is Mrs. Burwell who finally falls on her knees and begs her husband to stop beating Keckley. We cannot begin to compare her suffering to Keckley's, but out of this account evolve faint glimmerings of a sympathetic portrait. In her former mistress, Keckley shows us a white woman warped by her husband's perverse will to sexually dominate a female slave. Her sadism is horribly engendered by his lust for power.

We wonder how representative Mrs. Flint and Mrs. Burwell are. An unpublished study of the role of plantation mistresses in the lives of slaves shows mistresses to be responsible for only a small portion of punishments inflicted upon slaves. Yet the study, in which Elizabeth Craven surveyed nineteenth- and twentieth-century slave narratives, also shows that many incidents involving the cruelty of a mistress also concerned a female slave's alleged intimacy with the master. Clinton, who cites the study in *The Plantation Mistress,* summarizes Craven's findings: "When [male] slaveowners sexually harrassed or exploited female slaves, mistresses sometimes directed their anger, not at their unfaithful husbands, but toward the helpless slaves."[51] Jacobs and Keckley were victims of such mistresses who punished them for being who they were—attractive women who were also chattel. In writing about the white women who transferred their jealous rages to them, these black women evoke the autobiographical process as an avenue toward understanding and order. It is only through confrontation with the human evil of slavery that the freed woman can reorder experience, redefine her place in the world, and assert her rights to that place. By re-creating Mrs. Flint and Mrs. Burwell and their "cold, jealous heart[s]," these two black women rise in language from the ashes of their enslavement and create themselves anew—as individuated selves, as nonvictims. They perceive their relationships with their former mistresses as paradigmatic of the essential evil of slavery—the perversity of that "peculiar institution" which transformed victim into victimizer and severed potential bonds of sisterhood.

Such bonds shaped the early lives of Kate Drumgoold and Annie Burton, whose mistresses became mother figures in the chaos of the war and Reconstruction years. Drumgoold's portrait of her "white mother" is unadulteratedly sentimental.

Again and again throughout her narrative, Drumgoold extols the virtues of her mistress and gives her credit for everything she has accomplished in adult life. Born in Virginia near Petersburg, Drumgoold writes that she was barely old enough to remember the beginning of the Civil War. When her first mistress died, the girl's mother was sold to a man from Georgia. Drumgoold recalls her yearning for the lost mother, who was sold without her children's knowledge. ". . . the saddest thought was to me to know which way she had gone, and I used to go outside and look up to see if there was anything that would direct me, and I saw a clear place in the sky, and it seemed to me the way she had gone, and I watched it three and a half years, not knowing what that meant, and it was there the whole time that mother was gone from her little ones" (p. 5). Longing for her own mother, young Kate found maternal nurture in her mistress Bettie House.

Drumgoold's account of her early life is confusing because she relates events as she thinks of them, not as they occurred chronologically. She also uses the term *mother* to refer both to her real mother and to her mistress, and it is often difficult to determine which mother is which. When the war is over, her real mother returns to claim her and her sister. After many trials they are able to get to Brooklyn, where they set up housekeeping. After her mother's death, Drumgoold hires herself out in Brooklyn and eventually becomes a teacher. Throughout her narrative, she refers again and again to her "dear white mother," for whom she will always have "the kindest feeling" (p. 11). She credits her mistress with her religious training and writes of the white woman's carrying her to church on horseback when she was three. Drumgoold characterizes her mistress as a ministering angel who cared for her through sickness after sickness and who died from an illness incurred while nursing young Kate. ". . . she was more like one of the heavenly host than she was like us who are sinful creatures," Drumgoold writes. ". . . Lord, lead me on day by day, and help my feeble life be formed like her's" (pp. 16–17).

It is the mundane details of her mistress's care for young Kate that make Drumgoold's account of their relationship heartwarming. Her "white mother" refuses to call her a slave.

She buys her a ten-dollar hat and a horse named Charlie Engrum. She teaches Kate to ride and saves her breakfast when she takes early morning rides. When the doctor prescribes castor oil for typhoid fever, Kate's mistress secretly mixes it with molasses and butter. Never a cross word passes the white mother's lips, even when young Kate interrupts her prayers. The Betty House of Drumgoold's depiction is truly a fairy godmother, a powerful all-loving mother whose nurturance sustains the young black girl whose own mother was snatched away. Glowing with beneficence in Drumgoold's description, Mrs. House also becomes in this account the embodiment of "streams of God's providence" which bathe the black race in hope for the future. *A Slave Girl's Story* is very much one of those later slave narratives which Foster calls "cheerleading exercises" for continued progress and optimism. Drumgoold's descriptions of her "white mother" are part of that optimistic spirit. They may also reflect black and white women's opportunities for personal autonomy in antebellum Petersburg.[52] More than anything else, the relationship of young Kate and her mistress illustrates the capacity of human beings, particularly women, to cross racial barriers with kindness and empathy. In this sense, Drumgoold's autobiography, though highly sentimental, is what she claims it to be: a "delightful study" not only of a slave girl but of her recognition of the capacity of maternal love to cross racial lines.

Annie Burton's mistress is far from being such a paragon of female virtue. After a quarrel with young Annie's mother, her childhood playmate, her mistress has the black woman whipped for the first time. Annie's mother runs away from the plantation near Clayton, Alabama, leaving her three children. When she returns to claim them after the war, the mistress refuses to give them up. Under their mother's directions, the three children flee and are reunited with her. Yet Burton's account of these events of her childhood is noticeably lacking in bitterness toward the white woman who kept her and her brother and sister during their mother's absence. Actually, the author's depiction of her mistress is part of a central tone of ambivalence which characterizes this narrative. Throughout her story she gives lip service to the romantic legend of "happy, carefree childhood days on the plantation," but opposes her own rosy epithets with hard facts of whippings, hangings, and family separations which illustrate a disruptive, dehumanizing society (p. 3). Obviously Burton's "young life in the great Sunny South" was not as sunny as it could have been. It is somewhat puzzling that she persists in labeling it as such.

Her first memories of her mistress are of the white woman's indignation at young Annie's white father, who refuses to recognize the mulatto child as his. Burton relates that whenever her mistress sees him riding by, she takes Annie, then four yearrs old, out upon the piazza and exclaims, "Stop there, I say! Don't you want to see and speak to and caress your darling child? She often speaks of you and wants to embrace her dear father. See what a bright and beautiful daughter she is, a perfect picture of yourself. Well, I declare, you are an affectionate father" (pp. 7–8). Burton recalls that her father's response was to "whip up his horse and get out of sight and hearing as quickly as possible. . . . I never spoke to him, and cannot remember that he ever noticed me, or in any way acknowledged me to be his child" (p. 8). Burton's vivid account of this incident shows the psychological impact of such a rejection. The incident itself reveals a certain cruelty in her mistress, who uses Annie with no regard for the child's feelings to try to shame her white father. One wonders also at the mistress's motives. Could her repeated insistence on provoking this white neighbor reflect her anxiety that Annie might have been fathered closer to home? Such suspicions could have led to the quarrel between mistress and Annie's mother which resulted in the black woman's whipping. Since we can see these events only through Burton's young memories, our knowledge is limited.

With a father who would not acknowledge her and a mother who deserted her, it is not surprising that young Annie found some sense of family feeling in her relationships with her mistress and her mistress's daughters. After the war when the slaves left the plantation, Annie and her brother and sister continued to work side by side for their former owners. There is an underlying sense of familial closeness in Burton's description of the division of labor: "My mistress and her daughters had to go to the kitchen and to the washtub. My little half-brother, Henry, and myself had to gather chips, and help all we could. My sister, Caroline, who was twelve years old, could help in the kitchen" (p. 10).

Burton reports one whipping received probably from the hand of her mistress, but her account renders the event as far from earthshaking: "One day [after the war] mistress sent me out to do some churning under a tree. I went to sleep and jerked the churn over on top of me, and consequently got a whipping" (p. 11). Interestingly, in her other accounts of whippings, Burton does not make clear who is administering the punishment. At one point she writes that the overseer gave the whippings, but in relating the actual punishments, she merely writes that someone "was whipped." Nor does she elaborate on the severity or duration of the punishments. Those accounts are, of course, in stark contrast to those of Keckley, who counts every lash.

Burton does describe two other nurturing relationships between black and white southern females. In one, a white woman cares for young Annie; in the other, Annie's mother shares food and shelter with a white woman. Burton's accounts of these two relationships balance each other in illustrating a strong sense of female community after the war. In 1866, when Annie's mother and her children moved into the town of Clayton, Annie was hired out to a wealthy lawyer's wife, Mrs. E.M. Williams. "Mis' Mary," as Burton calls her, taught her to memorize and recite poetry. Mis' Mary became a second mother to the black girl in her charge and made certain maternal decisions in her behalf, often in concert with Annie's mother. The white woman also worked with Annie's mother to provide proper chaperonage to parties (this often to Annie's chagrin) and to teach her honesty and prepare her for the future. Burton writes: "I owe a great deal to Mis' Mary for her good training of me, in honesty, uprightness and truthfulness. She told me that when I went out into the world all white folks would not treat me as she had, but that I must not feel bad about it, but just do what I was employed to do, and if I wasn't satisfied, to go elsewhere; but always to carry an honest name" (p. 15).

Roles of nurturance are reversed in Burton's recollection of the difficult times right after the war. She writes that after her mother regained her children, she housed them in a hut. As night fell and hard rain began falling, a white woman and her three children knocked and asked for refuge. Though the black mother had only small amounts of hoe cake and soup, she divided that meager amount with the white family. Burton recalls the mutual compassion each woman felt for the other and particularly her mother's show of kindness. As they talked late into the night, the two women seemed to gain strength from each other. Burton writes that after the children went to sleep, "the two mothers still continued to talk, setting down on the only seats, a couple of blocks. A little back against the wall my mother and the white woman slept" (p. 44).

This picture of the sleeping mothers, black and white, both displaced and left destitute by the war, is a moving study in sisterhood through mutual suffering. It is a picture which embodies Drumgoold's and Burton's visions of cross-racial female nurture. Slaves only in their prepubescent years, Drumgoold and Burton never had to contend with that two-headed dragon of the slave South, the lecherous master and jealous mistress. Reared in a time of confusion and family disruption, both turned to white women for stability in their young lives. Unlike Jacobs and Keckley, who had the misfortune of being born two generations earlier, these two southern black women experienced white womanhood as a source of strength and female community and as a sustaining force in their lives.

The autobiographies of two former border-state slaves, Lucy Delaney and Amanda Smith, reflect more diverse attitudes toward their former mistresses. Both slave narratives were published in the early 1890s and both have a strong religious flavor. Yet Delaney's *From the Darkness Cometh the Light; or, Struggles for Freedom* (1891) is, as its title suggests, also an account of struggle against white oppression. Her struggles, like those of her mother, often took the form of verbal and physical confrontations with unreasonable mistresses. Smith, on the other hand, developed in early life, also through her mother's example, a sisterhood with white women through shared religious experience. In *An Autobiography: The*

73

Story of the Lord's Dealing with Mrs. Amanda Smith the Colored Evangelist (1893), Smith describes her and her mother's love for the religious "Miss Celie," their friend, fellow worshiper, and mistress, who eventually became their avenue to freedom. Delaney's and Smith's opposite attitudes toward the white women in their lives provide significant commentary both upon the diversity of the mistress–slave woman relationships and the powerful influence that black mothers exerted, by instruction and by example, in the formation of their daughters' relationships with the white community in general and white women in particular.

Delaney was born to an intelligent, aggressive black woman who herself had been born free in Illinois and then kidnapped and sold in Missouri. Polly Crocket Berry was a central figure in the life of her younger daughter Lucy as she grew up in slavery in St. Louis. Unlike Drumgoold and Burton, young Lucy had no need for a white surrogate mother. Having been born free, Polly Berry was more versed in the ways of the world than many slave women. One of Delaney's earliest memories is of her mother's instructing her older daughter Nancy to run away to Canada while accompanying their mistress on a trip to Niagara Falls. When Mrs. Cox returns to St. Louis without Nancy, she sends for Lucy's mother to inform her of her daughter's escape. Delaney depicts the scene as evidence of the masks which slaves wore in dealing with their masters and mistresses. She remembers that

> Mother was very thankful, and in her heart arose a prayer of thanksgiving, but outwardly she pretended to be vexed and angry. Oh! the impenetrable mask of these poor black creatures! how much of joy, of sorrow, or misery and anguish have they hidden from their tormentors!
>
> I was a small girl at that time, but remember how wildly mother showed her joy at Nancy's escape when we were alone together. She would dance, clap her hands and, waving them above her head, would indulge in one of those wierd [sic] negro melodies, which so charm and fascinate the listener.[53]

When Delaney's mother, a volatile woman, does lift her mask on another occasion to respond with rage to Mrs. Cox's severity, the Coxes summarily auction her off to the highest bidder despite the fact that she has a twelve-year-old daughter. Interestingly, Delaney seems to blame Mrs. Cox, rather than her mother's master, for this callous act; she describes her mother as having been "sold away from her child, to satisfy the anger of a peevish mistress!" (p. 22). As her daughter re-creates her, Polly Crocket Berry is a daring woman, though. She soon escapes, makes her way North, is recaptured, returns to St. Louis, and sues for her freedom on grounds that she was born free. A jury decides in her favor and she takes up residence near her still-enslaved daughter.

When Lucy is sent to work for Mrs. Cox's sister Mrs. Mitchell, she patterns her relationships with her new mistress after her mother's with Mrs. Cox and takes an aggressive stance when unfairly chastised for failing to wash the clothes properly. When Mrs. Mitchell calls her "a lazy, good-for-nothing nigger," she retorts angrily, "You don't know nothing, yourself, about it, and you expect a poor ignorant girl to know more than you do yourself; if you had any feeling you would get somebody to teach me, and then I'd do well enough!" (p. 25). Since Delaney's mother had often told her that she "would not die a slave," she recalls that she "always had a feeling of independence" and refused to be mistreated by her mistress. She writes rather proudly that in one instance when Mrs. Mitchell tried to whip her, "I rebelled against such government, and would not permit her to strike me; she used shovel, tongs and broomstick in vain, as I disarmed her as fast as she picked up each new weapon" (p. 27). This war of wills is depicted as a peculiarly female battle. When Mr. Mitchell refuses to control Lucy, his wife vows, in an outraged show of power, to sell her. But, again, Lucy reacts according to her mother's directions and runs away. Although she is later jailed for seventeen months during the lengthy legal action in which her mother sues to have her declared freed, in 1844 she is eventually emancipated as the daughter of a free woman and begins her new life with her mother, who, she writes, "clung and fought" until her daughter's "freedom was established by every right and without a questioning doubt!" (p. 45).

Polly Crocket Berry teaches her daughter to defy the authority of the slaveholding establishment and the mistress as the epitome of that establishment. By her own example this black mother shows how to defy white woman's control and how to use the ambivalent feelings toward slavery of this border-state white community to gain legal freedom. In all of the power struggles between slave women and their mistresses depicted in these narratives, only Lucy Delaney and her mother both defy their mistresses and then exert their rights to that defiance through the courts. Delaney's re-creation of her mother's bravery and determination in battling the white women in their lives reflects her pride in her own courage and success—a success decidedly more possible in antebellum Missouri than in antebellum Mississippi or other states of the Deep South, where white woman's power was more staunchly supported by the patriarchy.

Amanda Smith's early childhood experiences with white women in Long Green, Maryland, also reflect a strong maternal influence, but in the direction of cross-racial female nurturance and devotion between slave woman and mistress. Instead of showing young Amanda how to rebel against white women, Mariam Matthews Berry is represented by her daughter as the paragon of devoted service. Smith reports that her mother's young mistress, "Miss Celie," was as devoted to Mariam and her family as Mariam was to her. Their bond is their common religiosity. When "Miss Celie" is "wonderfully converted" at "an old-fashioned, red-hot Camp Meeting . . . in the old-fashioned way; the shouting, hallelujah way," only Mariam, who was similarly converted two years before, can tolerate her mistress's company. Celie's family thinks she has "lost her mind" when she begins each day praying and shouting. But Amanda's mother and grandmother meet Celie in the dairy for secret prayer sessions, despite instructions to avoid encouraging their young mistress in her religious bent. When "Miss Celie" falls sick with typhoid fever and is on the brink of death, her last request is that the family allow Amanda's free father to purchase Mariam and her children; and Celie dies, Smith recalls, with her head upon Mariam's breast and with the motherly black woman singing hymns to soothe her young mistress as she breathes her last.[54]

Just as Mariam serves as a black mother figure to young white Celie, Smith describes her own obverse relationship with "old mistress," Celie's mother, as one involving warm nurturance of a young black girl by an older white woman. Yet, as Smith writes her autobiography years later, she seems to have suspicions about the motives of her "old mistress":

> She was very kind to me, and I was a good deal spoiled, for a little darkey. If I wanted a piece of bread, and if it was not buttered and sugared on both sides, I wouldn't have it; and when mother would get out of patience with me, and go for a switch, I would run to my old mistress and wrap myself up in her apron, and I was safe. And oh! how I loved her for that. They were getting me ready for market, but I didn't know it. I suppose that is why they allowed me to do many things that otherwise I should not have been allowed to do.   (p. 22)

This isolated comment is rather strange since Samuel Berry, Smith writes, was eventually allowed to buy his family's freedom as Celie had requested, and since Smith goes on to write further about her childhood devotion to her "dear old mistress." "I would follow her around. Sometimes she would walk out into the yard and sit under the trees, and I would draw the chair after her; I was too small to carry it. She would sit down awhile, and I would gather pretty flowers. When she got tired she would walk to another spot, and I would drag the chair again. So we would spend several hours in this way" (p. 22). Whatever her suspicions later in life, Smith acknowledges that she "was too young to have any trials of [slavery]" (p. 22). When Amanda was eight and her father was allowed to purchase his family, the Berrys moved almost immediately to Pennsylvania. What memories she had of the cross-racial female relationships of her youth are thus deeply grounded in the ideal of a shared religious closeness. In Smith's *Autobiography,* black woman and white woman—her mother and Miss Celie—thwart a materialistic patriarchy much like Stowe's Eliza and Mrs. Shelby, with genuine faith in the active power of Christian sisterhood. Whether in secret prayer sessions at the dairy or in songs and promises at the deathbed, these two southern women, as they exist in Smith's memory, comfort and support each other in a relationship of mutual regard.

Although, significantly, Smith's Miss Celie is a pariah to her own white family, some plantation mistresses would have relished the perception of themselves as Christian influences upon their women slaves. As Sudie Duncan Sides and, more recently, Catherine Clinton have shown, mistresses often felt very deeply their obligations to nurse, direct, and indoctrinate the slaves under their care. Letitia Burwell, who claims she "never saw a discontent face" among the one hundred slaves on her parents' Virginia plantation, writes that her mother and grandmother were constantly concerned about the needs of their slaves—"what medicine should be sent, whom they should visit, who needed new shoes, clothes, or blankets—the principal object of their lives seeming to be in providing these comforts." She feels a deep debt of gratitude to white southern women of the past. "For what courage, what patience, what perseverance, what long suffering, what Christian forbearance, must it have cost our great-grandmothers to civilize, Christianize, and elevate the naked, savage Africans to the condition of good cooks and respectable maids!"[55] Burwell's remarks illustrate Sides's and Clinton's findings from other white women's autobiographical writings: that, above all, white southern women, like white southern men, viewed slaves primarily as chattel and as childlike, dependent, inferior human beings. Sides concludes that the white southern woman accepted slavery, not because she liked it, but "because it provided her with a meaning for her life which she might not have otherwise." Ironically, Sides's research indicates that slavery made the plantation mistress feel "Christian" because she could teach slaves "principles of brotherly love, kindness, humility, long suffering and redemption as taught by Christ." House servants often "got what passed for love" from white women as long as they were "willing not only to act subordinately but to be subordinate to whites." Sides shows that the mistress's professed love of slaves was often narcissistic: the white woman had the image of herself as "kind, generous and Christian. The slave's love was a reenforcement of her own view of herself, the self she wanted to be."[56] Sallie A. Putnam of Virginia emphasizes what she saw as a reflective quality in mistress-slave relationships of the period: "Our slaves . . . were our confidants in all our trials. They joyed with us and they sorrowed with us; they wept when we wept, and they laughed when we laughed. Often our best friends, they were rarely our worst enemies. Simple and childlike in their affections, they were more trustworthy in their attachments than those better versed in wisdom."[57]

Other writings indicate that what the mistress may have seen actually mirrored in the black woman was a sexual self long repressed under the nineteenth-century white mantle of purity. The black woman's stereotypical associations with passion and with lack of inhibition were often viewed by white women as a threat, both socially and psychologically. The southern lady knew she must repress her sexuality or be considered immoral. As she repressed her own sexuality, she also may have felt compelled to reject an outward symbol of it, the black woman. On a subconscious level, the white woman recognized the slave woman, willing or unwilling, as potential sexual competition and as a direct embodiment of the double standard. When women like Mary Chesnut rant over the evils of miscegenation, they focus their rage upon black women as well as white men. Yet their anger may also be directed toward a social system that does not allow them sexual expression. They seem to see in black women an indigenous but lost physicality which has been drained from them as part of their training for the pedestal. They are both attracted to and fearful of that sexuality, and their feelings for black women reflect that ambivalence. In actuality and in language, they strive to "control" black women, unconsciously seeing them, perhaps, as embodiments of their own sexual selves, which they, of necessity, must deny and repress.

The mammy myth seems to arise from these perceptions. To render the black woman sexless is to remove psychological and social threats to the image of the southern lady. In their diaries and memoirs, white Southern women of the period show genuine affection for nonsexual and therefore nonthreatening mammy figures and, at the same time, betray resentment and fear of black women whom they associate with unrestricted sexuality. In their writings, many create nurturing black women who are so selfless that it is impossible to believe in them as flesh-and-blood individuals. A Louisiana woman whose family fields along the Mississippi River were "dotted with busy and contented slaves" tells of her servant Charlotte, a trusted member of the family. "Her zeal in our service never flagged," writes Eliza McHatton Ripley; "she had no higher ambition than the faithful discharge of her daily duties."[58]

In her later reminiscence, *Social Life in Old New Orleans,* Ripley devotes one whole chapter to extolling mammies. Entitled "A Monument to Mammies," the chapter immortalizes her own black female house servants and those of other white families. She recounts close personal relationships between white and black women. Her cousin Mrs. Chinn is said to have burst into tears in describing the death of her mammy, who "died holding the hand of the sorrowing mistress, her last words, 'My work is done. I tried to do my best.' " Ripley's own Mammy Charlotte, an old woman, is said to have met her at the door when she first entered her husband's home as a bride and proved a great "comfort" and "real help" during the writer's "sunny life in the plantation home and in the dark days of the war, too." Yet Ripley's comment about another mammy is more revealing about the nature of white woman's perceptions of the black. She writes, "Every boarder in that big house knows mammy, but I doubt if one of them knows her name; I do not."[59] Susan Bradford Eppes's mammy meant safety, comfort and nurturance after a long journey; she writes that "memory calls up Mammy's tender touches as she divested us of travelling apparel, bathed us gently and laid us in our little bed in all its gleaming whiteness. Nothing like that, where we had been, and surely nothing like the goodnight hug Mammy gave us ere she blew out the light."[60]

Sides categorizes the writings of white southern women of the period into two groups: diaries actually kept before, during, and after the Civil War, and memoirs, written at a later date, that dealt with those same years.[61] Like the slave narratives written before and after the war, these two types of writings have structures, themes, and purposes which influence how these white women express their feelings about black women and about slaves and slavery generally, and how they re-create their cross-racial relationships—whether of the hour before or of the past several decades. Sides believes that the memoirs are less reliable as historical documents for all the obvious reasons—fading memory, the human tendency to remember only the positive, the wish to appear in the best light in one's family history, along with the fact that many were published toward the end of the nineteenth century and thus were influenced by that period's sentimentalization of the Lost Cause and appeal of southern agronomy in the face of growing industrialization.[62] Such writings tend to defend slavery, Sides writes, rather than examine relationships within the system. She argues that the actual diaries and journals have an immediacy and honesty (presumably about racial as well as other issues) that the retrospective writings do not, and contain "an explicit and generally negative view of slavery" or an acceptance of the slave society with "no question of its right or wrong."[63]

Book-length, published autobiographical writings of neither category, however, lend themselves to such a neat dichotomy. Like the longer, published women's slave narratives, these white women's books may be examined, in most cases, as more consciously sustained literary endeavors than shorter unpublished manuscripts. Many women prepared their own journals for publication and, like Mary Chesnut, Cornelia McDonald, and Eliza Andrews, carefully edited and rewrote sections. Such writings are a fascinating combination of spontaneity and retrospection. On the whole, though, the diaries, memoirs, and combinations thereof reflect within each subgenre a vast range of feelings for slaves in general and black women in particular. With only a few albeit significant exceptions, the writers of these autobiographies, usually plantation mistresses of social standing, remake their own cross-racial female relationships without creating correspondingly human portraits of the black women in their lives. In these white female writings, real black women often become impenetrable stereotypes whose humanity eludes their creators, blinded as they may have been by assumptions of black inferiority, or fearful as some may have been of confronting their own culpability in an inhumane social and economic system. Significantly, though, only a few white women diarists and writers of memoirs of this period *failed* to write about black women, and those who did usually concentrated their writings on Civil War battles and Reconstruction hardships, rather than upon plantation life and personal experience.[64]

Clearly there was no one Old South or single white female experience of the period. Considered here are eighteen writers of nineteen autobiographies of the period, representing life in eight of the eleven Confederate states. Whether these white writers express their feelings about black women and slavery in momentary jottings or well-edited memoirs, and *regardless* of their stances on secession or slavery, most of these autobiographies reflect their creators' extremely ambivalent feelings toward black women. The same pen might sentimentalize nurturing relationships with shadowy mammy figures and express outright disgust for black women. Only three of these seventeen white women writers exhibit sensitivity both to the degrading horrors of slavery and the particular difficulties of individual slave women. Of these three, Cornelia McDonald and Mary Blackford were Virginians who lived comfortably (until the war) but were not brought up with the greater wealth associated with Deep South plantations. (Wealthy women, women such as Susan Dabney Smedes of Mississippi, Catherine Devereux Edmondston of North Carolina, and Susan Bradford Eppes of Florida, were accustomed to a way of life that involved hundreds of slaves and thousands of acres.) Also, as L. Minor Blackford, the editor of his grandmother's writings, points out, antislavery sentiment was not unusual in Virginia during this period.[65] Kate Stone, the third writer who shows sensitivity to black women, does not fit this profile, however. She was brought up on Brokenburn, a large cotton plantation in northeast Louisiana which boasted 1260 acres and 150 slaves.

Despite differences in location and economic position, Stone and Blackford are linked by strong maternal influences; their mothers impressed upon their daughters the importance of considering the feelings of their slaves. The mother of McDonald, who was perhaps the most compassionate of these three writers, died when she was fifteen and is not mentioned in her daughter's diary. McDonald's kindheartedness and sensitivity to the plight of slave women, particularly slave mothers, seem to evolve more from her own maternity; she was the mother of seven during the difficult war years and, like Stowe, was acutely cognizant of the slave society's disruption of black families.

Other white southern women, both diarists and writers of memoirs, express strong racist sentiments. Two who seem particularly vehement in their antiblack feelings and actions were Edmondston of North Carolina and Eppes of Florida. Edmondston, whose diary was composed from 1860 to 1866 but not published until 1979, was the daughter of wealthy landowners on both sides of her family. She often depicts black women as lazy and insolent and refers to black children as "little monkeys."[66] Eppes, who grew up in the Florida cotton belt ten miles north of Tallahassee, wrote her reminiscences (her "diary" is a literary invention) as "a bitter and unreconstructed Southerner" (p. xxi). She too was the daughter of a powerful and distinguished family of ardent secessionists. Her father, Dr. Edward Bradford, a descendant of the famous New England family, invested much time in her education and probably influenced her thinking on many subjects. Her aversion to blacks may well be related to the murder of her husband, Nicholas Eppes, by three black men in 1904. Like the Carolinian Edmondston, Eppes writes of "insolent" black women who refuse to work and she mentions that at age nineteen she used a leather whip on a group of black children. Interestingly, she may have been influenced in her relationship with black women also by her mother, whose temperament resulted in the flight of Eppes's "dear black mammy" Lula (pp. 84–85).

Other white women writers of autobiographies—the great majority—fall somewhere between the sensitivity to black women shown by Stone, McDonald, and Blackford and the disavowal of black humanity by Eppes and Edmondston. From Virginia to Florida, Texas to Georgia, white women who write of the Old South express a common and central ambivalence toward black women which seems to have no correlation to economic status or location. Most of these women were in the upper economic and social echelons of the Old South, and the realities of their lives must have had little in common with those of their women slaves. In their diaries or retrospective writings they re-create the Old South in terms of their own internalized stereotypes of what its men and women should be and do. Some, not all, of these writings are nostalgic visions of an agrarian Camelot rather than actual representations of a real and painful world. All, from the best writings of Chesnut and McDonald to the cloying picturesqueness of the lesser writers, maintain a tone of incredulity at the irrevocable loss of a familiar and much-cherished way of life, the fractured and diminished world of the South.

Diarists expressed both pro- and antislavery sentiments, and their feelings about "the peculiar institution" understandably affected their portrayal of the black women in their purview. Women like Edmondston and Sarah Morgan Dawson of Louisiana believed that slavery was an essentially benevolent system for contented "Cuffee," as Edmondston called blacks. "And to think old Abe wants to deprive us of all that fun!" Dawson complains. "No more cotton, sugar-cane, or rice! No more old black aunties or uncles! No more rides in mule teams, no more songs in the cane-field, no more steaming kettles, no more black faces and shining teeth around the furnace fires!"[67] Edmondston, whose diary is replete with irritation at the "laziness" and "insolence" of slave women, approves in particular of the benefits of the plantation nursery system. "Fat, healthy, well fed, greasy little wretches," she writes, are placed in "a nursery independent of their Mamy's and Daddies [sic] household arrangements" (p. 23). She believes that the plantation system can take better care of the "little monkeys" than their own mothers and fathers, an assumption based upon the notion that physical nurturance, as if they were livestock, is the only significant factor in black children's environment. Like Dawson, she laments the passage of a way of life and the necessity of secession. Though surrounded by hundreds of slaves, she fails to see slavery as an issue that should evoke such a national struggle. "This glorious Union," she mourns, "broken up for the sake of a few negroes!" (pp. 36–37).

Dawson, Edmondston, and Eliza Andrews, a Georgian who years after the war disavowed the system she defends in her diary, seem to be both repelled and fascinated by the excessive emotional and sexual powers they associate with black women. Dawson writes in consternation that her Bible class for slave women becomes a wild scene of repentance, "kissing and reconciliation" (p. 89). As more and more items are confiscated by Yankee troops, she worries that her clothes will be worn by black women. She writes that she would rather burn them: "Fancy my magenta organdie on a dark beauty! Bah! I think the sight would enrage me!" (p. 178). Particularly as the war closes, Andrews and Edmondston seem to fear the stereotypical sexuality of black women who consort with Yankee soldiers. These white women, constrained by Victorian standards of behavior, have lost power and physical freedom simply by being on the losing side of the war. In their day-to-day jottings, they express bitterness, and perhaps also fear, by their emphatic disgust at the "indecent exhibitions" of the females of "an inferior, savage race."[68]

Miscegenation in the aftermath of war sickens Edmondston, who writes that such behavior "disgusts & revolts my whole nature" (p. 552). Edmondston feels that slavery placed the greatest burden on the slaveholder. "Cuffee," as she calls the black race, "is more contented and in better subjection" than the rest of the world may realize. As the mistress of a huge plantation, she was almost totally blind to the plight of the overworked and overbred slave woman, whom she views as a laboring mechanism that should never break down. She reflects this attitude in her description of one of her female slaves: "Viney was sorting seed corn, under heavy complaint as usual. I wish I could for once see a hearty negro woman who admitted herself to be such over 40, one who was not 'poorly, Thank God!' To be 'poorly' is their aim & object, as it ends in the house & spinning. Viney I know has real cause for complaint, but she makes the best of it!" (p. 20).

Interestingly, Edmondston wants devotion and nurturance from black women, but cannot comprehend a cross-racial female relationship as being one of mutual kindness and affection. She writes scathingly of favored women servants, "including negroes, servants of widows & single Ladies" who have become "terribly insolent" (p. 173). In an October 1865 entry she writes that during a severe liver ailment of three months' duration she was "nursed in a most devoted & affectionate manner by my maid Fanny. Her faithfulness was a subject of remark by every one who saw her. At times she actually wept over me. . . ." Yet she then goes on to criticize Fanny for leaving her to follow her husband and tend a sick child. She cannot understand how the black woman could forsake her mistress for her own family (pp. 717–18). Edmondston's blindness to black individuality and family ties and her expressions of distrust may indeed be factors of her economic status; as a wealthy manager of a large prosperous plantation, she stood at an extreme distance from the black experience. Yet other writings such as those of Kate Stone, who also helped manage such a plantation even farther South, make it impossible to generalize about the connection of economic status to racial attitude. The only apparent difference between Edmondston's and Stone's backgrounds seems to have been the kindly influence of Stone's mother.

Regardless of background, many of the diarists, writing on the spur of the moment and at a younger age than the retrospective writers, reveal powerful conflicts about the sexuality of black women. "Bad" black women obsess Emma Holmes, a twenty-two-year-old Charlestonian when she began her diary. Holmes moved in the same circles as Mary Chesnut and, like Chesnut, was "a believer in aristocracy."[69] Apparently she did not write the diary for publication but rather as a personal journal of her observations and feelings during the historic period in which she lived (p. xxiii). There is a sense of immediacy, a literary breathlessness, about the diary, in contrast to the more measured, carefully composed retrospective writings of Smedes and Chesnut.

Holmes does not write about black women with much frequency, but her remarks reflect an equation of black womanhood with miscegenation. In comments on black women in general, she denounces their sexual behavior with white men, describes several scenes of debauchery, and repeatedly decries such activities. Yankee soldiers, she seems to think, spend much of their time when not fighting in "dreadful . . . revolting" debauches with black women (p. 102). Closer to home she writes of fellow passengers on an omnibus: "two Jewish youths & their two negro female servants, one a respectable old 'mauma' but the other a girl with whom they seemed on the most familiar & intimate terms, while she took out the worth of her $5 by carrying a live goose. I thought *miscegenation* had already commenced—disgustingly" (pp. 359–60).

Black women, Holmes feels, should dress soberly and not flaunt themselves in finery. She approvingly describes Rachel, the servant of some friends, as nonsexual,

> a most respectable old Virginia maumer . . . among the very few who wear the respectable & becoming handkerchief turban, so familiar to low country eyes, and she looked so homelike it did me good to see her. The other negroes at church were all in the most ludicrous & disgustingly tawdry mixture of old finery, aping their betters most nauseatingly—round hats, gloves & even lace veils—the men alone looking respectable.   (p. 428)

Interestingly the finery described in this entry of 2 April 1865 is that probably worn before the war by white women. In their "white" garments these black women become embodiments not only of forbidden sexuality but of a shattered southern social structure. As the editor of her diary points out, Holmes and her family were prominent members of the southern aristocracy, and the primary significance of her writing lies in its vivid depictions of "the impact of war on the Southern elite" (p. xvi). In her diary Holmes attempts to control her own vision of these black women by what was, in April of 1865, wishful thinking. She writes, "If I ever own negroes, I shall carry out my father's plan & never allow them to indulge in dress. It is ruin body and soul to them" (p. 428). Ironically, one is reminded of Holmes's earlier entries about the beauty of young white women in their party finery: "The girls all looked remarkably prettily, their floral ornaments were beautiful . . ." (p. 350). But "the colored ladies" mean only one thing to Holmes: "O Heavens, the mind and heart sickens over the revolting thoughts—miscegenation in truth, & in our city!" (p. 429).

Like many white women of her generation in North and South, Holmes never married. She was locked into patterns set by societal expectations of women of her race and class, yet the chaos and bloodshed of the terrible struggle denied her the positive aspects of her socially prescribed role—marriage, home, and family. In her diary she projects unexpressed bitterness at her own white female entrapment upon black women, whom she saw with limited vision as embodiments of sexual and social freedom. Re-created in her threadbare finery, the young attractive black woman is everything that Holmes can never be.

Among the writers of journals and diaries, Blackford of Virginia and Stone of Louisiana seem unthreatened by black female sexuality. Blackford and Stone are also unusual in that they use their journals to express sympathy for the plight of black women who were "prey of the brutal lust of their oppressors."[70] As indicated by the title of her journal, "Notes Illustrative of the Wrongs of Slavery," Blackford believed as her mother and father had, that "property in human beings hardens the heart, dims, ay blinds, us to human rights and human suffering" (p. 39). She began her journal, which she kept from 1832 to 1866, because of an incident involving one of her husband's women slaves, the family cook, whose husband worked on an adjoining plantation and was sold by his master to a slave trader without notice. Blackford describes the slave woman's sorrow as her husband came to take leave of her:

> The poor wife is almost heartbroken for, as he is sold to a Negro trader, there is no probability of their meeting again in this world. She says, "if he was prepared, I would rather have seen him die than going off with those handcuffs on."
>
> I offered to let Jane be sold to go with him that they might not be seperated, [sic] but the young man who acted as agent for the Trader told me candidly that that would not secure the end I desired, for they would be sold wherever they got the highest price for them.
>
> The frequency of these sales and the high prices offered by the Traders and above all the deadening effects of Slavery upon the feelings have steeled the hearts of the people to its enormity.

Blackford goes on to describe the plight of a young black woman in a slave trader's group "whom the trader kept in the capacity of his Mistress until, either from weariness of her or in the hope of gain, most probably from both, he sent her along with the rest to be carried South and sold, probably in the New Orleans market, where a branch of this inhuman traffic is to sell pretty girls for Mistresses for white men: These command a *very high* price" (p. 2).

Like Harriet Beecher Stowe, whom she greatly admired, Blackford views the disruption of family ties and the black woman's sexual predicament within the institution of slavery as the worst of its evils. In her most moving exhortation against slavery she writes:

> Think what it is to be a Slave!!! To be treated not as a man but as a personal chattel, a thing that may be *bought* and *sold,* to have *no right* to the fruits of your own labor, *no right* to your own wife and children. . . . Deprived by the law of learning to read the Bible, compelled to know that the purity of your wife and daughters is exposed without protection of law to the assault of a brutal white man! Think of this, and all the nameless horrors that are concentrated in that one word *Slavery.* (p. 47)

L. Minor Blackford writes that his grandmother's sentiments were absorbed from her parents, particularly from her mother, and that she "was brought up to look upon slaves as human beings whose hard lot deserved not contempt but sympathy, to look upon them as persons capable of selfless devotion and worthy of deep affection. This was the attitude of her mother, the great influence in her life" (p. 3). Mary Blackford's father, John Minor, who built the estate Hazel Hill near Fredericksburg for his family, introduced a bill into the Virginia Legislature for the emancipation of slaves. He died leaving his wife Lucy with children to support and an estate in debt. Instead of selling the slaves to pay their debts as was the custom, Mary's mother sold Hazel Hill because she could not bear to sell those who had served the family faithfully through the years. L. Minor Blackford writes that his grandmother had a close personal relationship with a black woman hired from her owner to take care of the eight Blackford children. Mary Blackford and "Mam' Peggy," as she was called, maintained an affectionate friendship which lasted for sixty years. Unfortunately, the family history *Mine Eyes Have Seen the Glory,* which includes portions of Mary Blackford's journal, does not include segments which deal with that relationship. However, L. Minor Blackford does write that in their declining years they cared for each other and kept a running battle about the locations of their graves, Mam' Peggy being determined that she would not be buried at her mistress's feet (p. 257).

Kate Stone's antislavery sentiments are expressed only in the retrospective preface to her journal *Brokenburn,* but her day-to-day accounts implicitly reflect concern for the slave women who inhabited her family's large cotton plantation in northeastern Louisiana. Like Holmes, Stone was in her early twenties during the war years, yet her journal entries, unlike Holmes's, show the continuity of her many daily associations with black women and reflect the writer's sincere interest in the affairs of slave families. Like Blackford, she was greatly influenced by her mother's humane treatment of the women who managed the household chores. Although her mother protected the family slaves from cruelty and saw that they were cared for, still, Stone writes in retrospect, "there were abuses impossible to prevent. And constantly there were tales circulated of cruelties on neighboring plantations, tales that would make one's blood run cold. And yet we were powerless to help.

". . . I have never regretted the freeing of the Negroes. The great load of accountability was lifted, and we could save our souls alive."[71]

Stone's diary, which she began in 1861 at age twenty, is replete with everyday incidents of interaction with black women. She reports visiting the quarter "to see old Aunt Annie who is sick. Took her some little delicacies and read a psalm" (p. 24). She is well informed of the events in the slave quarters, and she seems concerned about death and sickness, particularly as they affect slave women. One entry describes the death of a child: "Another death among the Negroes today—Jane Eyre, Malona's baby. The little creature was lying in its mother's lap laughing and playing when it suddenly threw itself back, straightened out, and was dead. . . . This is the third child the mother has lost since Mamma bought her, and she seems devotedly attached to her babies. This is her last child" (p. 87). Another just as personal account is of a birth: "Courtney gave birth today, little girls, the first twins born on Brokenburn. Good luck to them" (p. 38). What sets Stone's journal apart is the absence of derogatory remarks about blacks in general and black women in particular. In the journal of her early adulthood, she writes sympathetically of slaves; and although she does not decry slavery as she does in later years, her entries are unusual in that they reveal in a young white southern female a surprising sensitivity to the humanity of black women and, perhaps more significant, a knowledge and an acceptance of their daily lives and roles in the slave community.

In its direct treatment of the issue of southern white guilt, Stone's retrospective preface, written in 1900, is as unusual as her journal. Her daily dealings with the black population of Brokenburn apparently made her sensitive to the many discomforts, difficulties, and actual torments of slave life. In her preface, almost forty years later, she remembers the heavy uncomfortable shoes that slaves had to wear; she recalls the names and features of all the women house servants; she wonders how the black cooks managed the difficult load of cooking three enormous meals day after day for such large households as hers. Her roots, she remarks, were six generations of southern slaveholders. Yet, slavery, she realizes, even under the best of owners,

> was a hard, hard life: to toil six days out of seven, week after week, month after month, year after year, as long as life lasted; to be absolutely under the control of someone until the last breath was drawn; to win but the bare necessaries of life, no hope of more, no matter how hard the work, how long the toil; and to know that nothing could change your lot. Obedience, revolt, submission, prayers—all were in vain. Waking sometimes in the night as I grew older and thinking it all over, I would grow sick with the misery of it all. (pp. 7–8)

She raises the issue of moral accountability with what can only be described as personal anguish. "Always," she writes, "I felt the moral guilt of it, felt how impossible it must be for an owner of slaves to win his way into Heaven. Born and raised as we were, what would be our measure of responsibility?" (p. 8).

The older Stone's discomfiting questions about moral accountability—personal and societal—were seldom echoed in retrospective writings of white southern women. As Sides points out, those memoirs, particularly in the last years of the nineteenth century, tend to present slavery in a rosy, sentimental glow which re-creates plantation life of the Old South as a lost Camelot peopled by chivalric soldiers, brave belles, and docile slaves. Many of these reminiscences attain or at least approach the quality of polemic tracts designed to show generations to come that their southern white ancestors were not "inhuman wretches," but "men brave, courteous, true" and "women sensible, gentle, and retiring," as Letitia Burwell, the descendant of nine generations of Virginia planters, puts it (p. 59). In general, such women characterized the Afro-American as a "menial race," believed that "no people held in bondage ever received so many benefits," and argued that the evils of slavery "were far greater to the slaveholder than to the slaves."[72] In remaking the Old South of their youths, these retrospective writers, regardless of locale or economic status, tend to re-create black women into antithetical stereotypes: They are long-suffering, nurturing female Uncle Toms, mammies who infantilize their white charges (Susan Eppes's "Mammy Lulu" still puts her to bed when she is nineteen); or they are female embodiments of what Ralph Ellison would call the "bad nigger" in American literature[73]—prostitutes, thieves, murderesses. Often in these writings black women of both types become living "proof" that white racism and the slave society had their merits.

In *Memorials of a Southern Planter,* Mississippian Susan Dabney Smedes not only constructs an image of the devoted mammy from a real black woman, but endows her with a voice to praise her Dabney owners and extol the patriarchal system which enslaved her for so many years. This creation of the sympathetic voice of a devoted, nurturing, nonsexual black woman is part of Smedes's larger avowed purpose of these 1887 memoirs, to "throw a kindly light on Southern masters."[74] Blacks and whites in the Dabney household, which included four thousand acres and five hundred slaves, are depicted as members of one happy family. "The bond between master and servant was, in many cases, felt to be as sacred and close as the tie of blood," she writes (p. 34). As a flesh-and-blood example of her thesis, she presents the venerable Mammy Harriet, who helps tell the family history and praises, to the dialectal rhythms of Smedes's pen, the innumerable virtues of her white family. There is no evidence that Smedes's assertions of kindnesses to the slaves on the Dabneys' large Mississippi plantation are unreliable. Yet her *Memorials* clearly falls into the category of southern reminiscence that was motivated, as Sides suggests, by the desire "to appear in the best possible light to one's descendants," and influenced by "the human tendency to remember the best."[75] As her editor points out, Smedes "seems never to have questioned either the legality or the morality of the institution of slavery" (p. ix), and in fact depicts her father's plantation Burleigh as the patriarchal system at its best. Although her mother taught her plantation management, the strongest influence in Smedes's life seems to have been her father, Thomas Dabney. After the untimely death of her husband eleven weeks after their marriage, followed shortly by the death of her mother, Smedes returned to Burleigh to become its mistress. Her avowed literary purpose, as the title of her memoirs indicates, was to immortalize her father as a kindly benevolent master whose slaves were allowed to visit the Big House on social calls, who nursed slaves through sickness, and who refused to move slaves out of his purview for fear they would not be looked after. She likens her father to a king who, in managing his "kingdom," must of necessity possess wisdom, tact, and patience (p. 102). Memoirs such as these are cloaked in "a haze of romance"[76] and nostalgia, not only for the southern past, but for a way of life irrevocably lost.

In such nostalgic treatments of the southern past, black women such as Mammy Harriet take on multiple and complex symbolization. The mammy, as Clinton suggests, was created by white southerners as "the positive emblem of familial relations between black and white . . . a trumped-up figure in the mythologizing of slavery," and in her maternal benignity came to be an acceptable symbol to whites of black power.[77] Though Clinton views the mammy as a sexual image as well, with "warm bodies to serve white needs," to white women like Smedes she may well have been an obverse reflection of the sexually alluring black woman—and thereby a non-threatening and noncompetitive figure. In her associations with home and motherhood, the mammy may be also a black counterpart of "true womanhood," a reinforcement of the Victorian cult of domesticity, just as the stereotypical sexuality of the young black woman presented a denial of its values. This may explain the surge of mammies in the nostalgic literature of the South.[78] The legendary mammy of ante-bellum times had questionable basis in fact, but embodied a positive black alternative to female sexuality "in the great Sunny South." In this symbolization, the mammy becomes the black counterpart of the southern lady on her pedestal. Both female figures are nonsexual, nonthreatening stereotypes that suited a chivalric, patriarchal slave South and its literature.

In the early pages of *Memorials*, Smedes writes that Mammy Harriet, who grew up with her father, Thomas Smith Gregory Dabney, sits beside her as she writes. Smedes transcribes Mammy's stories about the family, which consist mainly of praise for her masters and mistresses and depict the closeness of the races under the institution of slavery. Mammy Harriet is allowed to give the account of the Dabneys' move from Virginia to Mississippi and to tell how, when given the choice, she leaves her husband to follow Thomas Dabney on the premise that "ef you got a husband or a wife who won't go to Mississippi, leff dat one behind. Ef you got a good marster, foller him" (p. 35). Mammy Harriet's main role in Smedes's memoirs, it seems, is to reinforce the thesis that the Dabneys were the best of masters and mistresses and that slavery provided the best of worlds for the Dabneys' black family. The black woman, as quoted by Smedes, tells the story of the journey to Mississippi like a saga of a trip to the Holy Land, with the faithful black pilgrims "follerin' our marster" (p. 40). She speaks of her beloved "Miss Mary," her master's first wife, as "a lady to de tips o' her toes" who lets her wear her wedding gloves, slippers, and veil and provides her own parlor for her wedding. This same Miss Mary was to throw away a huge bowl of molasses when a roach fell in it and "neber let her people eat what she would not eat" (p. 43).

In Mammy Harriet's account of life with the Dabneys, slaves die with white arms around them. She recounts warm stories of the love between mistress and slave woman. She recalls running to tell Miss Mary that one of her favorites, Granny Harriet, is dying: "Missis put on her bonnet an' went to her jes' as fast as she could. When Grannie see her she could not speak, but she hold out both arms to her. Missis run into her arms an' bust out cryin'. She put her arms roun' Grannie's neck, and Grannie could not speak, but di big tears roll down her cheeks. An' so she die" (p. 47).

Mammy Harriet shares Smedes's view that blacks are inherently inferior to whites. She approves the master's assertions that blacks cannot help certain things—such as sleeping long hours and eating too much fried fish. All of her statements are reinforcements to or texts for Smedes's assertions that antebellum life was wonderful for the Dabney slaves. Together, Smedes and her re-creation of Mammy Harriet become in *Memorials* a biracial female chorus extolling the virtues of the patriarchal slave culture. "Quoting" Mammy Harriet for pages, Smedes views her as a positive symbol of the system she is defending and perhaps also as a nonthreatening black woman whose sexuality is neutralized by her white viewpoint. Like Mary Eastman's Phillis, Mammy Harriet, a real black woman, is devoted to her white folks. One cannot help but wonder, though, whether in a sense she too is a fiction. Are her monologues not products of Smedes's wishful thinking, of her need to have a reassuring black voice echoing her assertions that all was indeed well within the slave culture of her youth?

In a similar characterization, Louise Wigfall Wright, daughter of a Confederate senator, re-creates the old slave Sarah, keeper of the Wigfall plantation in Marshall, Texas, as the epitome of loyalty. Wright presents the incredible *exemplum* of Sarah's maintaining the Wigfall home for four years during the war while the family was away. The black woman was put in charge of the family silver. Wright writes with pride that "when we returned, not a single piece was missing; though, in the meantime the War had ended, and she was free to come and go as she chose, and could easily, in the lawlessness of the time, have decamped with her prize, with no one to gainsay her."[79] And likewise, another wealthy and highly placed white woman, Ellen Call Long of Tallahassee, daughter of a two-term territorial governor, paints in retrospect a highly sentimental portrait of a black woman nurse. She recalls a visit in which she watched "little Floridians" with their

> "mammy," the superior nurse, who supervised the noisy crew, whom she petted and scolded in the same breath. It was a beautiful relation, this of the black nurse; a mother-lieutenant, whose authority scarcely slackened in the presence of parents; mutual devotion and dependence, making fast friends of the two. The very dress of "mammy" was picturesque; a white cotton and blue checked apron . . . was checked like a chessboard, and her head was enveloped in a white handkerchief, that contrasted strongly with her black skin, and it did duty as often wiping the tears of her little flock. . . .[80]

When a black woman does not fit the mold of the non-threatening mammy, she may be "punished" by being depicted as Ellison's "bad nigger." Writing about urban war experiences, Sallie A. Putnam of Richmond uses male slaves to illustrate loyalty, usually on the battlefield, and females to show treachery and disloyalty during war times. She writes disapprovingly of a mistress's returning from prayer meeting to find two of her maids, "reared, trained, and belonging to her, missing" along with many of her valuables and pieces of clothing. She decries such "thievish depredations" and seems shocked that "confidential servants, brought up in the house of their mistress" could be so disloyal as to choose freedom over bondage and take items necessary for their welfare (pp. 264–66).

Yet in these memoirs, the ungrateful, dishonest, or promiscuous black woman—the epitome of Ellison's pejorative characterization—is almost nonexistent. The reasons for this omission are surely complex. Interestingly, though, Smedes, Wright, and Long may have had similar motivations in sentimentalizing black women and the institution of slavery. All three were of wealthy families, and all were strongly attached to their fathers. Smedes's book is a memorial to Thomas Dabney, and Wright not only admired her father but enjoyed the social position generated by his political affiliations during the war. Long's mother died when she was ten, and she worshipped her father Richard Keith Call, choosing to stay in Florida with him when her husband moved to Texas, and dedicating her book to his memory. Both father and daughter were antisecessionists, yet years later Long writes that "slavery and the South is the school in which the negro is restrained from vice, and trained in the ways of men and humanity" (p. 65). This is an opinion most likely shared by Governor Call, who owned several plantations near Tallahassee, one of which he ceded to his daughter. Long presents what she calls "a sensible picture of slavery"—the "well regulated plantation" where "everything prospers . . . and goes on in perfect order" (p. 164). She goes on to paint an idyllic picture of black existence in such an order, second in pleasantness only to Smedes's. In such congenial depictions of slavery in the form of black women and the essential benevolence of good plantation management, all three of these women achieve a common end: they re-create their fathers, the masters of such a system, in a beneficent light. This is Smedes's avowed purpose in writing her *Memorials*, and it seems to be a motive for Wright and Long. In creating black women who nurtured and protected the patriarchy, they reaffirm its essential morality and present their own fathers as kindly patriarchs within a benevolent system.

Even those writers of reminiscences who opposed slavery depict black women in stereotypical modes and seem not to have known them well as individuals. One wonders at the *lack* of personality traits, excepting loyalty and disloyalty, by which these white women depict the black women in their lives, particularly as compared to the vivid characterizations of white women in the female slave narratives. The truth of the matter may be simply, and sadly, that blacks of either gender were of importance to many white women only in terms of their abilities to render services and reflect white self-images. The threats that black women posed to white came only in the forms of disloyalty and sexual competition. Many white women may have been blind to individual characteristics of black women, except as they explicitly reflected the presence or absence of those threats.

One such opponent of slavery, Constance Cary Harrison, whose grandfather was the first person in Virginia to manumit his slaves, writes in her *Recollections Grave and Gay* of 1911 that she had "drunk" in her "mother's milk—who inherited it from her stern Swedenborgian father—a detestation of the curse of slavery upon our beautiful Southern land" and had "early found and devoured" *Uncle Tom's Cabin.* Yet she emphasizes the ill effects of slavery upon white rather than black women. Those "pretty languid creatures from the far Southern States had never put on a shoe or stocking for themselves"; their idea "about owning and chastising fellow-beings who might chance to offend them was abhorrent. . . ."[81] For all her hatred of slavery, Harrison fails to re-create believable portraits of blacks, male or female. Her descriptions of plantation life have the same rosy glow as those of Smedes, Eppes, Long, Gay, and Burwell; and her few portraits of black women are affectionately condescending and indicative of scant acquaintance with the reality of the person behind the white-imposed stereotype. She gently derides the "portly cook," who buries her husband one week and remarries the deacon who walked her home from the funeral the next. Her use of dialect is cloying and her anecdotes about "the colored folk" seem designed to support the recollections she has of wondering whether slaves "could be happier free" (p. 142).

Another Virginian who felt what she called "the reproach of human slavery," Sara Agnes Rice Pryor re-creates in her memoirs two portraits of loyal black women. Her portraits of Mammy Grace and Aunt Jinny stress the nurturance these two women lovingly bestowed upon their white masters and mistresses. Pryor recalls, somewhat wistfully, the comfort she derived from these two women as she grew up on a large country estate near Richmond. She, like many southern white women, seems to have enjoyed being infantilized. Mammy Grace, she writes, insisted on "a personally superintended bath" for each young person in the family, no matter how old; and after the war Aunt Jinny, "full of sympathy and resource," welcomes her white folks back to their devastated home and gives comfort, food, and bedding.[82] To Pryor and Harrison, at least in retrospect, slavery was reprehensible; at the same time, Harrison's condescending treatment of black women suggests the premise of white superiority, while Pryor ignores the individual personalities of black women to describe their nurturing role. The black woman is presented in both memoirs as a comical or maternal façade, behind which there is no human being of real substance or seriousness.

Between these white women's journals and memoirs is a hybrid subgenre which combines the spontaneity of the journal form with a retrospection suggested by the passage of time and careful editing and revision. Two of the South's most memorable female autobiographies, those of Cornelia McDonald of Virginia and Mary Chesnut of South Carolina, are of this hybrid type. Not surprisingly, since both women were intelligent, acutely sensitive to issues of race, and strongly opposed to slavery, their retrospective journals provide crucial insights about cross-racial relationships between black and white women of the Old South. Their writings also indicate the diversity of racial attitudes within the same anti-slavery ideology, and suggest also how white attitudes may be related to economic and social position. McDonald, wife of a Winchester lawyer, lived a fairly comfortable but far from luxurious life. She came from a family which was less than affluent. At the war's outset, she was left with seven children and constant troop movement through her region. Chesnut suffered through the war as well, but on a more superficial level. She had no children and was the wife of the influential James Chesnut, son of one of the wealthiest planters in the state. In much of her writing, her concerns are more political and social, while McDonald's are child- and family-centered. Chesnut's position and concerns place her at a farther remove from the black experience. McDonald, acutely sensitive, artistic—she painted as well as wrote—and deeply religious, suffered emotionally from the war and seemed to find in the black women around her a common ground of pain and despair.

McDonald began her journal at the request of her husband, who wished to be informed of each day's events during his absence from their Winchester home throughout the war years. McDonald writes that she faithfully made daily entries, but lost part of the journal during a move in 1863. In 1875 she tried to recollect the incidents recorded in the first part of the diary (March through November 1862) "and to write them again as nearly as possible like the original."[83] Her writings, then, are combinations of original jottings and recalled events in diary form rendered as if they were original. Like Chesnut (and Stowe), she detested slavery and perceived it as a white male's institution. In her introductory remarks to the journal, she writes:

> I never in my heart thought slavery was right, and having in my childhood seen some of the worst instances of its abuse, and in my youth, when surrounded by them and daily witnessing what I considered great injustice to them, I could not think how the men I most honored and admired, my husband among the rest, could constantly justify it, and not only that, but say it was a blessing to the slave, his master, and the country; and (even now I say it with a feeling of shame), that the renewal of the slave trade would be a blessing and benefit to all, if only the consent of the world could be obtained to its being made lawful. (pp. 11–12)

McDonald differs from Chesnut and most of the other white women considered here, because of her intense compassion for black women. She seems to care genuinely for individual women and to depict them *as* individuals with selves commensurate to her own. Two stories of the tribulations of black women, both in the rewritten section of her journal, show McDonald's sensitivity to the despair of those who were forced by war or by their owners into desperate straits. She writes of her children's two nurses, Catherine and Lethea, with compassion and sorrow, finding common maternal ground with these two black women, who nurtured her children as well as their own. For Catherine, who runs away to follow the Yankee soldiers, McDonald has only concern. She knows that Catherine will have difficulty surviving with two young children and after much searching finds her "making her way painfully along the road from Harpers Ferry, with her baby in her arms and little Manuel following her, the picture of

100

famine and grief . . . and when I saw her gaunt figure approaching the house with her poor baby on her arm and the other little one clinging to her ragged skirt, I could not believe the starved, forlorn creature could be my trim-looking, neat nurse" (pp. 80–81).

McDonald becomes even more concerned about a slave woman whose services she rents when the woman's owner decides to sell her. In the retrospective section of her journal, she records daily arguments with Lethea's owner, who wants to sell the woman "to prevent her leaving with the Yankees." McDonald is particularly fond of Lethea because she helped her to nurse her infant daughter Bess, who had died only a few weeks before and whom McDonald mourned deeply. She shares with the black woman the experience of motherhood, and she knows the pain of the separation of mother and child. She recalls fighting the owner's insistent request, believing "it is downright perfidy to deceive the poor creature into consenting to go." She mourns the fact that her husband is gone and that she does not have the money to buy Lethea. It is significant that years after the fact, as McDonald remakes the reality created in the lost portion of her diary, Lethea's tragedy still haunts her.

The intensity of her sorrow for the black woman and distress at her plight remain fresh. In a 12 October 1862 entry she writes: "I cannot endure the thought of her grief; to be torn from her husband and perhaps from her children. Her image will be always associated with that of my lovely baby. She held her and my darling loved her. . . . It is like giving up the last of her. To me it seems as if all the flowers of life are withered, and nothing left but the bare, bitter, thorny stems" (p. 97). Further entries sensitively re-create Lethea's suffering:

> Oct. 15   Another painful scene with Lethea's owner. Poor Lethea must go. It is dreadful to see her tears and distress. I went up stairs into a room where she was busy tacking down a carpet. Her tears were falling on her hands as they held the hammer. . . . I could not tell her she had to go, dreading to witness her sorrow, but turned away, and waited for some other time.

> Oct. 19   Poor Lethea has gone. When she saw there was no

hope, she submitted humbly and quietly. She came to my bedside in the early dawn to say "good bye." She wept and wrung her hands. Margaret was with her, but her other child was not to go.

Oct. 20 . . . I would not have believed that the sorrow of a poor servant and her departure would have made me so sad. I thought of that beautiful and sad lament of Jeremiah. "Weep not for him that dieth, neither bemoan him; but weep for him that goeth away, for he shall return no more, nor see his native country." (p. 98)

More than a decade later, Lethea and her sorrow haunt her former mistress, and we sense McDonald's feelings of help-lessness and guilt in regard to the black woman's plight. Cor-nelia McDonald, kind-hearted though she was, was surely no Mrs. Shelby who helps Eliza fight a mercenary institution and win. Lethea must go, and McDonald, thirteen years after the fact, still feels her culpability in the black woman's tragedy. Although she re-creates both black women as victims, this is perhaps not only because they *were* but also because she, unlike so many other white women of the Old South, genuinely felt a bond of common womanhood and common humanity with these slave women whose sorrows filled her memory.

Like McDonald, Mary Chesnut combines the diary and memoir, but by a more complex artistic process. Her actual Civil War journal was not meant for publication, and her "diary" was actually written twenty years after the war, in 1881–1884. C. Vann Woodward's 1981 edition, entitled *Mary Chesnut's Civil War*, incorporates parts of the original journal with the retrospective "diary," which was first published in 1905 and later in 1949 in an edition by Ben Ames Williams entitled *A Diary from Dixie*—a title that Woodward believes Chesnut would have disliked.[84] Woodward's edition provides a synthesis of the two forms of autobiography, the diary and the memoir, in a responsibly edited version of what Chesnut actually wrote during the war and twenty years later.[85] Chesnut's writings, so crucial to an understanding of the period and to the white southern viewpoint, also reflect a deeply ambivalent attitude toward black women, whom she equates not only with forbidden sexuality but with the status of motherhood which she, frustrated at her own inability to have children, envies and resents. There is a darkness at the core of Chesnut's feelings for black women, and her strange love-hatred of these women makes an appropriately in-conclusive conclusion for this chapter.

As Woodward points out, however, Chesnut shows "an unusual sense of responsibility toward the history she re-cords," particularly in light of the fact that the lapse of time between her first and last versions was "not merely the passing of two decades, but the most traumatic years in the history of the South (pp. xxvi–xxvii). One of her stated purposes in her revision of the eighties, Woodward finds in her correspon-dence, was what she calls "leaving myself out" (p. xxvi). To whatever extent she succeeded, Woodward attempts to right the balance by reinserting personal comments which previous editions have left unpublished. *Mary Chesnut's Civil War* thus captures the sweep and chaos of a society at war, as did Williams' *A Diary from Dixie,* but this new edition allows a closer view of the autobiographer—that interior perception of self which Pascal insists is essential to true autobiography.[86] In her journal Chesnut writes that she is "like a spider, spinning [her] own entrails" (p. 23). Woodward's edition allows us to examine the web of self that Chesnut has woven and then redesigned with art and imagination.

That web is complex and multistranded, and Chesnut's feelings about black women are part of its central complexity. It has become commonplace to point out that Chesnut sees miscegenation as the embodiment of the evil of slavery and of the double standard that allows the white southern male sexual freedom and marital infidelity while his wife and daughters are bound by the prohibitions of chastity. In her often-quoted diatribes against this aspect of slavery, though, Chesnut seems so intent on pitying the white women whose husbands are involved in these philanderings in the quarters that she has no sympathy left for the hapless black women who were their sexual victims. She views them instead as symbols of sex-uality, ironically, with freedoms not allowed respectable white women:

. . . we live surrounded by prostitutes. An abandoned woman is sent out of any decent house elsewhere. Who thinks any worse of a negro or mulatto woman for being a thing we can't name? God forgive us, but ours is a *monstrous* system and wrong and iniquity. Perhaps the rest of the world is as bad—this *only* I see. Like the patriarchs of old our men live all in one house with their wives and their concubines, and the mulattoes one sees in every family exactly resemble the white children—and every lady tells you who is the father of all the mulatto children in everybody's household, but those in her own she seems to think drop from the clouds, or pretends so to think.   (p. 29)

Chesnut's journal at this point reflects her intense feelings about the sexual repressions of white women that emerge in titillating talk: "Good women we have, *but* they talk of all *nastiness*—tho' they never do wrong, they talk day and night of [erasures illegible save for the words "all unconsciousness"] my disgust sometimes is boiling over—but they are, I believe, in conduct the purest women God ever made. Thank God for my countrywomen—alas for the men!" (p. 31).

Chesnut goes on in this passage to compare the system which lends itself to miscegation as "patriarchal. So it is—flocks and herds and slaves—and wife Leah does not suffice. Rachel must be *added*, if not *married*" (p. 31). Significantly, Chesnut moves to a discussion of her father-in-law, "Mr. Chesnut Senior," who she apparently believed had children by a slave named "Rachel" (p. 31, n. 5). She ends her diatribe with a bitter pronouncement upon black women: "And again I say, my countrywomen are as pure as angels, tho' surrounded by another race who are the social evil!" (p. 31). Intelligent though she was, Chesnut seems to blame black women for a social evil only white men could instigate and focuses her bitterness at its victims rather than their victimizers. The intensity of that bitterness and its misdirection may also derive from her complex reaction of envy and admiration toward what she conceives as a female sexual freedom—an actual acting out of the "nasty talk" of white women, who substitute the sexual talk for sexual freedom. Also Chesnut's feelings for black women are related to her own presumptions of white superiority. Slave owners are martyrs to their responsibilities to these inferior beings, she believes, and southern women work harder than missionaries in seeing to the needs of blacks, who are "dirty, slatternly, idle, ill-smelling by nature (when otherwise, it is the exception)" (p. 245). Sneering at northern abolitionists, she concludes: "The best way to take negroes to your heart is to get as far away from them as possible" (p. 307).

In slaves generally, Chesnut, a member of the wealthy planter class, also senses an incipient capacity for violence. In Camden, South Carolina, during the early stages of the war, she writes: "A genuine slave-owner born and bred will not be afraid of negroes—quand même. Here we are mild as the moonbeams and as serene. Nothing but negroes around us— white men all gone to the army" (p. 234). Yet she protests too much. Again and again throughout her narrative she comments on the inscrutability of slaves and seems to fear what Faulkner would later depict as the "great balloon face" of blackness that so enraged and frightened Thomas Sutpen. She associated blackness with death: "I am always studying these creatures. They are to me inscrutable in their ways and past finding out.

"Dr. Gibbes says the faces of the dead grow as black as charcoal on the battlefield, and they shine in the sun.

"Now this horrible vision of the dead on the battlefield haunts me" (p. 114).

Chesnut particularly fears female house slaves because of their positions of trust and their proximity to the white family. Though she seems genuinely fond of her maid Molly, she is deeply shocked by the murder of her Cousin Betsey Wither- spoon, who was killed by her maid Rhody and several other slaves. ". . . the bloody story haunts me night and day," she writes, and she tells and retells the gory details of the murder and the strange looks in the black woman's eyes as she tries to clear up suspicions. What bothers Chesnut particularly is that she cannot understand why Rhoda, whom her cousin had treated well, would cold-bloodedly murder "that innocent old lady." She writes,

Hitherto I have never thought of being afraid of negroes. I

had never injured any of them. Why should they want to hurt me? Two-thirds of my religion consists in trying to be good to negroes because they are so in my power, and it would be so easy to be the other thing. Somehow today I feel that the ground is cut away from under my feet. Why should they treat me any better than they have done Cousin Betsey Wither-spoon? (p. 199)

What Chesnut never seems to recognize, except perhaps subconsciously in her fear of black inscrutability, is the enormous frustration and explosive rage engendered by the simple fact of being a slave. Insightful though her remarks are otherwise, she seems blind to what it must be like to be a slave. She goes on to tell the story of Mrs. Cunningham, whose slaves hanged her from a tree to make it appear that she had committed suicide. In her horrific descriptions of these murders, Chesnut reveals a profound fear of slaves, particularly of female slaves who have admittance to the boudoirs of their mistresses. She knows "if they want to kill us, they can do it when they please—they are noiseless as panthers." When she writes, "we ought to be grateful that any one of us is alive," she seems to refer to white women who remain on the plantations during the war at the mercy of their slaves (p. 211). She consoles herself with thoughts of her own slaves' loyalty— "nobody is afraid of their own negroes"—yet the Witherspoon case which so haunts her shows, above all, that some southern women would do well to be more fearful. Yet Chesnut ends this passage in a declaration of faith: "my Molly and half a dozen others that I *know*—and all the rest I believe—would keep me as safe as I should be in the Tower of London" (p. 212).

Molly does seem to be the one black woman whom Chesnut trusts implicitly, and perhaps for good reason. Molly tells her mistress when the overseer is cheating her out of butter and hams. During the war Molly and her mistress go into the butter and egg business together and make enough to subsist upon. Chesnut describes how Molly takes care of her when she becomes ill in Columbia and how she races out for the doctor when her condition worsens. Another description, of an unexpected gift from Molly, shows Chesnut's affection for the black woman yet at the same time her blindness to

Molly's affection for Molly's husband, Lige, and children: she writes, supposedly from Columbia, "My Molly will forget Lige and her babies, too. I asked her who sent me that beautiful bouquet I found on my center table. 'I give to you—'twas give to me.' And Molly was in a moment all wriggle-giggle blush—golden crown blushes" (p. 336). When one of Molly's children becomes ill on the Camden plantation, Chesnut seems a bit piqued that Molly insists upon going home to take care of the child when Molly's "mother, the best woman in the world, is given nothing else to do but take charge of Molly's children" (p. 353). Yet she strongly approves Molly's actions later in her narrative, when she recounts how the black woman gave Chesnut courage on a grueling journey to visit her own dying mother. The two women are harassed by a drunken man, but Molly eases her mistress's spirits by vowing to wallop the man if he comes near her (p. 462).

Chesnut has fond feelings for the Molly who protects and nurtures her. Yet she has little real sense of Molly's own identity as a person with other affections. When Chesnut walks into a scene in which an enraged Molly is striking her own daughter for carelessly hurting her baby sister, Chesnut writes that she simply cannot understand what the fuss is about and that she resents that kind of behavior when she is tired. She describes Molly as

> looking more like an enraged lioness than anything else, roaring that her baby's neck was broken. Howling cries of vengeance. And the poor little careless nurse's dark face had an ashen tinge of gray terror, and she was crouching near the ground, like an animal trying to hide, and her mother striking at her as she rolled away. All this was my welcome as I entered the gate. It takes these half-Africans but a moment to go back to their naked, savage animal nature.   (p. 642)

Chesnut actually seems to see Molly as a black subordinate self adjunctive to her own white personality. When Molly shows how much members of her own family mean to her, Chesnut reacts with exasperation and resentment.

Significantly, her adverse reaction often is prompted by Molly's affection for her own children. Chesnut, embittered by her own childlessness, resents black women's associations with fertility. Obviously, Chesnut feels deeply that she has missed an important part of womanhood. In a section of journal which she deleted from her book, she calls herself "a childless wretch" and becomes deeply wounded by a remark made by her father-in-law in which he equates a woman's usefulness with the number of children she produces. Later she writes wistfully, "women need maternity to bring out their best and true loveliness" (p. 105). Apparently, though, she means white women, for she equates childbearing for black women, who have "no end of children and no beginning of husband," with propagation of a breed of parasitic human beings who depend on whites for sustenance (p. 54). The fertile black woman, for Chesnut, becomes what Jung calls the negative image of Great Mother.[87] As a white woman who has been denied her sexuality and the opportunity to bear children, whether through her own barrenness or her husband's, she views fertility in black women as deeply threatening. These slaves, who she feels are less than human, can produce children while she cannot. "They rapidly increase and never diminish in numbers," she writes direly (p. 77). And it is to her the bitterest of ironies that while they do so, she and her husband, an only son, will have no children to carry on the family name and inherit the Chesnut estates.

To Chesnut, black woman is the emblem of the hidden evil of slavery, adulterous miscegenation, that "sorest spot" that Harriet Beecher Stowe did not touch when she made Legree a bachelor. For Chesnut, the real hurt and indignity of this sexual evil of the slave society is not the black woman's violation but the white woman's shame. In Molly she finds the maternal nurturance she needs in the chaos of the Civil War South, but though she seems to love the Molly who takes care of her, she fails to see her as a human being whose own family is central to her life—a life which excludes the white world. More than anything Chesnut views the black woman as the embodiment of her own fears and disappointments. She equates white womanhood with slavery. In the black woman she sees sexual freedom and maternal joy. What she does not see is that the black woman's sexuality and fertility often led to her greatest indignities and deepest pain. What she does not see is the black woman as a *self* correspondent to her own—as an organic, a separate personality.

Exactly what makes her vision different from that of McDonald (or those of Edmondston and Eppes from those of Stone and Blackford) is still unclear; yet many of the same factors—maternal and paternal influences, locale, economic and social status—seem to influence these white women's racial attitudes in important yet not easily measurable ways. Yet Chesnut's ambivalence toward black women and her inability or unwillingness to acknowledge their humanity may be approached as a paradigm for this paradoxical pattern of connection and rejection in southern racial experience, a pattern that would absorb those literary artists who sought to recreate that experience in modern American fiction. In these autobiographical writings, from both white and black female perspectives emerge instances of sisterhood in the face of common suffering, moments when these women crossed lines of resentment and pain to minister to one another. For the most part, though, those color lines blinded white women to the humanity of their black sisters and built in black women massive layers of hatred for those fair ladies who would not, or could not, see their suffering. Traces of this blindness and hatred remain. Catherine Clinton writes that America is still "haunted by the rattling of the chains."[88] It is perhaps these peculiarly female chains, those of the body and those of the mind, which rattle loudest. And it is surely in these intense and deeply personal female writings that they may be heard to reverberate most insistently.

CHAPTER III

"Twin Sistered to The Fell Darkness"
CLYTIE, ROSA, AND THE MYSTERY OF RACISM

Then she touched me, and then I did stop dead.
ROSA COLDFIELD

This is the terrifying, hopeful, hopeless, epiphanic moment in Faulkner's *Absalom, Absalom!* in which black woman confronts white, acknowledges her as womankind and humankind, and seeks mutual recognition. It is a moment of pulsating stasis which plunges straight to the depths of that chasm between races which made sisterhood in the Old South, and by implication any human kinship, the matter of a moment's recognition shattered by fear and antipathy. In her rejection of Clytie Sutpen, Rosa Coldfield reflects the darkness of the white self which rejects human connection with the black Other and is doomed to say tragically and hysterically, as Rosa does to Clytie, *"Take your hand off me, nigger!"*[1] Faulkner's creation of Rosa and Clytie's moment of connection and rejection is perhaps the most powerful example in the canon of what Walter Slatoff finds to be Faulkner's "sense of life as conflict, tension, and frustration"—an intensely ambivalent perspective which burdens his fictional world with more ambiguity and complexity than the real one and makes his writing an intensification of conflict for conflict's sake, and thus "a deliberate quest for failure."[2]

Yet Clytie's confrontation with Rosa in the white woman's headlong rush to participate in Judith Sutpen's grief for Charles Bon and the unresolved tensions of that confrontation are more in touch than Slatoff acknowledges with the often bitter reality of relationships between black and white women of the nineteenth-century South. The early women's slave narratives show black women reaching for a sense of humanity and recognition from the white women who controlled their lives. Like Clytie, they were disappointed, often bitterly so. The southern lady herself, the chaste object of white male gynecolatry, developed a simultaneous loathing of and yearning toward black female sexuality, which in *Absalom* is embodied not in Clytie herself but in the idea of Sutpen's lust for her mother. Like the real Mary Chesnut and the fictional Rosa Coldfield, many southern white women were afflicted with an inability to recognize their black sisters' individuality and humanity. Their blindness is the blindness of the country which sends the young Thomas Sutpen to the back door without hearing what he has to say. It is "a country all divided and fixed and neat with a people living on it all divided and fixed and neat because of what color their skins happened to be and what they happened to own" (p. 221). As Rosa remembers and reenacts this moment between her and the black daughter of Sutpen, she and we feel the paradoxical power of racism as an implacable, irrational, self-defeating force with a mind of its own. Clytie is the only person who sees and respects Rosa as woman and as self. Rosa knew, and knows, the value of such a human response. Yet in this moment with Clytie and thereafter she cannot bring herself to acknowledge the black woman as an equivalent self.

It is this human unwillingness to acknowledge the humanity of others which is at the very heart of the novel and which links the terrifying irrationality of racism to the excessive rationality of Sutpen's code of expediency. Time after time, the people of *Absalom* reject and destroy their fellow human beings. The balloon-faced slave at the door of the mansion sends Sutpen to the back. Sutpen himself refuses so much as to raise an eyebrow in acknowledgment of his own son. Judith and Clytie cannot mother Charles Etienne because they cannot see him as a person in his own right. Rosa's rejection of Clytie is echoed in Sutpen's refusal to think of Rosa—or of any white marriageable woman—as more than a vehicle of gestation, a mare or bitch to fulfill his design. This is the puzzle of *Absalom*. It is part of the "universal mutual experience, the anguishes and troubles and griefs of the human heart" of which Faulkner spoke at West Point,[3] this inability or unwillingness of one human soul to recognize equivalent humanity in others. It is the flaw of the Old South that led to its destruction.

Yet with Faulkner, and particularly with *Absalom*, issues are not so clear. The "message" of the novel is also epistemological. Like Quentin, Shreve, Rosa, and Mr. Compson, we can never really know the past. There is no fourteenth way of looking at the blackbird that is more accurate or real than the thirteen others. We nibble at the edges of truth. As Quentin and his roommate Shreve McCannon attempt to piece together the fabric of the lives which Thomas Sutpen and his children lived, we and they realize the futility of such a quest. Sutpen's saga emerges from such a realization, but also from a mutual need of all the narrators to confront the past. None of the versions of Sutpen's dream to build an empire out of southern soil and his ultimate failure is entirely accurate. Yet the story which emerges becomes cumulatively powerful because of the faltering, *human* way it is told.

In the imaginations of Rosa Coldfield, Mr. Compson, Quentin and Shreve—and in our own—Sutpen and the southern past become syntheses of many stories, all of them complex, baffling, terrifying. Sutpen, as he emerges from the voices of others, builds his plantation but sees his dynasty collapse through his unwillingness to recognize his own son, Charles Bon, because of his black blood. That one act results in Sutpen's son Henry killing Charles to prevent his marriage to their sister Judith. Sutpen's last attempt to continue his male line results in his own grisly death, again because he cannot view a human being as anything more than means to an end. When young Milly Jones produces a daughter instead of the son Sutpen so desperately wanted, he treats Milly like an animal which failed to breed correctly. Her grandfather Wash

Jones, Sutpen's only friend, cuts him down with a scythe because of this, Sutpen's last failure in human relations. Yet all these events are filtered through many consciousnesses decades later. None is reliable. Many times we are at third and fourth removes from the truth. Sutpen's life is a crashing boulder which pulls with it, tragically and terribly, other lives. His story is more than a story; it becomes a part of the lives of those who tell it. Even Quentin is deeply affected years later by Sutpen's story and what it implies about an evil which is peculiarly southern and at the same time terrifyingly universal. The burden of that knowledge makes him "older at twenty than a lot of people who have died." He—and we—join Mr. Compson in saying, "It's just incredible. It just does not explain. Or perhaps that's it: they don't explain and we are not supposed to know" (p. 100).

Nor does the relationship between black and white women consist of Rosa and Clytie's relationship only. In the commonality of purpose and shared determination to endure which binds Judith and Clytie Sutpen, Faulkner also portays true affection, mutual recognition, and sisterhood—literal and metaphorical—between black and white women. Judith and Clytie grow up as sisters and together endure what life and the men in their lives force them to endure. Each of the narrators who attempts to reconstruct the lives of these two Sutpen women pictures them as sisters in the deepest sense. When Mrs. Compson asks Judith if she plans to commit suicide, her answer is, "No, not that. Because somebody will have to take care of Clytie, and father, too, soon . . ." (p. 128). Likewise, Judith, whom we come to know through her humane actions and her willingness to suffer if suffer she must, overcomes the barrier of sexual competition to allow the octoroon her time of mourning for Charles Bon. She treats the exotic, emotional woman with grave kindness when she comes to Sutpen's Hundred, just as later she would take care of Charles Etienne and die doing so. Her acceptance of Bon's mistress and of her implicit sexuality contradicts Mr. Compson's judgments (Mr. Compson is wrong about a great many things, particularly as they concern women) that such women's "white sisters of a mushroom yesterday" always reject the "female principle" in "moral and outraged horror" (p. 116) and that Judith herself lived by "the ruthless Sutpen code of taking what it wanted provided it were strong enough" (p. 120). We know the impenetrable Judith by her deeds, and they surely support Cleanth Brooks's assessment that Judith is "one of Faulkner's finest characters of endurance—and not merely through numb, bleak Stoicism but also through compassion and love."[4]

In Judith's relationships with Clytie and with the octoroon, Faulkner holds out the possibility of the expansive heart, the loving impulse, the human commitment. This is particularly true of the physical and spiritual sisterhood of Judith and Clytie. Bleak though their lives are, Clytie and Judith become in their closeness twin emblems of human unity and cross-racial female bonding. It is their relationship, their common bonds of suffering, which make that "scratch" on "the block of stone" Judith perceives as life. They, more than any other characters in the book, embody Judith's belief in human interconnectedness as visualized in her metaphor of "the strings . . . all in one another's way like five or six people all trying to make a rug on the same loom only each one wants to weave his own pattern into the rug; and it cant matter, you know that, and yet it must matter because you keep on trying or having to keep on trying . . ." (p. 127).

Yet the more apt metaphor for cross-racial relationships of the novel and of its time and its place is Rosa Coldfield's vision of herself and Clytie as being *"twin sistered to the fell darkness"* (p. 140). *Absalom* is about the failure of human relationships. It is about people and their failure to love, to acknowledge the humanity of others, and to follow Faulkner's own injunction that they be better than they know how to be. Rosa's is such a failure. She rejects the humanity of the only person who acknowledges her own. Her obsession with Clytie as black and as woman becomes a driving force in the novel. Behind that obsession is surely suggestion of her own sense of guilt and, through that suggestion, the implication of a more expansive, a finer sensibility than the rigid, bitter woman she becomes.

Rosa vents her fury at Sutpen for rejecting her humanity, but her despairing anger is self-directed as well. She focuses her rage at Clytie, and she pits her will against that of the black woman. Yet it is she and Sutpen and their mutual inhumanity that she sees mirrored in Clytie. We see, if Rosa does not, that her failure to respond to Clytie's humanity is part of the tragedy and enigma of what has made her life what it is—an "abstract contradiction" of openness, joy, and human connection. Rosa's failure to respond to Clytie is the paradoxical tragedy of the Old South itself, and of all its white women who could never move beyond their own shackles of racism to feel the humanity in their black sisters' touch or the need for connection and recognition it signified. It is as a failure, then, that we view Rosa and Clytie's volatile antithesis of sisterhood. In that antithesis Faulkner probes the paradox of racism as a source of the intense ambivalence with which white southerners, including himself,[5] regarded the Afro-American. It is the puzzle of Rosa's failure to respond to Clytie's humanity that makes this the cross-racial female relationship in *Absalom* that is most worthy of closer scrutiny.

Rosa herself is an anomaly to the dichotomous confines which some critics have employed to categorize Faulkner's female characters. She is rigid old woman and vulnerable virgin. She is perverse and pitiful, cruel and caring, active and passive. She is the force which drives the past into the present, which insists on the telling of the tale, which must know why. She is, in short, the perfect example of Faulkner's insistence that "no person is wholly good or wholly bad"[6] but a complex mixture of the two. It is Rosa Coldfield's conscious rage and subconscious guilt which press the story to its terrifying end. She is both artist and participant. It is she who insists not only that the story be told, but that it be *understood*. The failure that everyone, including the reader, has in understanding the haunting meaning of the past is even more powerfully ironic because of her angry insistence that Sutpen's human failures, and by implication her own, be clearly delineated and dealt with. Rosa Coldfield is no ghost, as David Miller would categorize her.[7] Nor does she embody the passive pro-creativeness of the female principle that, according to Brooks and Sally Page, informs Faulkner's perceptions of women.[8] She is a complex character whose rapacious yet infinitely pitiful outrage evokes bafflement and ambivalence. Rosa's complexity and the complexity of our response to her reflect the limitations of archetypal approaches to her and to other of Faulkner's more complexly drawn women characters, as well as the restrictiveness of categorizing Faulkner himself as either misogynist or gynecolatrist and his women as reflections of that dialectic.[9]

The active pressure that Rosa exerts on the story also defies the concept that the active male principle balances female passivity in Faulkner's works.[10] Rosa is many things, but she is far from passive. It is her stubborn insistence on knowing and on telling which is the controlling force in *Absalom*. Page's assertion that by age ten Rosa "has abdicated existence" is not borne out by the facts. Although she is, as Page says, one of Faulkner's women excluded from "the procreative role set aside for woman by the natural processes of life," she is far from being "idle" and "useless."[11] Rosa provokes action rather than being its "goal and end"; she does live by "codes of honor"; she struggles to discover reality and herself.[12] In an important sense, *Absalom* is more Rosa's book than anyone's. She evokes the epistemological process, and she pays with her life for what she comes to know.

Rosa's driving need is not so much to discover the nature of the "something . . . living hidden in that house," but to know herself—to *understand* why her life has turned out as it has. She finds in Clytie an objective correlative for the intense ambivalence, the love and the hate, she feels for herself as white southern woman trapped by gender, history, culture, and her own racism. Rosa may intuit Clytie as a female shadow-self,[13] the product of pure sexual passion which young Rosa envisions, but never experiences, during her "summer of wistaria" at age fourteen. In chapter 5—much more Rosa's story than Sutpen's—Rosa describes the *"root and urge"* of her own developing sexuality. She knows her sexual self is now *"gnarled forgotten,"* but her *"moment"* did exist, she insists, *"when the entire delicate spirit's bent is one anonymous climaxless epicene and unravished nuptial— . . . a world filled with living marriage like the light and air which she breathes"* (pp. 144–45).[14] Yet Miss Rosa speaks from a citadel of "longly thwarted old female flesh" (p.

14). Her root never came to flower. "An ironical symbol of chaste Southern womanhood,"[15] she is in metaphorical opposition to the stereotypical sexuality of the black woman exemplified in Mr. Compson's perception of the octoroon as embodying

> a female principle which existed, queenly and complete, in the hot equatorial groin of the world long before that white one of ours came down from trees and lost its hair and bleached out— a principle apt docile and instinct with strange and ancient curious pleasures of the flesh (which is all: there is nothing else) which her white sisters of a mushroom yesterday flee from in moral and outraged horror. . . . (p. 116)

Although Clytie, like the old Miss Rosa, is more of an androgynous character, she is to Rosa not only a Sutpen, but an emblem of the culture which opposes love and sexuality, and bisects female sexual functions and attitudes by race. Rosa sees Clytie not as individual but as the implacable force of the slave South which dehumanizes and devours. Clytie exudes an "extrasensory perception" which Rosa herself calls "*a brooding awareness and acceptance of the inexplicable unseen, inherited from an older and purer race than mine*" (p. 138).[16] Yet just as it is impossible to know the past in *Absalom,* it is impossible to know the real Clytie. We see her only through the distorted lens of other eyes. She is ultimately impenetrable. From the outside her loyalty seems to be to her Sutpen heritage. She "lives selflessly and with dignity."[17] She is an example of the complexity of Faulkner's depictions of blacks: they are, as Ralph Ellison says, neither "good nigger" or "bad nigger" but a complex exploration of the white southerner's guilt and conflict about race.[18]

Clytie's significance to Rosa cannot be overstated. As Lee Jenkins points out, in the minds of many real and fictional whites, the black is an embodiment of "the very idea of contamination and of the idea that the mind is divided against itself." To Rosa, Clytie is at least partly an example of the impact of the black on the white mind, "the harbinger of the idea that the dark, irrational, and instinctual dimension persists in its threatening potential as a force which overcomes reason and light or infiltrates and compromises them."[19] Rosa sees Clytie as evidence of the "dark dimension," especially as it relates to pure sexuality. Perhaps the closest study of the Rosa-Clytie relationship, Régine Robin's "*Absalom, Absalom!*" in *Le Blanc et le noir chez Melville et Faulkner*, suggests that Rosa's aversion to Clytie, like that of many white women of the Old South toward their black sisters, is based on fear of female sexuality. Rosa, much like Emma Holmes, sees the black woman as emblematic of a loss of sexual control in which she as white woman is not allowed to indulge. Clytie, writes Robin, "est conçue comme une couleur et incarne toutes les forces sexuelles qui effraient Rosa dont les instincts, les impulsions, les désirs sont en ébullition. Tandis qu'elle essaye de les combattre et de refouler cette partie d'ellemême qu'elle juge noncivilisée, elle transfère sur la femme noire le principe du mal et de l' enfer."[20]

Throughout her narrative Rosa associates blackness with sex and with loss of control, which both repel and fascinate her. Her descriptions of blacks are sexually suggestive. She speaks of Sutpen's "wild negro," who allows young Judith to let the horses run away on the ride to church (p. 25). His "wild negroes," she reports, fight "naked . . . to hurt one another quick and bad"(p. 29). Her descriptions make Quentin envision Sutpen's slaves as "wild niggers like beasts half tamed to walk upright like men, in attitudes wild and reposed" (p. 8). Significantly, she ties Judith and Clytie to this wildness and lack of restraint. She pictures them watching the fights unmoved. Yet, as Faulkner is careful to have Mr. Compson point out, Rosa does not mention the two black women among Sutpen's slaves, as if such an explicit connection between sex and race were more than she could consciously acknowledge. It is the specter of miscegenation embodied in Clytie which so horrifies her. To the young Rosa—whose only real love is an imaginary one, whose vicarious pleasure at sixteen is to sew unskillfully and painstakingly Judith's trousseau, whose ever-present need is to control passion—Clytie's face and touch become tangible evidence of a loss of that control.

In their first confrontation she sees in Clytie the horror of miscegenation and of the whole social structure which, as Mr.

Compson says, divides women into "ladies or whores or slaves" (p. 114). Clytie becomes Rosa's own divided self and the divisiveness of southern culture which relegates passion to the dark sphere, the black woman. In a flash she sees at once what Eric Sundquist calls "the ruinous divisions" of the South,[21] which allow the Sutpens of the country to engender black bastards for recreation, as casually as they might fight with their slaves, and sire white heirs with the most intense care and concern. She tells Quentin that her confrontation with Clytie brought her into the world of reality. It becomes the initiation experience that Brooks says Faulkner's women do not have.[22] Although Rosa does not deny the truth of her epiphany, she does reject its bearer.

Rosa has been said to fear and despise Clytie.[23] Yet her feelings are more ambivalent, and they change with age. It is important to envision Rosa as a young woman in the 1865 confrontation with Clytie. Although the old Rosa describes her youthful feelings, the young Rosa—layered through perceptions of the old—often seems older than she is. Her descriptions of the onset of puberty are rendered in such a mature voice that it is the older Rosa we see as we listen, not the inarticulate young girl. Rosa associates herself with Judith, who is four years older, and often seems older than she is. She sews a trousseau at age sixteen; she learns how to cut down her aunt's old dresses; she becomes parent to the father when he repudiates life and shuts himself in the attic. Her sister Ellen asks her, a seventeen-year-old, to take care of Judith, who is twenty-one. In her early years she was not allowed to act like a child and spent her childhood lurking at corners behind closed doors, becoming the object of what Mr. Compson calls the "outraged female vindictiveness" of her unbalanced spinster aunt and the puritan rigidity of her father. Her aunt shows her the duality of human nature by teaching her to hate men and then deserting her to elope with one. The Rosa who meets Clytie on the stairs in 1865 is a young woman whose upbringing has both sheltered and exposed her. She knows how to sew and how to feed a crazed father and herself. She knows how to hate Sutpen but she knows very little about what it is in him which repels her.

As Thadious Davis points out, we come to know Clytie through the older Rosa: she "achieves life primarily through Rosa Coldfield's imaginative construction of her."[24] As Davis so astutely suggests, each narrator in *Absalom* invents his or her concept of "Negro" and in so doing succeeds in a self-defining process that expresses the limits of his or her "imagination, personality and humanity,"[25] It is in this sense that Rosa actually creates Clytie, exerting in talk the control which she cannot have in life. Though the scene is one of recognition, it is also one of struggle—of the volatile, violent, and inexplicable force of racism which pits white and black women into deathlock struggles in life and in literature. The scene, revised four times to intensify its power,[26] is a paradigm of the bitterness of southern racial experience. And there is, for the white, no turning back from the path of racism finally taken. This is part of "the reality" into which Rosa Coldfield awakens. The poignancy of the scene is that of the southern racial experience itself. It would have been the easy thing for the white woman to respond to the black. It is the hard thing for affection-starved, nineteen-year-old Rosa Coldfield to reject Clytie's acceptance of her as woman—truly as *Rosa*. What seems to haunt Rosa, and Faulkner, is why she could not reach out across racial barriers to a common humanity with a common soul.

Miss Rosa says that at first she felt Clytie's presence only as "*that inscrutable coffee-colored face,*" with its implacable and immobile force. When Clytie orders her not to go up the stairs, she recalls her and Clytie's glaring at each other "*not as two faces but as the two abstract contradictions which we actually were*" (p. 138). The order itself pits black woman and black will against white. Clytie repeats the order: "*Dont you go up there, Rosa*" (p. 138), and evokes in Rosa strongly conflicting responses. On one hand she feels that it is "*the house itself that said the words*"— the house which Sutpen built and created as part of himself. Clytie's orders are Sutpen's own. At the same time Rosa recognizes the meaning of her given name, coming from the mouth of a black woman who should be calling her "Miss Rosa."[27] Rosa recognizes that the older Clytie might be calling her Rosa because she is still young, but she knows intuitively that *"that was not what she meant at all"* (p. 139). What Clytie does mean is a recognition of Rosa as woman, as *self.* Rosa, that paradoxical combination of childishness and age, knows now as she did then that Clytie *"did me more grace and respect than anyone else I knew; I knew that from the instant I had entered that door, to her of all who knew me I was no child"* (p. 139). Yet, her racism does not permit mutual recognition, mutual respect. She recalls: *"'Rosa?' I cried. 'To me? To my face?'"* (p. 139).

Clytie attempts again to exert her will, and for that moment of *"furious immobility,"* Rosa *feels* Clytie as woman, as black, as human *force,* as individual with self commensurate to her own. She feels the breaking down of racial barriers, the impact of

> that black arresting and untimorous hand on my white woman's flesh. Because there is something in the touch of flesh with flesh which abrogates, cuts sharp and straight across the devious intricate channels of decorous ordering, which enemies as well as lovers know because it makes them both—touch and touch of that which is the citadel of the central I-Am's private own: not spirit, soul; the liquorish and ungirdled mind is anyone's to take in any darkened hallway of this earthly tenement. But let flesh touch with flesh, and watch the fall of all the eggshell shibboleth of caste and color too. (p. 139)

This is the moment of simultaneous tension and resolution in which white and black women connect in an electrifying way. It is a connection which echoes through Rosa's psyche and memory and reverberates, as Davis says, "all tensions between black and white, between classes and races that have been used to define the South and to establish the major concerns of the novel."[28] Clytie's touch is, as Robin suggests, the touch of life; of *feeling*; of human connection: "Clytie, mère spirituelle, forme et initie Rosa qui découvre l'essence de la vie; les sens. Cette révélation se manifeste par la main de la femme noire qui canalise les préjugés raciaux de Rosa pour les annihiler."[29] Under that *"black arresting and untimorous hand,"* Rosa stops dead, and at the same time comes to life. She feels Clytie's blackness, womanhood, and individuality all at once in the black woman's *"furious and unbending will."*

It is at this point that Rosa denies Clytie the human recognition the black woman has given her. Rosa's denial is furious, emphatic: *"Take your hand off me, nigger!"* (p. 140). This is a difficult passage to analyze, perhaps because Faulkner, through the older Miss Rosa, seems to be both rendering the denial and analyzing it on several different levels. There are layers of meaning and of levels of involvement in this passage. The younger Rosa is depicted *in medias res*, totally submerged in the confrontation; the older Rosa looks back on her own epiphany and the horror of her kinship with the evil of Sutpen in Clytie and in herself. Faulkner too is much involved in this episode, in which he seems to be seeking a psychological insight into the dark nature of racism. The older Rosa says that she did not cry to *Clytie*, to "*it,*" Clytie's "*furious and unbending will.*" She spoke "*to it through the negro, the woman*" and says she expected no answer "*because we both knew it was not to her I spoke*" (pp. 139–140). The older Rosa tells Quentin that she cried out of "*shock which was not yet outrage because it would be terror soon*" (p. 140).

In that moment the younger Rosa and Clytie stand linked as women in a "*furious immobility, the two of us joined by that hand and arm which held us, like a fierce rigid umbilical cord, twin sistered to the fell darkness which had produced her*" (p. 140). Rosa's fear is that "*fell darkness,*" to which she acknowledges kinship. The older Rosa knows that she too is irrevocably chained to a darkness of the mind and spirit that Sutpen represents. She recalls that she always instinctively feared Clytie and felt in her touch a terrible participation in "*some cumulative over-reach of despair itself*" (p. 140). Yet in the articulation of her epiphany— "*And you too? And you too, sister, sister?*"—she implicitly acknowledges her own sisterhood with Clytie and with the dark side of her self and her culture.

Rosa's cry, in youth and age, is Faulkner's as well. Like Quentin's last words, her anguish and her recognition of that anguish resonate beyond the text into that deeper indefinable realm which becomes "*more true than truth.*" Just as David's cry, "Absalom, Absalom, my son, my son!" both defines and expands to mythic proportions the horror of parental failure and grief, Rosa's fearful, questioning acknowledgment, "*And you too? And you too, sister, sister?*" resounds through the American consciousness. It is the recognition and culmination of southern white guilt and black pain. And it connects the two in an electrifying way. Therein seems to lie the source of Rosa's racism and deep opposition to Clytie. The "reality" that the older Rosa "wakes into" in relating this encounter is the paradoxical tension between love and hate in human relationships and within the self. It is the nightmare, the "terror in which you cannot believe," that human kinship in black-white relationships can revert to horror, fear, hatred.

This is the mystery of racism. It is the mystery, the unaccountability which Faulkner probes and releases in this encounter and in Miss Rosa's attempt to understand it. In this sense, Clytie's "*face . . . was its soul's own inquisitor,*" her "*hand . . . the agent of its own crucifixion*" (p. 142). Racism erupts out of the peculiar intensity of human encounter and the fear such an encounter produces. The implication here is that racism is unavoidable; it is in the very nature of things. Paradoxically, it is the very interconnectedness of human beings that results in hatred and fear of the racial Other. Sundquist believes that this scene is evidence of Faulkner's own guilt as a white southerner.[30] It is surely a scene which haunts Quentin and Miss Rosa alike and dramatically focuses Sutpen's rejection of his black son and Quentin's despair. And it is one which embodies the paradoxical specter of racism in the relationship of two women who are bound as sisters in one electrifying moment of interconnection. As such, it offers little hope for true sisterhood between white and black women, and by implication for eventual human kinship between the races in the South. Rosa and Clytie are forever caught in confrontation, in a quivering tension which defies resolution.

Through the years they remain, as Rosa says, "*open, ay honorable, enemies*" in a house doomed by violence, deception, and rapacity. When Miss Rosa recalls her stay with Judith and Clytie during the war and after, she describes Clytie as

> *so foreign to me and to all that I was that we might have been not only of different races (which we were), not only of different sexes (which we were not), but of different species, speaking no language which the other understood, the very simple words with which we were forced to adjust our days to one another being even less inferential of thought or intention than the sounds which a beast and a bird might make to each other. (pp. 153–54)*

The women remain "three strangers," but paradoxically Miss Rosa's description of their time together at Sutpen's Hundred betrays a warmth of feeling for black and white woman alike. This is the first and only time Rosa Coldfield lives in a communal atmosphere and becomes part of a group, rather than a peripheral, lonely creature hovering around corners and behind doors. Each of the three women had her own particular jobs to do. Together, Miss Rosa recalls,

> *we grew and tended and harvested with our own hands the food we ate, made and worked that garden just as we cooked and ate the food which came out of it: with no disinction among the three of us of age or color but just as to who could build this fire or stir this pot or weed this bed or carry this apron full of corn to the mill for meal with least cost to the general good in time or expense of other duties. It was as though we were one being. . . .* (p. 155)

Rosa recalls this period in images of warmth, growth, and fellowship among the three women. She speaks of their sitting around the fire at day's end, the "*talk of a hundred things,*" their planting and harvesting of the earth.

In Rosa's mind, Clytie is part of the female triumvirate which ekes subsistence from the earth. Yet again in 1909 as she tells of this earlier time, Rosa cannot recognize Clytie's humanity. Instead of faithful sister and fellow sufferer, Clytie is the dark Other: "*the very pigmentation of her flesh represented that debacle which had brought Judith and me to what we were and which had made of her (Clytie) that which she declined to be just as she had declined to be that from which its purpose had been to emancipate her, as though presiding aloof upon the new, she deliberately remained to represent to us the threatful portent of the old*" (pp. 156–57). One of the questions concerning Miss Rosa's narration here is whether her antipathy toward Clytie is something she felt as a young woman as she lived the experience she tells, or whether it is embellished by Sutpen's affront after the war and the festering hatred she has nursed during the ensuing years. Despite her mixed blood, Clytie is a member of the Sutpen family. She is the emblem of its dark side; yet she is also a reminder to Rosa that she herself has no family—that Sutpen's failure to see her as a human being cut her off from familial relationships which she might have had and which Clytie, from the beginning of her life to its end, never lacks.

There is no doubt about Rosa's feelings for the Clytie who in 1909 again bars her way up the stairs of Sutpen's Hundred. Rosa is dead wrong when she describes Clytie as "*holding fidelity to none*" (p. 156). Though we know Clytie only through the perceptions of others, we know her above all to be fiercely faithful to her Sutpen heritage. Just as she tried to protect Judith from Rosa in 1865, she attempts to bar Rosa's path to Henry. Interestingly, Quentin, who reconstructs the encounter, fails to see in the aged Clytie the qualities of strength and indomitability that Rosa describes time and time again. He remembers her as a "tiny gnomelike creature" with "worn coffee-colored face" and "doll-like hand" (p. 368)—clearly a less imposing figure than the woman Rosa sees in 1865 as a force of "*rocklike and immobile antagonism*" that became greater than Clytie herself and "*seemed to elongate and project upward*" (p. 137). Quentin feels their connection strongly. He describes them as moving toward the confrontation as if they knew it had been ordained. On the way out to Sutpen's Hundred, Quentin remembers, Miss Rosa whimpered, "She's going to try to stop me . . . I know she is" (p. 364). Clytie, he feels, seems to know "that this hour must come and that it could not be resisted" (p. 369).

This scene varies from the 1865 confrontation in many ways. One which is overlooked is that Clytie, as Quentin recalls, did not call Rosa by her correct name. Twice, and somewhat pathetically, she called her "Rosie." First she caught Rosa's arm and said, "Dont you go up there, Rosie." Quentin recalls that when Rosa continued to walk toward the stairs, "Clytie said 'Rosie' and ran after the other again, whereupon Miss Coldfield turned on the step and struck Clytie to the floor with a full-armed blow like a man would have, and turned and went on up the stairs" (p. 369). Though Quentin may have forgotten what Clytie actually said, it is unlikely that "Rosie" would have been his own slip of the tongue, since he is continually correcting Shreve's "Aunt Rosa" to "Miss Rosa," and seems concerned that Rosa's correct name be used. It is possible also that Clytie, old as she was, may have forgotten or misspoken. Yet Faulkner's sensitivity to nuance gives us pause. It certainly seems possible that Clytie's misuse of Rosa's name is significant, that it shows above all a giving up, a verbal emblem of the impossibility of human recognition between Rosa and Clytie—a kind of last-gasp sign that Clytie's trying is over. This is certainly borne out by Rosa's reflexive, violent response—the blow from white woman to black which is as old as the slave-holding South itself. As Quentin intuits, it is truly the black woman "who owns the terror,"

Yet it is Quentin's as well, for he inherits that same terror of violence, of failure, of horror. This is the terror which erupts at the end of *Absalom* into the horrifying vision of Clytie framed in the window of the burning house of Sutpen—"the tragic gnome's face beneath the clean headrag, against a red background of fire, seen for a moment between two swirls of smoke, looking down at them, perhaps not even now with triumph and no more of despair than it had ever worn, possibly even serene above the melting clapboards before the smoke swirled across it again" (p. 376). The picture is that of the crucifixion as Clytie looks down through the window. Robin writes that "l'image de la croix. . . . donne une dernière touche divine à Clytie."[31] But it is a fiery cross upon which she dies, a peculiarly southern cross—and one which Rosa herself actually lit.

Yet Rosa, who to Clytie *is* the terror, still wants to own it. We are left with the repellant picture of her "struggling with silent and bitter fury, clawing and scratching and biting at the two men who held her" as she fights to enter the blazing house (p. 375). It is this vision of Rosa Coldfield in front of Sutpen's Hundred, "struggling and fighting like a doll in a nightmare, making no sound, foaming a little at the mouth," which becomes more of a terror than the lurking idiot Jim Bond, who at least howls "with human reason" (p. 376). It is in this scene that one sees Rosa's heart of darkness. Both women are dying. But it is only Clytemnestra, serene in the window, who remains psychically whole. Rosa's determination to conquer the only person—male or female, black or white—who truly touched her, connected with her, shows above all the terrible power of racism, its mystery and its treachery. It is a power which supplants paternity, brotherhood, and sisterhood. It is the terror that Quentin holds in his mind's eye when he lies panting in the cold New England dark, swears he doesn't hate his homeland, and isn't sure why not.

The force and resonance of *Absalom, Absalom!* are created out of that terror and out of Faulkner's as well as Quentin's response to it. Both Quentin and his creator are heirs of the patriarchy, and both seem to feel that inheritance as a destructive force. As Faulkner has shown us, we can never know the past, but neither can we escape it. Although we do not know the extent of Faulkner's readings in women's autobiographies of the Old South,[32] Rosa Coldfield and Clytie Sutpen are nonetheless powerfully connected to these real women of the past, their writings, and their South. Just as Quentin is a son of his country, so are they daughters of theirs. Together they become in Quentin's mind—and in ours—a metaphor for the brutalizing and destructive power of a racist society, and the lingering vestiges of that power in our culture.

Southern women wrote of their own time and their own cross-racial female relationships in order to redefine themselves and reexamine their own often contradictory feelings about their culture. Faulkner re-creates this autobiographical process in Rosa Coldfield's own remaking of the past. As she, like many real white women of the Old South, tells of her relationship with the black Other, we become, like Quentin, drawn into a threatening web of mutual terror and pain. We too become burdened, mired in the past; to free ourselves we too must deconstruct, analyze. In *Absalom* we find what we do not in the autobiographical and political writings about the Old South: in Rosa's words, we find fiction "*more true than truth*," more persuasive than polemics. *Absalom* and its biracial female experience become not a mere patterning of the reality of the southern past but an intense reverberation of the terror, power, and irrationality of racism past and present.

Rosa and Clytie's binding sisterhood of yearning, antipathy, and despair becomes "*the fell darkness*" both of and beyond southern racial experience. It is a darkness glimpsed only fleetingly in the autobiographical writings and polemic fiction. Yet in the context of these earlier works, Faulkner's

powerful fiction of the Old South achieves even more significant referential weight. *Absalom* forces us to *see*, as Conrad
would have it, to penetrate the relationship between human
need and human destructiveness through the metaphor of a
regional cross-racial female connection. In a significant way,
Absalom both re-creates and interprets the texts that come
before it. Clytie and Rosa's powerful and tragic sisterhood is
both epiphanic and exegetic. Not only does it dramatize the
intensity of racial encounter as cultural experience but it becomes the vehicle through which we may interpret that experience in the American literary consciousness. Forever frozen
in a quivering tension of connection and rejection, of request
and refusal, Clytemnestra Sutpen and Rosa Coldfield make us
feel the mystery of racism. They make us know its power as
human evil.

CHAPTER IV

Sapphira and Her Slave Women
CATHER AND HER PROBLEMATIC SOUTH

In *Absalom, Absalom!* the truth of the past remains eternally nebulous. Moral issues do not. Faulkner leaves little doubt as to the destructiveness of Sutpen's callous disregard for the humanity of others and of Rosa Coldfield's intense bitterness toward Sutpen, Clytie, and herself. *Absalom* is about the failure of a man, his progeny, his country. It is a story of moral blindness, of an "innocence" which is both terrible and tragic. It would be inaccurate and inappropriate to draw such moral conclusions about Willa Cather's last novel, *Sapphira and the Slave Girl,* published four years after *Absalom.* Like *Absalom,* *Sapphira* is a novel of the slave South; it is retrospective (Cather heard the story as a child but wrote it in her sixties); it probes the complexity of human motivation that produces the evil act; it seeks understanding of that human complexity in what Cather calls "the irrecoverable past," in the stories about people whom one can never really know, never really *see into.*

Yet *Absalom* lends itself to a critical exuberance, to hyperbole. *Sapphira* is instead a fragile novel about which it is easy to say too much, to say it too fervently, to be too sure.[1] It is a vast distance which separates the heated intensity of Yoknapatawpha from the cool deliberateness of this Virginia novel. This book of Cather's age is the repository of a measured assessment of the past in a unique synthesis of clarity and complexity which resists analysis. What is created is, as Cather would have it, "felt" experience. The insistence upon referential meaning in such an experience is as deadly to an analysis of *Sapphira* as "the spirit of the 'idea' " is to Cather's art.[2] *Sapphira and the Slave Girl* is the perfect example of what Cather felt art should be—"the novel démeublé." It is both simple and complex: actually its complexity is rendered through a deceptive surface of simplicity and calm. It suggests rather than describes, emphasizes feeling over seeing, employs a translucent language and structure that evokes rather than delineates the imaginative experience.

The illusiveness of that experience has puzzled critics. Several see the novel as a failure, as artistically and morally incoherent. John H. Randall complains that the principal act of the book, Nancy's movement to freedom, is undercut and that in mid-novel Cather reverses the values upon which the book is based. Sapphira Colbert is first perceived as wicked, but then, in a disconcerting (for Randall) turn of affairs, becomes the protagonist. There is, he feels, "a blurring and a complete loss of definition of moral issues" in *Sapphira and the Slave Girl* that makes the book an inconsistent and a puzzling failure.[3]

Randall articulates the central paradox of the book: Cather's ambivalent depiction of Sapphira, the crippled southern aristocrat who imagines that her miller husband, Henry Colbert, is enamoured of one of her young slave women, Nancy. In the first two-thirds of the novel, Sapphira, like Harriet Jacobs's Mrs. Flint, is the embodiment of white female rage at the specter of miscegenation in her own yard. She wakes in the night imagining Nancy in the miller's bedroom. Afflicted by dropsy, she sees in the lithesome, exuberant girl the youth and health that she herself will never regain. Although Cather depicts Nancy as a sexual innocent, Sapphira, like Emma Holmes and other real white women of the period, perceives the slave girl as the stereotypical, sexually available black woman and has little doubt that Henry has succumbed to her desirability. Interestingly, Sapphira is more aware of young Nancy's sexuality than the slave girl herself or Henry Colbert seems to be.

Yet Sapphira is concerned mainly with power. She views her

husband's affection for the "yellow girl" as an undercutting of
her power over him in their relationship which, as he himself
puts it, makes her "the master," him "the miller."[4] Though
Nancy is the mulatto daughter of her favorite slave, Till,
Sapphira mistreats the girl shamefully. She hits her, forces her
to sleep on a pallet outside her door, and throws her in the path
of Henry's rake of a nephew, Martin Colbert, who tries repeatedly to rape her. As Josephine Jessup puts it, Sapphira "should
reveal herself as one of the meanest women in fiction."[5] Her
cruelties to Nancy so sicken Sapphira's daughter, Rachel
Blake, that she finally helps Nancy escape Sapphira's and
Martin's clutches. Henry Colbert, who has genuine affection
for the slave girl and is opposed to slavery strangely does little
to help Nancy except to provide money for her escape.

Yet, even more strangely, after Nancy's escape Sapphira
eventually forgives her own daughter for her part in it, approaches death with dignity and grace, and so becomes the
heroine of the novel. She is eulogized eloquently by Till,
whose daughter she attempted to ruin; and years later Till's
loving report of her mistress's last days places Sapphira in a
glowing light as the novel ends. Yet this white woman who
exerted her power over a female slave so unmercifully never
really sees the error of her ways. She murmurs at the end of the
novel that "we would all do better if we had our lives to live
over again" (p. 269), but in her case, that admission is certainly
an understatement. Also, as David Stouck points out, Sapphira's evil is ultimately beneficial to Nancy, who obtains a
good position and a family of her own in Canada. Sapphira's
unfounded jealousy and mistreatment become the *"felix culpa"*
which propels Nancy into a better life. At the end of the book,
Stouck says, we admire and sympathize with Sapphira.[6]

The epilogue of the novel, set twenty-five years later than its
main action of 1865, gives us cause to do so. All that remain of
Sapphira and Henry are their monuments in the Colbert
graveyard and in Till's memory. Nancy comes home for the
first time in expensive clothes and with tales of life among the
rich. Till tells the stories of Sapphira's last days and her reconciliation with her daughter Rachel. Yet the epilogue also presents problems with consistency. Until this point, the story is

presented by what we think is an omniscient narrator. In the epilogue we discover for the first time that the narrator is an individual who actually knew these people. We are given a first-hand account from the five-year-old girl who witnessed the real-life reunion of Nancy and Till and listened to Till, the repository of Dodderidge and Colbert history, tell of Sapphira's last days. Cather herself heard the story of Nancy and witnessed the reunion. William Curtin has raised the question of internal consistency in this narrative technique. He finds the novel a failure, not because it is autobiographical, but because "the narrative technique does not make clear the relation of the narrator to the story."[7] Cather herself decided that she had made an artistic mistake by bringing herself into the story.[8] In the epilogue, fiction becomes fact with startling suddenness. These inconsistencies in characterization and narrative techniques make *Sapphira,* which is smooth reading on the surface, an enormously difficult book to respond to emotionally or critically.

Yet these very inconsistencies provide interesting links to other works about the slave South, including autobiographical writings, polemic fiction, and *Absalom.* At the end of the novel Cather evokes the female autobiographical mode by remaking into *reality* that which has until this point been presented as fiction. Although this transformation is disconcerting, it does enlarge our perception of the complexities of the southern experience and the enduring qualities of cross-racial relationships. Nancy Till has become a legend to the young girl of the epilogue, whom we are led to believe is Cather. In the epilogue Nancy becomes the Everywoman of the slave narratives, who has asserted her own identity in a free land, who has *become* a person in her own right in reaction to the racist evil of her white mistress. Rachel Blake is the quintessential kind mistress, who, though she did not own Nancy, treated her as a kind mistress would—with human dignity. Rachel is the truly beneficent mistress that writers like Cornelia McDonald, Mary Blackford, and Kate Stone genuinely aspired to be, and that others like Mary Chesnut and Susan Smedes believed they were. Her relationship with Nancy has endured for twenty-five years and has even touched the life of the young white girl who relates the story of Nancy's homecoming.

The autobiographical section has another effect as well: it implicitly suggests the problematic nature of experience, the fact that stereotypical modes and single points of view, such as those used polemically by Harriet Beecher Stowe and Mary H. Eastman, often cannot convey the real nature of experience, especially southern racial experience. Like Faulkner in *Absalom,* Cather seems to be suggesting, particularly by her sudden change to the autobiographical mode, that we can never really know the past, yet at the same time we cannot escape it. The multiplicity of views we receive of Sapphira from the outside is similar to that of Thomas Sutpen and is antithetical to the monolithic impressions of Stowe's and Eastman's characters. Rachel, Henry, Till, Nancy, all have their views of Sapphira; and the first-person narrator in the epilogue technically provides the kind of respondent and chorus for *Sapphira* that Quentin and Shreve do for *Absalom.* The result in both novels is a filtering of the meaning of southern racial experience through the alembic of many voices and many listeners. This filtering transforms and intensifies that experience in the sense that the many sides of southern experience reflected in this paradigm of multiple knowing become synthesized and transformed in our own perceptions. We create our own vision of the past as we are forced to interpret the multiplicity which confronts us in the fiction. We thereby remake the Old South in response to fictional rather than historical reality.

The density that Cather achieves in her quiet portrayal of the slave South, however, contains elements which are in a sense more baffling and disturbing than the terror of *Absalom.* Like the pious Henry Colbert, Cather equivocates about the wrongness of slavery itself. At the end of the antebellum section of the book, Henry says to Sapphira that she has been good to "a great many folks" and that "sometimes keeping people in their place is being good to them" (p. 268). Though we cannot construe the miller's judgment as being Cather's own, she does show black characters as being unwilling or unable to accept freedom. Till, who was trained for service by a white surrogate mother, Mrs. Matchem, seems to find pleasure in serving Sapphira and never questions her role, despite the fact that Sapphira has married her to a eunuch. Nancy, who

135

has every reason to want freedom, loses her nerve at a crucial point in her escape and begs Rachel to take her home. Nancy, a mulatto, is described as having "a foolish dreamy nigger side of her nature" which Cather implies is irresponsible and unreliable (p. 178). Although she is cruel to Nancy, Sapphira takes good care of her slaves, laughs at their jokes, nurses them when they are sick. Like Susan Dabney Smedes's Mammy Harriet, Till, the stereotypical mammy in her old age, tells of the freeing of the Dodderidge slaves and how many had to be chased away because they did not wish to leave the farm. The story of Tap, the happy black youth, becomes an Eastman-like *exemplum* of what happens to young, exuberant blacks who are cast from the patriarchal umbrella that keeps them out of trouble. During the Reconstruction, the happy-go-lucky Tap is hanged for a pool-hall murder, despite the efforts of Back Creek farmers who attest to his good character before a "Yankee jury." The young narrator of the epilogue observes, "Mrs. Blake and Till always said it was a Yankee jury that hanged him; a Southern jury would have known there was no real bad in Tap" (p. 290).

Cather has been described as having racial attitudes typical of "an elderly midwesterner in the thirties, that is to say, a theoretical belief in complete equality and a practical acquaintance with Negroes only as servants or laborers."[9] We do not think of Cather as a southerner. Edward Bloom and Lillian Bloom call her "a Southerner by birth, a Midwesterner by adoption, and a cosmopolitan by instinct."[10] When she was nine, her family left the tranquility of home, "Willowshade," in Back Creek Valley, Virginia, for the prairies of Nebraska, which she immortalized in *O Pioneers!* and *My Ántonia*.[11] She returned to her birthplace over a half-century later, in 1938, when she was beginning to think about writing what would be her last novel, and her only book about the South.[12] Yet the Blooms' theory that Cather left the South "too young to absorb deeply the southern tradition" may be questioned. It was Cather herself who said that the only important things that happen to a writer happen before adulthood. The Blooms' assessments of *Sapphira* as the depiction of "a barren social order" and Cather's re-creation of southern culture as possessing "rigidity and static quality"[13] do not address the central inconsistencies of the novel or the moral tension between the slaveholder as protector and as tormentor. Clearly Sapphira Colbert is not a little Eva, but neither is she a Marie St. Clare or a Rosa Coldfield.

What is interesting about this novel is Sapphira's moral ambiguity, which implies Cather's assessment of slavery as a complex, problematic phenomenon. "The peculiar institution" produced order, something which Cather sought more and more as she grew older. Particularly before and while she was writing *Sapphira,* she was undergoing great emotional trauma with the deaths of close friends, her parents, and her brother. Like most Americans during the thirties, she was deeply concerned about war and the Depression. *Sapphira* was released the day Pearl Harbor was bombed. Cather found her Virginia years, Edith Lewis writes, full of "great richness, tranquil and ordered and serene." As Lewis also points out, however, Cather's attitude toward the land of her birth was deeply ambivalent; and she "felt something smothering in the polite, rigid social conventions of that Southern society."[14]

Sapphira seems to have begun as "a complete history of manners and customs of the Shenandoah Valley" from which Cather is reported to have cut "a good six pounds" not essential to her story.[15] Particularly in its cross-racial female relationships, the novel is a study of how societal expectations may mold moral character. We are reminded of one of Cather's favorite women writers, Jane Austen, and her Emma Woodhouse, who is governed by social expectations and unconsciously does evil deeds because of her desire to manipulate people to fulfill such expectations. In Cather's novel, Sapphira Colbert's good and evil sides are developed and perpetrated by the institution of slavery, which allows her both to abuse and nurture her chattels. Her relationships with three of her women slaves—Nancy, Till, and Jezebel—reflect her own capacity for good and evil, and by implication, the mixed nature of all human beings. Above all, *Sapphira,* much like *Absalom,* is a study of the very human consistency of evil, and its ever-present cohabitation with the human rage for order, the desire for power, and the need for recognition. The troublesome aspect of *Sapphira* is that as it suggests the mixed nature of human motivation and conduct, it also implies that evil can be without serious consequence, that the black woman of the slave society could indeed escape North from a cruel mistress with no serious emotional scars, that slavery usually had no grave and irrevocable psychological effects upon the enslaved.

Biographical approaches to the novel, however, suggest that Cather may have been writing more about her own experience than about the slave South. Recently critics have examined Cather's characterization of Sapphira as the author's attempt to come to terms or make peace with her own domineering mother, who died shortly before Cather began to write *Sapphira*. In seeking freedom from Sapphira's repression, Nancy has been seen as a fictional embodiment of Cather herself as she attempts to resolve her conflicting emotions about her mother—a woman who is described as "having punished disobedience with a rawhide whip" but possessing "a great capacity for life."[16] Sandra Seltzer feels that the central antagonism of the novel is between Sapphira and Rachel, a "strong and willful mother and an equally strong and willful daughter."[17] Though such biographical interpretations may have validity, Cather would have disliked them. She disliked those women writers who were too often, she felt, "so horribly subjective" and engorged their fiction with "drivelling . . . contemptible feminine weakness."[18]

As a fictional character, Sapphira is far from such a woman. The more obvious comparison is between the author and Sapphira herself. Cather, fiercely independent, was burdened in her later years with inflammation in the tendons of her wrists and had to have either one hand or the other immobilized for long periods.[19] This was a particular burden for a woman who insisted, as Randall says, "on complete self-sufficiency and self-reliance."[20] The real reason, we are led to believe, that Sapphira suspects Henry and Nancy is her intense frustration at her own physical incapacity. Cather's empathy with her strong-willed female character who must face disability and death may account in part for her ambivalent portrait of Sapphira and the mixed nature of Sapphira's relationships with black women.

Sapphira is, as E.K. Brown says, "wholly the slave-owner."[21] Yet she is not as "cold and calculating" as Elizabeth Sergeant would have her,[22] particularly not in her associations with the slave women Jezebel and Till. Cather depicts a firm, deep attachment between "Miss Sapphy" and Jezebel, who is also a fierce, strong woman facing disability and death. At the end of her life Jezebel, who has worked for Sapphira most of her life, seems closer to her mistress than to her own people. They are linked by age and pain and the ever-deepening shadow of death. They are united by the past and their mutual work. Sapphira brings the old black woman mock-orange blossoms for her pillow, and they talk of life and growth, of past plantings and transplantings of the trees, shrubs, and flowers they grew together. Unlike Nancy, Sapphira is not shocked by Jezebel's grisly joke about wanting "a li'l pickaninny's hand" to eat. When Jezebel dies, Sapphira selects one of her own nightgowns for the corpse and instructs the cook not to skimp on the food for Jezebel's relatives. Everyone agrees that "Miss Sapphy" gives Jezebel a "beautiful laying away." Jezebel's pride and her savage refusal to be mistreated in her early life become a purer, more sympathetic form of Sapphira's refusal to give up control of her own life and those of others. Jezebel's life is a commentary on Sapphira's. Patricia Fleming even suggests that Jezebel is Sapphira's double and expresses the white woman's need to assert herself in the face of disability and death.[23]

Like Jezebel, who fought the slave traders who captured her, Sapphira tries to exert control. It is unthinkable to her that she herself might become the slavish object of manipulation: "The thought of being befooled, hoodwinked was unendurable" (p. 106). Jezebel cannot control her own life because she is a slave. In relationships with whites, Sapphira, because of her sex and her disability, can exert control only through subterfuge. Cather's initial description of Sapphira suggests the woman's rather sinister ability to manipulate others. As she attempts to persuade Henry to agree to sell Nancy (she owns the slaves, but as a woman cannot sell them without her husband's permission), Sapphira is described as frighteningly unattractive. She has "very plump white hands," a "bland voice" and "small mouth," "pale-blue eyes," and a "deformity of the ankles" (pp. 6–9). Her own daughter Rachel, who interrupts Sapphira as she strikes Nancy with a hairbrush, sees in her mother's face "placid self-esteem" and hears in her voice "a kind of false pleasantness" (p. 15). Jezebel's life shows a more honest form of rebellion—a pure need for self-determination which has been polluted both in Sapphira's obsessive need to control the lives of others and in the system which gives her the power to exert that control.

In her relationships with blacks, Sapphira usually is able to exert the direct control that she wishes to use on whites but cannot. "The peculiar institution" is eminently suited to Sapphira, who is above all egocentric. The most terrible instance of her self-absorptive control of her slaves is her refusal to allow Till a sexually normal marriage. She marries her off to Jeff, a "capon man," simply because it would be inconvenient for her favorite maid to be, as Lizzie puts it, "havin' chillun all over de place,—always a-carryin' or a-nussin' 'em" (p. 43). Till's only apparent sexual rebellion, which produced the half-white Nancy, may not have been so much a rebellion against white sexual repression as an acquiescence to its male rather than female form. Till, particularly the old Till of the epilogue, is cast in the mammy mold of Smedes, Ripley, and Eppes. She has internalized the white values of her surrogate mother, Mrs. Matchem, and, like Smedes's Mammy Harriet, is the black female voice created by a white female consciousness to extol the slave culture and white women. Merrill Skaggs's theory that Cather deliberately evokes southern stereotypes in *Sapphira* only to puncture them works well with Sapphira and Nancy, but not with Till.[24] She is the epitome of generous black servitude and obviously the characterization of a white writer who not only sees her only in relation to her white folks, even when most of them are dead, but also creates her as the satisfied product of at least a partially benevolent system.

Interestingly the novel opens with Sapphira's attempt to sell Till's daughter, and closes with Till's glowing eulogy for her "Miss Sapphy." It is difficult to take Till seriously as a black woman. About forty when the novel opens, she echoes Sapphira's aristocratic values and worries remarkably little about her mistress's mistreatment of Nancy. She instructs her daughter to "smile right, an' don't go shiverin' like a drownded kitten" when she serves Sapphira, and that all will be well: "In all Loudoun County Miss Sapphy was knowed for her good mannahs, an' that she knowed how to treat all folks in their degree" (p. 45). When Sapphira takes Nancy for her Easter visit to Winchester, Till worries not about how her daughter will be treated, trusting to "the Dodderidge manners," but feels "slighted and left behind." Like Sapphira, Till is an aristocrat by temperament: "She liked, as she said to herself, to live among 'folks,' not among poor farmers and backwards people" (p. 69). She feels that the finer accomplishments she learned from Mrs. Matchem—"keeping the brass and silver bright, the stores of bed linen and table linen bleached"—are lost on the mill farm on Back Creek (p. 69). Rachel Blake, who becomes more of a mother to Nancy than her own, recognizes that

> Till had been a Dodderidge before ever she was Nancy's mother. In Till's mind, her first duty was to her mistress. Ever since Mrs. Colbert had become an invalid, Till's position in the house was all-important; and position was dear to her. Long ago Matchem had taught her to "value her place," and that became her rule of life. Anything that made trouble between her and the Mistress would wreck the order of the household. (p. 219)

Till's tie to Sapphira is so close that Nancy must turn to Rachel for help in escaping the degenerate clutches of Martin Colbert, whom Sapphira has invited for a visit so that he may ruin Nancy. Rachel, who has herself taken on the mantle of servitude in caring for the poor and downtrodden in the area, is much more active in Nancy's behalf than Till, or than Henry Colbert, whose equivocal contribution to Nancy's escape is to leave some money in his pocket for Rachel to take for that purpose.

One of the problems with the epilogue is the falsity of Nancy and Till's reunion. Though Till obviously cares for her daughter (after her escape, she asks for word of her), that caring does not extend either to action on her behalf or to rejection of Sapphira's egocentric white value system. It certainly does not extend to outward rebellion. Cather seems to be opposed to slavery as a system; she has the well-meaning Henry and Rachel attest to the wrongness of "*owning*." Yet Till's devotion to Sapphira, like the tragic story of the freedman Tap, becomes in itself an endorsement of established order and of a sense of decorum achieved in antebellum life under the hierarchical relationships required by slavery. Sapphira's evil never seems to touch Till, and we wonder why.

At the end of the book, old Till ironically has become the family matriarch. She is the keeper of the family treasure and legend. The child of the epilogue visits Till's cabin and sees the Dodderidge-Colbert keepsakes:

> They were stowed away in a pinewood chest with a sloping top. She had some of the miller's books, the wooly green shawl he had worn as an overcoat, some of Miss Sapphy's lace caps and fichus, and odd bits of finery such as velvet slippers with buckles. Her chief treasure was a brooch, set in pale gold, and under the crystal was a lock of Mr. Henry's black hair and Miss Sapphy's brown hair, at the time of their marriage. The miller himself had given it to her, she said. (pp. 291–92)

With the child as her audience, Till builds a legend around Sapphira's last days and imbues her mistress with grace and dignity in the face of pain and death. Despite growing weakness and discomfort, the Sapphira remade in Till's imagination "wouldn't give in, an' she never got out of temper" (p. 293)— surely a contrast to the Sapphira who beats Nancy with her hairbrush and sets the lascivious Martin after her like a hound to the fox. Till fondly recalls lighting her mistress's candles in the parlor and watching Sapphira as she sat alone and smiling in her wheelchair. She is, in Till's mind, heroic in death and does not ring the bell for help although there must have been moments of pain and struggle. Till fantasizes that, at her death, Sapphira went away with "fine folks" waiting outside for her in the arbor. To the end Till believes in Sapphira as a southern lady. The book closes with her pronouncement on her beloved mistress: "She oughtn't never to a' come out here. . . . She wasn't raised that way. Mrs. Matchem, down at the old place, never got over it that Miss Sapphy didn't buy in

Chestnut Hill an' live like a lady, 'stead a' leavin' it to run down under the Bushwells, an' herself comin' out here where nobody was anybody much" (pp. 294–95).

In her elevated devotion to Sapphira, Till becomes a black voice for the white aristocracy of the slave South. As such, she is less than believable. While Sapphira in her self-centered maliciousness and graceful dignity becomes an interesting and a complex character who evokes the mixed human condition, Till, the creation of a white artistic consciousness, is only a voice of the slavocracy—and an unconvincing one at that. Yet the two women are remarkably alike in their love for order, fine things, aristocratic people; their mutual egocentricity, so strong that it interferes with nurturance of their own daughters; the lack of fulfillment in their heterosexual relationships and their apparent indifference to that lack. Sapphira becomes Till's desirable white Other, the shadow self that she yearns toward, makes, and remakes in her tales of Sapphira's life and death. Still, Till does not ring true as a fictional character. She is more of a caricature than a complex identity. Her devotion to Sapphira, the woman who deprives her of her sexuality and her child, has troubling implications. Till's unquestioning desire to serve her white folks and eulogize her mistress, combined with Nancy's triumphant return to the land of her birth, subtly suggests that slavery had no permanent ill effects upon the enslaved.

Although Cather's characterization of Nancy is more fully drawn, the young black woman is never presented as a complex individual in her own right. Like her mother, Nancy wants to please. One has the impression, in fact, that had Sapphira not persecuted her so vigorously, she would have grown up to be as devoted to her mistress and to the institution of slavery as Till is. Nancy seems childlike throughout. There is an implicit contrast between her inability to cope for herself and the self-sufficiency of Rachel Blake at about the same age. We are told that Nancy is older than seventeen-year-old Rachel was at the time of her marriage. Whether Cather means to imply that slavery makes children of blacks or whether her distinction is based on race, we are never certain. Certainly the most meaningful relationship in the novel is that of the fright-

143

ened, childish Nancy and the maternal Rachel, who spirits her North and actually forces her into the action that will save her from Sapphira's evil. Rachel, who is associated with spring and growth, becomes the powerful, life-giving mother to the young black woman. She not only offers her the gift of life; she forces her to accept it. Nancy and Rachel's journey North to freedom is a movement toward individuation for the black girl. Unwilling and afraid, she is propelled by her white "mother" into new birth of self, in a new life and a new land. Rachel Blake's parting words to Nancy connect the two women through time and space as she calls, "Goodbye, Nancy! We shall meet again" (p. 239).

When the two meet twenty-five years later, they seem to realize in a flash what they have meant to each other. The child narrator reports: "Tears were shining in the deep creases on either side of Mrs. Blake's nose. 'Well, Nancy, child, you've made us right proud of you,' she said. Then, for the first time, I saw Nancy's lovely smile. 'I never forget who it was took me across the river that night, Mrs. Blake'" (p. 283). This reunion is perhaps more moving than the inarticulate one between Nancy and her real mother. Yet it is still clear that Cather builds the relationship between Nancy and Rachel on the presumption of Nancy's inability to take care of herself, her inability even to know what she wants. Despite her chance for freedom and self-determination, she begs Rachel to take her home, saying that she would rather cope with Martin Colbert's lasciviousness than "to belong nowheres!" (p. 237).

Though the title would indicate otherwise, there is little direct interaction between Sapphira and her slave girl. In the second book Cather places Sapphira and Nancy together on the journey to Winchester, but by sending them on their journey and dwelling on Till's disappointment at not being included, she passes up an obvious opportunity to show their interaction. The most compelling action of the book is Nancy's struggle against Martin Colbert, Sapphira's pawn. Rachel recognizes, though Till and Henry Colbert will not, that Sapphira has brought Martin to the Mill House for the purpose of ruining Nancy. Cather creates an unusual situation in that she has the jealous white mistress use the sexual degeneracy of the southern white man to punish the black woman. Interestingly, Sapphira's attempt to ruin the slave girl implies recognition of Nancy's innocence—and therefore a negation of her suspicions about Nancy and Henry.

Suggestions of Cather's lesbian tendencies and her adolescent inability to accept herself as female open avenues of speculation about Sapphira's motives for hurting Nancy as reflections of Cather's feelings about her own sexuality. Cather seemed to fear heterosexual sex and produced in her novels, as Blanche Gelfant puts it, "a gallery of characters for whom [she] consistently invalidates sex."[25] Randall finds many fictional illustrations of the "extreme danger Willa Cather felt to result inevitably from sexual passion" and points to a long line of unhappy marriages in her fiction which suggest the author's feeling that "permanently satisfying relationships between men and women are impossible."[26] As an adolescent Cather insisted upon dressing as a man, much to her family's dismay; and her close relationships throughout her life were with women. Sapphira's rage at Nancy is motivated by the jealous fantasy of a sexual relationship which does not exist. Actually, in this novel we find one woman trying to rape another. The seductions and attempted rape in which Sapphira directs lustful Martin may be ramifications of Cather's own rejection of heterosexual relationships, her apparent desire to be a man, and the conflicts she seemed to feel about sex.

The vividly sensual scene in which Martin Colbert tries to pull Nancy down from the cherry tree suggests the intensity of that conflict. The scene, replete with the lush sensuality of the cherry tree and Nancy's innocent sexuality, is perhaps the most vivid in the book. As the young woman cavorts among the cherries up in the branches, below Martin seeks to woo her with songs and joking talk. Nancy responds happily to his teasing tone until he pulls her legs down from the tree and wraps them around his face as he stands upon a chair under the tree. Still Cather concentrates upon the sensuality of the scene. As the black girl begs to be released, Martin murmurs, "Pretty soon.—This is just nice.—Something smells sweet—like May apples" (p. 181). Throughout, the episode is depicted as seduction, not attempted rape, even though Martin uses force to pull Nancy partly down from the tree and seems intent upon using further force if need be. Nancy's scream brings help before he has a chance. Behind Martin and his actions is always the specter of Sapphira, who has brought him to the Mill House for that very purpose and who surely must be considered the perpetrator of Nancy's attempted rape. It is interesting that Cather places the attempted rape in such a vivid sensual setting, depicting Martin more as ardent impassioned suitor than rapist. Nancy in this scene becomes much like the cherries, a delectable object to be consumed and enjoyed, and the tone of the episode is less than serious; it is gently playful and aesthetically vivid. Martin's actions are of little consequence, not so much because he does not succeed in raping Nancy but because in this scene he becomes the playful, admiring suitor rather than the rapist. His association with Sapphira, moreover, as well as the light-heartedness of the scene, makes him seem almost feminine. He is transparent; we see through him to Sapphira's grim determination, reminiscent of Harriet Jacobs's Mrs. Flint or Elizabeth Keckley's Mrs. Burwell, to violate Nancy physically and psychologically.

Like Sapphira in her obsessive need to ruin Nancy, Cather also felt an obsession to destroy the female part of her artistic imagination. To Cather, the feminine meant sentimentality and mawkishness, and she sought to crush anything about herself or her writing which she considered soft or trivial, traits she associated with women writers of the period. She wrote derisively of women writers and associated the female sphere with the trivial. "I have not much faith in women in fiction," she wrote in a particularly scathing book review in 1895. "They have a sort of sex consciousness that is abominable. They are so limited to one string and they lie about that."[27] Sapphira and the Slave Girl and the intense relationship implied by the title seem to embody these related sexual and artistic conflicts of its author. Just as Nancy's growing sexuality is an enormous affront to the old and ill Sapphira, Cather's own femaleness also seems to have been an affront to her as individual and artist. In Sapphira's mind, as in the minds of many white women writers of the Old South, black female sexuality deserves violation. Cather does not approve of Sapphira's actions. Yet she too at times in her life tried to destroy the female in her own psyche and in her art.

As fictional characters in a historical setting Sapphira and Nancy are, above all, mistress and slave. Sapphira's whiteness is important because it gives her control through ownership. Brown suggests that Cather's primary interest in creating her fiction of the Old South was to show "what slavery has done to individuals."[28] Yet, just as slavery does not ruin Nancy's life, it has not made Sapphira more egocentric. It has simply allowed her, like Marie St. Clare, to indulge that self-centeredness to its fullest degree. As Stowe points out and Harriet Wilson's *Our Nig* dramatizes, women like Sapphira and Marie also resided in free states, where they abused indentured servants with great vigor. Above all else, Sapphira wants control. Recognizing the relationshp between sex and power, she is threatened by Henry's affection for Nancy, not so much because of a fear of their sexual involvement, but because their relationship is a direct affront to her own power over them both. She controls Henry as surely as she does her slaves. His response to Nancy places him outside the realm of her control and into a relationship from which she is excluded.

Sapphira's peculiar brand of evil emerges from a union of her own egocentricity and the institution of slavery. That same union, Cather indicates, can also produce happy slaves and the comfort and ease of a traditional social order, which is not perfect but not totally repressive either. Rachel Blake protests that social order. ". . . it ain't right," she says, yet at the same time she recognizes that Sapphira's associations with her slaves are often happy and comfortable and that "she believes in it, and they believe in it" (p. 221). Clearly Cather indicates in the novel that freedom is better than slavery, but also that it is a mixed blessing. Nancy's movement is, as the miller knows, "from the dark lethargy of the cared-for and irresponsible; to make her own way in this world where nobody is altogether free, and the best that can happen to you is to walk your own way and be responsible to God only" (p. 228). Strangely, Sapphira's evil releases her slave girl to the responsibilities of a world of partial freedom. Sapphira remains enslaved to her deteriorating body but frees herself from bitterness toward her own daughter for her part in Nancy's escape. Interestingly, Sapphira's decline begins with Nancy's release, and yet in a strange way she is irrevocably connected to Nancy and her movement from slavery to freedom. Sapphira too approaches release in the freedom from pain which will come with death. Sapphira, who has been so terribly evil, is redeemed and set free by her acts of kindness and consideration at the end of her life. In this fiction, which is above all *her* story, we ourselves free Sapphira from blame. We as readers are urged to forgive her just as she forgives Rachel.

In the context of the black and white female autobiographical writings of the nineteenth-century South, Sapphira becomes, at once, the black woman's nightmare of the jealous, cruel mistress and the mistress's view of herself as a woman of good will trapped in a system which denies her sexuality and humanity. Hers is a complex characterization which encompasses the good and evil that people do and what they are within the good and evil societies they build and destroy. This is Cather's last fictional look at experience, and we have the sense that she, like Quentin, tries to see more in her own southern past and in the "felt" experience of life itself than she succeeds in conveying. In Sapphira, as we know her through her relationships to black women, Cather creates "the inexplicable presence of the thing not named, of the overtone divined by the ear but not heard by it, the verbal mood, the emotional aura"[29] which she believed was valid artistic representation of complex human experience. We feel this complexity in Sapphira and her capacity for good and evil. We do not feel it in Till's devotion to white values, in Rachel's simple kindness to her mother's slave girl, or in Nancy's overnight emergence from child to adult.

Sapphira and the Slave Girl is not so much the "chronicle of a time that will never again be recaptured"[30] as it is a limited anatomy of Sapphira and her equivocal human qualities that nurture such inhumane institutions as chattel slavery. In Sapphira's oppositions and in the implication of the novel—that slavery often brought as much benefit as harm to the enslaved—Cather renders the southern racial experience as essentially problematic. Like Faulkner, she avoids closure, or certainty about the nature of the past. Yet, unlike him, she does not seem burdened, frustrated, or terrified by her inability or unwillingness to know the past fully. This is the troubling aspect of Cather's fiction about the Old South and its women. She acknowledges and re-creates the ambiguity of cross-racial relationships between southerners of the period, particularly between southern women. Yet she seems to accept that ambiguity quietly and passively, almost unquestioningly. In this regard, her novel is much more like the white female autobiographies of the period than fictions about it. Like Mary Chesnut, Cather does surely see the paradox of the southern female experience. Yet Cather, like the writers of wistfully nostalgic memoirs of the golden years in the antebellum South, creates a world in which evil does not hurt. In Cather's fictional Southland, the jealous mistress can repent; the beleaguered slave woman can escape; all can work for the good; all can be forgiven. In Clytie and Rosa, Faulkner gives us the bitter core of cross-racial female connection. In Sapphira and her slave women, Cather gives us the shell, perfectly formed, aesthetically pleasing, ultimately impenetrable.

CHAPTER V

Jubilee

THE BLACK WOMAN'S CELEBRATION
OF HUMAN COMMUNITY

> . . . I closed her eyes in death, and God is my witness, I
> bears her no ill will.

VYRY WARE

Margaret Walker's *Jubilee* is a novel of celebration and culmination, of vision and realism. Emerging out of the black folk and
autobiographical traditions, Walker's fictional treatment of the
Old South is above all, its creator writes, "a canvas on which I
paint my vision of my world."[1] Throughout her life as literary
artist and teacher, Walker has evoked her world, even her
fictional world of the slave South, as a place of possibility in
which the principle of "humanism" generates in persons of all
races vast potentials for love and fellow feeling. In a profound
sense, black literature emerges, she believes, from "the un-
broken tradition of humanistic values that did not spring from
renaissance Europe, but developed in Asia and Africa before
the religious wars of the Middle Ages." Walker's definition of
humanism synthesizes natural, religious, historical, and moral
elements. Hers is an organic philosophy of human life that
embodies "a recognition that we are part of nature and the
historical process, that we are implicit in the dynamic evolving
of mankind to ever higher planes of being, that all life must be

richly developed in spirit rather than mere matter, and that one must regard the sacred nature of a brother as one values his own privacy and his own inner sanctity."[2] What she calls her "new humanism" carries with it "a new respect for the quality of all human life" and therein must be squarely opposed to racism. Afro-American literature, she believes, "is a reservoir of black humanism." It is the standard-bearer of the values of "freedom, peace, and human dignity." It is what America, black and white, needs.[3]

Walker's humanism is a faithfulness to what she sees as "the living truth of the human spirit."[4] Her world, as she believes it is and as she creates it to be, is thus inhabited by a flawed human race with enormous capacity for moral insight and spiritual change which affirm rather than deny "humanist values." *Jubilee* suggests Walker's insistence upon an organic connection between "humanism" and religion, in which "even the highest peaks of religious understanding must come in a humanistic understanding—the appreciation of every human being of his own spiritual way."[5] In her novel those characters with the greatest of these capacities are black people who endure slavery, war, and Reconstruction to emerge in profound and steadfast solidity as wounded but victorious soldiers in the cause of individual freedom. Above all, *Jubilee* celebrates the ability of the southern Afro-American to move through the baptismal fire of the mid-nineteenth century and actually to become regenerated and whole through suffering. Yet the novel is about more than suffering and endurance; it is about freedom of self through the acknowledgment of a self-imposed bondage to the human duty of nurturance of others. And it celebrates that freedom in women and men of all races who bind themselves to one another in such a way.

Walker speaks of her novel as a culmination. It is a life's work which originated in the stories of her maternal grandmother, Elvira Ware Dozier, who kept young Margaret up past bed-time with tales of slavery times. Her own mother, Walker's great-grandmother, is the indomitable Vyry of *Jubilee*. Grandma, as young Margaret called her, would grow indignant when accused of telling the child "tall tales," and would retort, "I'm not telling her tales; I'm telling her the naked truth."[6]

That "naked truth," born of the black oral tradition, germinated in Walker's mind long before she actually began work on the book in 1934 at Northwestern. Walker put her project aside then, but throughout the years she worked on the novel intermittently, poring over Civil War histories and researching oral slave narratives whenever possible. In 1964 she began writing in earnest on the novel, which she would use as a dissertation for the doctorate at the University of Iowa. "On the morning of April 9, 1965, at ten o'clock," she writes that she typed the last words. "So, when I say that I have been writing *Jubilee* all my life, it is literally true. It has been a consuming ambition, driving me relentlessly."[7]

Yet *Jubilee* is a work of culmination in a more significant sense. It is a synthesis of folk tradition, imagination, and moral vision. It is at once realistic and visionary. Much like *Uncle Tom's Cabin, Jubilee* is a paradoxical, difficult novel.[8] As Arthur Davis suggests, Walker's characters, black and white, seem to be stereotypes based on southern myth.[9] Yet, like so many of Stowe's stereotypical creations, Walker's characters paradoxically spring into life and liveliness, surpassing their obvious symbolic designations. The heroine Vyry, who survives and endures white cruelty and oppression to return love for hatred, becomes not just the black Everywoman, but every human being who still believes, like Walker, in a "common humanity [which] supersedes race."[10] Walker's novel is about race and class in the South during the period before, during, and after the Civil War; and yet her writings and speeches throughout her life articulate her fictional messages: that, as Walker puts it, "history is not just one solid page of black and white,"[11] that racial reconciliation is possible, that love is redemptive and regenerative.

In its insistence upon resolution and forgiveness, *Jubilee*, published in the turmoil of the mid-sixties, may be seen as a natural culmination of American fictional and autobiographical treatments of the mid-nineteenth century—particularly the Civil War—and of the profoundly ambivalent relationships between black and white southern women during that chaotic period of history. As Phyllis Klotman points out, the novel presents history from the black woman's perspective. Vyry is the focus—moral, physical, and spiritual—of *Jubilee*. From the death of her mother Sis Hetta, in 1839, to news of the imminent birth of her fourth child at the end of the saga, we see the events of thirty years through the eyes of this larger-than-life black woman of the nineteenth-century Deep South.[12]

As is the case with women's slave narratives of the nineteenth and early twentieth centuries, Vyry's life *is* the book. Her movement from slavery through the vicissitudes of war to freedom parallels her burgeoning sense of who she is and what she stands for. All the while she gathers strength and self-knowledge and, as her white folks crumble under the barrage of war, she takes charge of their welfare as well as of her own and that of her children. Through this process of growth on southern soil, a process that in the slave narratives was usually the result of an escape North, Vyry—like real black women such as Harriet Jacobs—comes to know herself and her own capacities for endurance and love. *Jubilee* is a novel of Vyry's becoming. In its last pages, when she proclaims the message of Walker's humanism, one has the sense of immense possibility for this black woman who rejects racial bitterness as her southern heritage by revealing that she herself forgives the one white who mistreated her most shamefully, her mistress Salina Dutton.

Vyry's profession of forgiveness toward her dead mistress may be seen as Walker's recognition and release of much of the bitterness and hatred in relationships between black and white southern women of the mid-nineteenth century, in life and in literature. This is a fictional nineteenth-century black woman's gesture of conciliation, rendered by a real black woman writer of the volatile sixties. As such, it is a significant black acknowledgment of cross-racial female bonds of suffering that are so much a part of such white American fiction as *Uncle Tom's Cabin, Absalom, Absalom!* and *Sapphira and the Slave Girl. Jubilee* does not so much oppose violence and love as it presents them as catalysts for Walker's humanistic vision of life. Vyry's ability to love is born out of the violence in this fiction and is in its way as mysterious and powerful as Rosa Coldfield's racism. Vyry's willingness to help white women through the vicissitudes of war, poverty, and childbirth becomes, in Walker's vision, a peculiarly female regenerative process that saturates and dilutes racial bitterness through sisterhood and maternal nurturance. This process of conciliation is a harbinger of what Walker called in 1970 the "new consciousness" of a nonracist society.[13] *Jubilee* is, in fact, a supreme example of Walker's own assertion that "Afro-American literature is a reservoir of black humanism." It is perhaps also her exhibition of the "hope for a better world . . . founded on a new humanism instead of the old racism."[14]

At the same time *Jubilee* may be read as a moral resolution of fictional and autobiographical treatments of interracial relationships among nineteenth-century southern women. Walker's fictional construct of racial reconciliation is embodied in Vyry's charitable feelings for white women. Whether such a reconciliation opens this novel to Baldwin's earlier criticisms of oversimplification and distortion of reality, criticisms he directed toward other literature about blacks, is a pertinent issue.[15] Vyry's limited articulation of Walker's "humanistic values" does perhaps make life appear simpler than it is, although Randall Ware's opposing view may counter that simplicity to a degree. As a whole, though, Walker's philosophy of humanism complicates rather than simplifies life and renders fiction about race a more complex genre. History for Walker comes in shades of gray, as does its fictional mimesis. Paradoxically, issues of race lose clarity when considered in the light of Walker's humanism, yet such issues become even more urgent in such a light. Walker believes that specific white people have been unjust to specific blacks. She does not believe that all whites are evil, just as she does not believe that all blacks are good. Like that of Christ, Vyry's path is the hardest to follow because it is, at once, the most simple and the most complex.

Baldwin would perhaps chastise Walker for writing still another "everybody's protest novel" which imposes theological simplification upon the complexity of life. Yet Walker's vision of life has its own power. Speaking through Vyry's voice, she summons up the multilayered quality of that life, in which individuals of all races live in a mixed state of grace and disgrace, good and evil. Vyry's voice is the voice of good will, of duty, of a willingness to love and nurture. It is the articulation of some of our best human impulses. Yet it is Walker's vision rather than Vyry's voice that moves us. Vyry herself is a simple woman. She does not come to her decision to forgive past cruelties out of a fullness of consciousness which would make such a gesture psychologically dynamic. In this sense Vyry is different from Faulkner's Rosa Coldfield or Cather's Sapphira Colbert: she does not literally reflect in complexity of character the author's complexity of vision. Yet it is Walker's humanistic vision that remakes her own great-grandmother into the Christ-like Vyry. And, paradoxically, it is Vyry's very lack of complexity that illumines the awesome clarity and power of humanistic principles to transform human lives and relationships.

Vyry's is a black woman's voice in a black woman's novel. Yet it is a counterpoint to other voices in black and white literature about southern women during the crucial and difficult years of the mid-nineteenth century. Except for the slave narratives, these literary treatments of cross-racial female relationships during this time and in this place are all from a white point of view; and black women characters are either, like Stowe's Aunt Chloe or Cather's Till, presented stereotypically, or, like Faulkner's Clytie, they become inscrutable. What Robert Lively has pointed out concerning Civil War novels generally may apply to the four other American novels studied here—and particularly to Eastman's *Aunt Phillis's Cabin*: such white literary treatments, he writes, "have failed to enter slave minds or revivify slave ambitions; Negro characters have remained, for the most part, lacking necessary elements of unique individuality."[16]

Jubilee responds to these novels in the sense that it presents the slavery experience and cross-racial female relationships from the viewpoint of the black woman. Eight years after the publication of *Jubilee*, Walker said in conversations with Nikki Giovanni that she was still interested in "the black woman in fiction perhaps because I'm a black woman and feel that the black woman's story has not been told, has not been dealt with adequately."[17] The peculiarly female connection in *Jubilee* be-

tween natural creative principles of life and spiritual cre-
ativeness synthesizes much of what is positive in women's
relationships in the earlier novels and autobiographies. Walker
associates womanhood as it is personified in Vyry with burgeoning growth and fertility. Vyry's nurturance of white women is part of Walker's concept of creative physicality and
humanism. Such creativity, Walker wrote in 1980, "cannot
exist without the feminine principle, and I am sure God is not
merely male or female but He-She—our Father-Mother God.
All nature reflects this rhythmic and creative principle of
feminism and femininity: the sea, the earth, the air, and all life
whether plant or animal."[18]

In the same essay Walker suggests that the key to humanism
lies in the traditional female sphere and in the woman writer
who values that sphere. She sounds much like Stowe when she
writes a century later: "The traditional and historic role of
womankind is ever the role of the healing and annealing hand,
whether the outworn modes of nurse, and mother, cook, and
sweetheart. As a writer these are still her concerns. These are
still the stuff about which she writes, the human condition, the
human potential, the human destiny."[19] Vyry is such a woman
and such a symbol. And it is her connections with white
women—whether those women be cruel, helpless, or kind—
which reflect Walker's humanism and her own. It is also these
fictional bonds, formed under what Walker believes to be the
humanistic mantle of black fiction, that symbolically reconcile
the profoundly ambivalent feelings among these women of
this time and this region. The issue is whether this is a meaningful reconciliation, or a failure to acknowledge far deeper
and more painful conflicts.

Certainly Vyry's early struggles seem painful enough. The
novel opens with the death in childbirth of her mother Sis
Hetta, who had been since her early adolescence the concubine
of John Dutton, the master of the Georgia plantation. Two-
year-old Vyry is his daughter. After her mother's death, the
child is taken to the Big House, where she spends most of her
time trying to stay out of the way of Dutton's wife Salina, the
"Big Missy" of the plantation. Salina, instead of taking a
motherly role with her half-white stepdaughter, takes perverse

pleasure in tormenting the child, whose pale face is a flesh-and-blood emblem of her husband's infidelity. "Big Missy" Salina is a woman of steel, a real ogre reminiscent of Jacobs's Mrs. Flint, and yet she also is a fictional exaggeration of glorified white southern womanhood. The overseer Grimes describes her as

> a lady, . . . a fine, good lady. She nurses the sick far and wide, white and black. She knows how to handle niggers and keep a big establishment; how to set a fine table, and act morally decent like a first-class lady. She's a real Christian woman, a Bible-reading, honest-dealing, high-quality lady who knows and acts the difference between niggers and white people. She ain't no nigger-loving namby-pamby like that s.o.b. pretty boy she's married to.[20]

Salina's "Christianity" is in ironic contrast to her tortures of Vyry. When the child forgets to empty the chamber pot from the room of her half-sister Lillian, Big Missy throws the contents in her face. Soon after the death of Vyry's first surrogate mother, Mammy Suckey, the girl has the misfortune to break one of Salina's china dishes. Big Missy responds by hanging the child by her hands in a closet, where she loses consciousness. It is Lillian, Salina's daughter and Vyry's half-sister, who meets her father as he returns to the plantation with the words, "Oh, Poppa, come quick, Vyry's hanging by her thumbs in the closet and I do believe she's dead" (p. 37). Dutton rescues Vyry and forbids his wife to mistreat her, not so much on humane grounds but because "someday she'll be grown-up and worth much as a slave" (p. 37). Salina obviously associates Vyry with her husband's sexual appetites, and vows to "kill her and all other yellow bastards like her" (p. 37).

Just as the female principle is linked to creative humanism in *Jubilee*, so is the ideal of motherhood. The book begins and ends with the bearing of children. Sis Hetta dies in her attempt to bear a child, but Vyry at the end of *Jubilee* is expecting her fourth and has reconciled white and black interests through her willingness to aid in the delivery of other women's children. It is this maternal framework and emphasis which, by contrast, mark Salina, like Marie St. Clare, as an evil force. By all natural laws, the white woman, as the wife of Vyry's father, has certain maternal obligations to the mulatto orphan. In the southern context, it is understandable that she refuses to fulfill any natural obligations. But, instead of casting Vyry to the care of others and forgetting her, Salina tortures and torments her as if she, by being her mother's child, were innately guilty of some unforgivable sin. Like Cather's Sapphira, Big Missy becomes Jung's Dark Mother—a perversion of the generative principle, the primal threat to life and growth.

Young Vyry has two surrogate mothers: Mammy Suckey, whose death leaves her devastated, and more important, Aunt Sally, the Dutton cook, in whose cabin Vyry receives food and warmth, cooking lessons, and maternal affection. Without warning, the Duttons decide to sell Aunt Sally. As her black mother is dragged away sobbing pitifully, young Vyry cannot absorb the horrible reality of the experience. It is Big Missy, the Dark Mother, who shatters the child's dazed state: "Then Vyry found herself shaking like a leaf in a whirlwind. Salt tears were running in her mouth and her short, sharp finger nails were digging in the palms of her hands. Suddenly she decided she would go with Aunt Sally, and just then Big Missy slapped her so hard she saw tears and when she saw straight again Aunt Sally was gone" (p. 85). In contrast to Rosa Coldfield's slap which seems to seal the violent connection between white and black women, Big Missy's blow physically evokes separation—both between herself and the black-white child fathered by her husband, and between the child and her foster mother Aunt Sally. Rosa's slap is a recognition. Big Missy's is a rejection. Both blows embody in the space of a single instant the misuse of power by southern white women; both are indictments of that misuse and of its ultimate victimization of black women. Such epiphanic moments in *Jubilee* provide the novel with emotive translations of history, and thereby with a vividness and intensity which Walker does not achieve in her descriptive historical passages. Big Missy's separation of Vyry from her surrogate mother and the slap which irrevocably seals that separation confront us with the dark side of southern history and make us feel its terror.

Big Missy's cruelties occur in the first section of the book, which presents the antebellum period. The midsection, about

159

the Civil War, focuses on the general decline of the Dutton family. Salina loses husband, son, and son-in-law to the war. The only real grief she seems to feel is at the death of her son Johnny; yet she supports the Confederacy until its fall and then dies suddenly of a stroke, making good her wish never to see the slaves freed. The focus in this midsection is upon Vyry's resiliency and her care of the white women as their family disintegrates, a smoldering symbol of the waste and ruin of the Lost Cause. Vyry is also burdened with the care of two children by her marriage to Randall Ware, a free black who had gone North before the war.

As Salina loses control of the plantation and of herself, Vyry takes care of her half-sister Lillian and Lillian's children. After Lillian has lost her husband to the war and when her mother is also dead, she begs Vyry not to leave her alone on the plantation. Throughout this period directly after the war, Lillian gradually loses her mental powers, making it necessary for Vyry to take more and more control of the plantation. She single-handedly plows some land to plant vegetables, and persuades other black women on the deserted farm to help her plant food crops for themselves and the children, black and white, under their care. Lillian, who has lost brother, father, mother, and husband in close sequence, begins to lose touch with reality: she "seemed to pay less attention to what was going on around her as the days passed, but she smiled and gave her approval to their plans" (p. 277). When Lillian is attacked by Yankee soldiers and becomes permanently addled as a result, Vyry moves with her children to the Big House to take care of her white sister. As Lillian, a symbolic wreck of the Old South, sinks deeper and deeper into madness, Vyry—an emblem of the burgeoning New South—shelters and nurtures her. She becomes more of a concerned mother to her half-sister than the selfish Salina ever was, saving fresh eggs and buttermilk for Lillian in an effort to restore her health. Yet in spite of all her sister can do, Lillian slips further into permanent lethargy, rocking for hours, "apart from all around her" (p. 297).

Walker thus reduces this white woman, and Salina as well, to a state of utter powerlessness. Like Jacobs and Keckley, she as black writer exerts the ultimate control of language over white women of the past. In Walker's fictional construct, based upon her own heritage, these two white women who had such great impact upon her foremother's real life are re-created as either weak or wicked. Implicitly, Lillian's and Salina's loss of power becomes a symbolic reestablishment of the self-determination denied Walker's slave ancestors, and *Jubilee* a fictional reclamation of black female will.

As Walker strips away white female control, this midsection of the saga becomes the black woman's ascendancy. Vyry moves from the frightened slave child who ducks behind corners to avoid Big Missy to the mainstay of what is left of the white family. Her endurance is the thread which knits this section—and the whole novel—together into a rendering of the indomitability of the Afro-American heritage. Her loyalty to Lillian also shows the practical application of humanistic values to which Walker felt the black woman was particularly attuned. When it becomes plain that Randall Ware is not returning for her and the children, Innis Brown, who has helped her on the plantation, persuades her to marry him and to leave to find their own home. Yet Vyry will not desert Lillian without providing for her care. She sends for John Dutton's relative Lucy Porter to come for Lillian and waits until she arrives before leaving. Meanwhile she becomes Lillian's mother, nurses and sustains her as her mind dissolves with the old Confederacy. She has deep family feeling for her white sister, and she truly grieves for "Miss Lillian" as the white woman's mind wanders farther and farther from reality: "All this saddened Vyry. She felt terribly unhappy over Miss Lillian and it seemed so strange that things had turned out this way for the little golden girl she had always adored since she was a slave child herself growing up in the Big House" (p. 304).

Vyry's affection for Lillian remains throughout her years with Innis Brown. When she goes to visit Lucy Porter and her husband several years later, she weeps at Lillian's deterioration. To Lillian's repeated assertions, "I'm not crazy. I know who I am. I know my name. My name is Lillian," Vyry responds, "I know you ain't crazy, and I know you knows who you are. Honey don't you fret none. I knows you knows your name"

(p. 412). In her soothing words, Vyry shows her recognition of Lillian's former identity, and her kinship to her. She instinctively forgives her white sister for her thoughtlessness in the past years of slavery, and she mourns Lillian's loss of identity and sanity. Throughout her travels with Brown in their search for a permanent home, Vyry carries over that same openness and willingness to comfort and support white women of the merchant and sharecropper classes. Walker pictures many of the "poor whites" of rural Georgia and Alabama after the war as being in worse condition than Vyry and her family. Often, too, white sharecroppers are depicted as having intense resentment against the newly freed blacks because of the economic competition they present. Vyry and Innis become the victims of Klan violence and are forced to move when their house, which they built themselves, is burned down. Throughout these hardships, though, Vyry responds to the needs of white women while at the same time retaining her own sense of self. Nor does she let prejudice against blacks deter her from doing what she sees as her duty to fellow human beings who happen to be white.

When she and Innis find a white family still living in a sharecropper's shack that they have made arrangements to inhabit, Vyry recognizes poverty and actual hunger in the white wife and her six thin, ragged children. She immediately asks to be allowed to cook supper outside, and to her husband's astonishment, begins to make supper in a huge wash pot. Her preparations for the meal are ritualistic: "First she heated water from the well and scalded two big fat chickens. Then after she had dressed them she had Innis half-fill the big iron wash pot with water. Into this she put the cut-up chickens, a rabbit cut up, fat salt pork in hunks, a pan full of potatoes and onions, a jar of okra, tomatoes and corn mixture, salt and pepper, and let the pot boil a long time until the aroma of the food began to rise on the wind" (p. 348). Drawn by the smell of food, the white woman confides in Vyry that she and her family have eaten nothing but "fried meat grease and hominy since day before yestiddy" (p. 348). Always calling the white woman "ma'am," Vyry charitably feeds her and her family. She helps the woman circumvent her husband's pride by pretending that the whites are doing Vyry a favor by helping her eat an unplanned surplus of food.

In the morning, she again serves the white family hot food before they set out. In order to meet the white family's needs, she maintains a subservient pose, one which she was trained for as a slave. Yet, at bottom, her brief encounter with this poor white woman shows Vyry to be in control, just as she was in control with Lillian. Strangely, though, Walker depicts Vyry as unconcerned about gaining power in her relationships with whites. Vyry adopts a mode of behavior concerned only with ministering to the needs of others, regardless of race and regardless of the poses she must assume in order to do good. Her duty is to others; wherever that responsibility leads, she will follow.

In her relationship with another white woman later in the novel, Vyry becomes more assertive and less self-effacing. Her assertiveness comes perhaps from the knowledge that Mrs. Jacobson, her employer, is a self-sufficient woman who does not really need her in the same way that Lillian and the poor white woman did. In her characterization of Mrs. Jacobson, Walker seems to criticize the white woman for failing to see Vyry, who becomes her cook, as a wife and mother with her own responsibilities and as a person in her own right. Mrs. Jacobson is willing to help Vyry as long as it suits her purposes. She allows her to bring her three children to work with her and she is sympathetic to the idea of elementary education for blacks. She even promises to find a book for Vyry's daughter Minna. But when Vyry wants to quit her employment to help Innis with their house and farm, so as to allow her two older children the chance to go to school, Mrs. Jacobson becomes bitter and accusatory. She complains, "I understand how you colored people don't want to work the way you useta. What's more you won't work the way you useta. You expect everything to come dropping in your laps, houses and land and schools and churches and money, and you want to leave the white people holding the bag" (p. 373).

The message of Mrs. Jacobson's disgruntlement is that any white female relationship with a black woman must be predicated on her staying in her place as a servant and caretaker of white interests. Vyry breaks that code, and thereby reaps the wrath of her employer, who hitherto has been supportive. The old codes of slavery times are still operable as Vyry seeks a new life and new relationships with white women. Yet, again, Walker sees human behavior and morality in complex terms. When the Browns are burned out of their newly built house by Klansmen, Mrs. Jacobson offers Vyry the old job back in town and sends bedding and clothing to the distraught black family. Mr. Jacobson gives them money to travel on. Significantly, though, the influential Jacobsons do not offer to protect the black family against further trouble from local hoodlums and agree that the Browns have little choice but to move on. The Jacobsons treat the Brown family as a charity case. They give the Browns things that are simple to give; they withhold real support and friendship.

Small wonder that Vyry sinks into a depression after being burned out of her home and, soon after, losing a child at birth. What pulls her from her despair and lethargy, though, is a pilgrimage to Georgiana and "Miss Lucy" Porter, the relative who has taken over the care of Lillian. Recognizing the limitations of illiteracy and race in 1870, she makes the trip to get the Porters' help in recording claim to new property. Conscious of their debt to her for Lillian's care after the war, they agree to help her. Yet aside from the clerical help, it is just as much Lucy Porter's support and encouragement which cheers and sustains Vyry, who has realized with the loss of her house that the Reconstruction world is far from safe. Lucy counsels Vyry not to worry and insists that the Porters will make sure the Browns' land remains in their hands. Unlike "Big Missy" Salina, Lucy Porter seems to have a maternal feeling for Vyry and responds to her warmly and genuinely. Even their relationship, though, is based on the premise that the black woman needs the white woman to take care of her, that Vyry cannot function in the postwar society without a white sponsor. Though this may in fact be the case, Walker suggests that it does preclude true mutuality between the two women.

Yet Walker's ultimate vision of life is optimistic. She chooses not to explore the dark web of racism and ambivalence in cross-racial female relationships as Faulkner has done, or find in these relationships the problematic mixture of human nature as Cather pursues it in *Sapphira and the Slave Girl*. But in Walker's last spiritual vision of what is possible in these women's relationships, *Jubilee* powerfully suggests the infinite potential of human love through the regenerative principle and the overcoming of those dichotomous boundaries of race which so immured black and white women of antebellum, Civil War, and Reconstruction periods.

The events leading to this reconciliation begin ironically with Vyry's passing for white. When she and her family camp out near Greenville, Alabama, she begins to sell eggs and butter in town. Though she does not attempt to pass, having always thought of herself as black, she is treated like a white woman. Still leery about building a house in the area, she listens quietly to racist talk in order to gauge white feelings about blacks. Walker captures poor white sentiment in the monologue of an old woman who doesn't even have a dime to buy Vyry's eggs but, thinking that she is white, offers her a cup of water. Along with the water she shares her warped resentments of blacks' moving into the area:

> Them peoples ain't got no business in here, at all. They was much better off in slavery, and I says that's where they needs to be right now. Why, it's tore up our country just something awful! Instead of us prospering like we thought we was gonna after the war and everything, them grand rascals what the Yankees has brung down here ain't done nothing but set us back a hundred years. No telling when we'll git a living wage, and they even got the nerve of trying to open up mixed schools.   (p. 420)

With her pale features Vyry becomes privy to chilling talk of Klan tortures and murders, and peevish complaints that "niggers" have taken white folks' rights. Her hopes for making a home in the area fall.

It is her relationship with a young white woman and their common experience with the struggles of giving birth which reverse the force of racism that has swept the Browns from "pillar to post." On one of her trips into the white settlement, she becomes an emergency "granny" to this young woman and probably saves the baby by calming the mother and showing her how to give birth. She cares for the young mother and child, missing church on the following day to return to check on Betty-Alice Fletcher and her baby. She hushes Innis' complaints with an articulation of her philosophy, "I feels like it's my duty to help anybody I can wheresomever I can" (p. 429).

In a dramatic scene Vyry, who the Fletchers assume is white, listens to racist myths from the mouth of the white woman whose baby she has delivered. Betty-Alice parrots her husband's assertions that "all black nigger mens wants white women" and "nigger mens is got tails" (p. 430). When Vyry can stand no more she discloses her racial identity and the falseness of these myths. To the Fletchers and to Betty-Alice's parents, Vyry reveals in a flood of frustration and despair her feelings about the racism and violence she and her family have had to endure. Linked to the whole family and particularly to Betty-Alice through her participation in their regeneration in the birth of a child, she calls upon each of them to acknowledge her humanity and that of her family:

> . . . I does feel real bad and hurt down deep inside when I goes around and hears all the things the white folks is saying bout the colored peoples. What's so bad and what hurts so much is half the time they don't know what they talking about, they doesn't even much know us and what they saying is all lies they has heard and stuff they has made up. Me and my husband and my chilluns is been from pillar to post since the war. We ain't been ables to stay nowheres in peace. We's been in a flood and we's been burned out when six white mens purposely set fire to our brand-new house right in front of our very eyes. And it ain't nothing we done to them made them do it. We ain't even much knowed who they was. We's got us a place now out on the Big Road and we's been planning to build in this here community, but after all the terrible stuff I has heard just going round selling vegetables and eggs and stuff I'm scared for us to build, and I'm gwine tell my husband we's gotta be moving on. (pp. 432–33)

Mrs. Shackleford, Betty-Alice's mother, is the one who responds: "Well, I'm sho sorry to hear that. I can tell you is a good woman and a Christian woman, too. I thank God for what you done for my child and I wants you to know I wishes you well" (p. 433).

This *connection* between Vyry and the two white women, mother and daughter, through the common female experience of giving birth, results in meaningful interracial communication. Vyry thus extends the black circle of community, later embodied in the reconciliation of her two husbands at her own table, into a second, larger circle of interracial community. Walker's vision of peace, sympathy, and common goals linking all people into one human race becomes a reality of shared food and shared labor when the white members of the community, motivated both by good will and by Vyry's willingness to serve as community midwife, come to help the Browns build their long-awaited house. This is a moving and sweeping scene, and one which embodies Walker's celebration of creative humanism. The men in the community work together to build the house, while the women have a quilting bee. As they sew busily, Vyry moves among them "with her generous spirit of hospitality" (p. 440), she the seamstress sewing together black and white people and their lives and common goals. This quilting scene is a picture of the human race, the female human race, making the one and many patterns of life through love, sympathy, and sisterhood.

It is to this ideal of sisterhood, of human kinship, that Vyry speaks at the end of the book. And as she speaks, she takes on at the same time a mythic voice, Walker's voice, a profoundly caring voice. To Randall Ware's cynical view that whites only have use for blacks when blacks have something they want, Vyry responds that all people need one another, that Ware has "no God" in him and is obsessed with hatred. She bristles when Ware refers to her sister Lillian as stupid, and harshly criticizes his willingness "to try to beat the white man at his own game with his killing and his hating" (p. 482). At this, the climax of the book, Vyry returns to her childhood and "Big Missy" Salina, the first white woman in her life and the most treacherous. In her account of what she endured under this ogre of a woman and in her expression of forgiveness of such depths of human and female cruelty, Vyry shows herself to be truly a spiritual paragon. She tells Ware:

Big Missy was mighty mean to me from the first day I went in the Big House as a slave to work. She emptied Miss Lillian's pee-pot in my face. She hung me up by my thumbs. She slapped me and she kicked me; she cussed me and she worked me like I was a dog. They stripped me naked and put me on the auction block for sale. And worsetest of all they kept me ignorant so's I can't read and write my name, but I closed her eyes in death, and God is my witness, I bears her no ill will. (pp. 483–84)

These are marks of the suffering servant. Vyry's words are reminiscent of Christ's "Father, forgive them for they know not what they do."

Vyry's spirit of forgiveness is a fictional expression of the redemptive power of love. It is more what Walker thought her great-grandmother was than what she knew her to be. Walker admits this point:

Insofar as Vyry's lack of bitterness is concerned, maybe I have not been as honest as I should be, taking the license of the imaginative worker, but I have tried to be honest. My great-grandmother was a definite product of plantation life and culture. She was shaped by the forces that dominated her life. In the Big House and in the Quarters she was raised according to Christian ethics, morality, and faith, and she could not react any other way. Her philosophy of life was a practical one, and she succeeded in getting the things she wanted and prayed for. She realized that hatred wasn't necessary and would have corroded her own spiritual well-being.[21]

In reconstructing her grandmother in the simple and forgiving Vyry, Walker—writing most of her manuscript during the Civil Rights movement of the sixties—appears to suggest "black humanism" as an answer to America's racial conflicts. It is not so much Vyry's gesture itself which is significant, but Walker's association of this loving black woman and her simple act of forgiveness with the black writer's complex commitment to the humanistic values of "freedom, peace and human dignity." Like Vyry, but in a fullness of consciousness which she lacks, the black literary artist celebrates life and "the highest essence of human spirit."[22] This is what Walker means by humanism. By its very nature, such a vision embodies, at

168

once, the necessity to rebel and the willingness to reconcile. Vyry's act of forgiveness is not a passive acceptance of white cruelty, but an assertion of black self in the face of it.

Like Faulkner and Cather, Walker presents the volatile relationships of these black and white women as inextricable from the complex whole of the southern racial experience. Like that of the women's slave narratives, her point of view is that of the black woman. Though her white characters are often as stereotypical as Stowe's and Eastman's black ones and though her black heroine does not come to her moment of forgiveness and reconciliation in a fullness of consciousness, Walker's *Jubilee* transubstantiates Vyry's simple gesture into real vision. That vision is realized, significantly, in the southern black woman's forgiveness of the perverse and vicious cruelty of the southern white woman. In this sense *Jubilee* culminates more than one hundred years of American literary struggle with the paradoxical South and its women, fictional and real, white and black. At the same time, it celebrates the power of "black humanism" in a book that is part history and part fiction—a synthesis of life and literature.

As our great writers have shown, guilt at failure in human relationships is the inexorable white burden of southern history. In *Jubilee* the black woman's forgiving gesture suggests not so much an abatement of black pain or lifting of white guilt as a greatly simplified paradigm of Walker's belief that we can redeem ourselves by extending our sense of human community—whether white, black, male, female, southern, northern—in ever-widening circles. Baldwin would say perhaps that Vyry, like Uncle Tom and Bigger Thomas, "has accepted a theology that denies . . . life" rather than affirming its complexity.[23] And perhaps Vyry's gesture of forgiveness does come too easily. Yet it is undeniably significant that the black woman writer, descendant of a slave woman who suffered greatly at the hand of her mistress, renders that gesture and the vision of human community which it implies. It is she—as southerner, as Afro-American, as woman—who has a particular right, and perhaps also a particular need, to evoke such a vision. Robert Lively notes the truism, "historical fiction is more likely to register an exact truth about the writer's present than the exact truth of the past."[24] For Walker's present, and for our own, *Jubilee* illuminates, in a black woman's forgiveness of her white sister, a regenerative response to the southern past.

CONCLUSION

"The peculiar sisterhood" of the Old South casts a long shadow, and a dark one, upon the American literary and cultural consciousness. I would argue, in fact, that biracial female experience of the nineteenth-century South, particularly the mistress-slave woman connection, carries more power and resonance, more sheer metaphorical weight in American literature than any other cross-racial relationship. Because of the frequency, intimacy, and intensity of their connections, white and black women of the slave and Reconstruction South together become, in their own writings and in fictional representatives of their relationships, starkly compelling referents of the mind divided against itself. In modern fiction they become the *idea* of the terrible duality in human nature, the mysterious connection between human need for recognition and human desire to reject that need. In autobiography and fiction alike, this need and the desire to reject it become not just the external construct of the dynamics of racism, but are as powerfully realized as an internal psychological tension within the female psyche. By rejecting the humanity of another woman, as Rosa does Clytie's, one rejects one's own humanity. Racism is therefore, particularly in the case of these women of the Old South who are alike in so many ways, one of the darkest and most self-destructive impulses. When Rosa rejects Clytie, she rejects her own self as a full, caring, significant woman—as the "*Rosa*" of Clytie's defining voice.

My goal has been to open new avenues of inquiry rather than to rush toward any set of conclusions, however inviting

171

they may appear. As Faulkner and, in less obvious ways, others of these writers show us, we can never really know the past. But we can learn from trying to know it, through its own writers and through those of our own time, but especially through the often problematic relationships between them and the culture they both define and reflect. Cross-racial female connection of the Old South is indeed a "peculiar sisterhood" in a double sense, both in itself—what it *was,* or seemed to be—and in its referential weight—what it *became* in American literature. What seems apparent in both history and literature is that the contemplation, as reality and as metaphor, of biracial female experience of this period in southern history enables us to feel southern experience in a new way. It enables us to ask new questions, to become aware of both nuance and sweeping illumination arising out of a female context. It provides a peculiarly piercing vision of southern and human racial experience.

That vision arises, not from a single work or a single writer or a single encounter, but from mutual female experience as metaphor distilled and transformed through the alembic of a various American literary consciousness. This is a variousness of time, of literary purpose, of genre, of sex, of race, of creative insight. The female experience, as it moves through creation and re-creation, through this various literary consciousness, extends the circumference of the American mythic mind. It becomes, at once, southern racial experience, American racial experience, human racial experience. Traditionally women have been associated with feeling, with the power of the intuitive mind. In the case of racial experience, particularly that of the slave South, it is perhaps through feeling that we begin to know. As Kenneth M. Stampp says, "To understand the South is to feel the pathos in its history."[1] We begin to feel and thereby to know the South through Eliza's race across the ice, through Mary Chesnut's anger, through Kate Stone's anguished questions about moral accountability, through Harriet Jacobs' verbal lashings of a cruel mistress—through Rosa and Clytie's encounter upon the stairs, Sapphira's strange duality, Vyry's insistence upon forgiveness and human community. We even begin to know the South through falsity, through female stereotypes, through literary exclamations of sexual frustration, through black assertions of female self as separate from white Other. And what we feel, what we learn from these women, whether they be re-creations of self or fictional entities, is the intensity of human need and human connection and human terror embodied in racial encounter in the Old South and by implication in universal human experience, and the profound impact of racial encounter upon its literary interpreters.

Biracial female experience becomes a powerful micro-exposition of human pain and human connection, of the excruciating tension implicit in racial experience of the Old South. As such, "the peculiar sisterhood" serves as an entry into American literature that both interprets and concentrates the meaning of the southern past; that creates new critical relationships between works of the traditional canon and those outside of it; and that shows, above all, the ambiguous power of the idea of the Old South in the American literary consciousness. Yet, more than that, this literary sisterhood of biracial experience becomes a valid metaphor for human experience and for some of the most powerful of human emotions conveyed in literature. In this sense, female experience gives us insight into our literature, and that literature itself validates female experience in American culture. This holistic relationship between culture and literature is perpetuated by the seeking of new literary contexts through which we may know ourselves, past and present, and of new cultural contexts through which we may know our literary art more intensely and more creatively.

"The peculiar sisterhood" and its troubling, lingering impingements upon American culture and literature offer such a context, and suggest others. Surely it binds these American writers and their penetrations into the southern past. We are left in the end with a powerful sense of *connection*. In Rosa's blow to Clytie we feel the wrath of Keckley's Mrs. Burwell or Jacobs's Mrs. Flint; in Till's story of Sapphira's death we hear Smedes's Mammy Harriet extolling her mistress; in Vyry Ware's forgiveness of Salina Dutton we hear a fictional attempt at reconciliation of all that has gone before. Yet we are left with

Rosa and Clytie's encounter of the flesh. We are left with Rosa's terrible and ambiguous response to the black woman who asks for human recognition, for kinship, for sisterhood. We are left with the haunting question: *"sister, sister?"*

NOTES

INTRODUCTION

1. William Faulkner, *Absalom, Absalom!* (New York: Modern Library, 1966), p. 140.

2. Anne Firor Scott and Catherine Clinton find the plantation mistress's life of drudgery and heavy responsibility in ironic opposition to her elevated position in the popular mind. See Scott, *The Southern Lady: From Pedestal to Politics 1830–1930* (Chicago: Univ. of Chicago Press, 1970); and Clinton, *The Plantation Mistress: Woman's World in the Old South* (New York: Pantheon, 1982). For an excellent synopsis of the roles and conflicts of white southern women, see also chapter 1 of Anne Goodwyn Jones's *Tomorrow Is Another Day: The Woman Writer in the South, 1859–1936* (Baton Rouge: Louisiana State Univ. Press, 1981), pp. 3–50.

3. Recent historians of the Old South seem to agree generally that black and white women often were forced into these dichotomous roles. See John Blassingame, *The Slave Community: Plantation Life in the Antebellum South* (New York: Oxford Univ. Press, 1972), p. 82; W.J. Cash, *The Mind of the South* (New York: Knopf, 1941), pp. 87–120; Eugene Genovese, *In Red and Black: Marxian Explorations in Southern and Afro-American History* (1968; rpt. Knoxville: Univ. of Tennessee Press, 1984), pp. 112–21; Herbert Gutman, *The Black Family in Slavery and Freedom, 1750–1925* (New York: Pantheon, 1976), pp. 80–85; Kenneth Stampp, *The Peculiar Institution: Slavery in the Ante-Bellum South* (New York: Knopf, 1956), pp. 350–61; and Bertram Wyatt-Brown, *Southern Honor: Ethics and Behavior in the Old South* (New York: Oxford Univ. Press, 1982), pp. 296–98, 307–24.

175

4. Trudier Harris's *From Mammies to Militants: Domestics in Black American Literature* (Philadelphia: Temple Univ. Press, 1982) is one of the few studies with emphasis upon cross-racial female relationships.

5. James Baldwin, "Everybody's Protest Novel," *Partisan Review* 16 (June 1949): 578–85; rpt. Elizabeth Ammons, ed., *Critical Essays on Harriet Beecher Stowe* (Boston: G.K. Hall, 1980), pp. 92–101.

6. C.W. Larison, *Silvia Dubois (Now 116 Yers Old.) A Biografy of The Slav who Whipt her Mistress and Gand her Fredom* (1883; rpt. New York: Negro Universities Press, 1969), p. 63.

7. Harriet Wilson, *Our Nig; or, Sketches from the Life of a Free Black,* ed. Henry Louis Gates Jr. (1859; rpt. New York: Vintage, 1983), p. 105.

8. Zilpha Elaw, *Memoirs of the Life, Religious Experience, Ministerial Travels and Labours, of Mrs. Zilpha Elaw* (London: Published by the Author and sold by T. Dudley, 1846); Julia A.J. Foote, *A Brand Plucked from the Fire: An Autobiographical Sketch of Mrs. Julia Foote* (Cleveland: Printed for the Author by W.F Schneider, 1879); Jarena Lee, *Religious Experience and Journal of Mrs. Jarena Lee,* 2d ed. (Philadelphia: Published for the Author, 1849); Nancy Prince, *A Narrative of the Life and Travels of Mrs. Nancy Prince Written by Herself.* 2d ed. (Boston: Published by the Author, 1853).

9. As noted in Chapter 2, this is not to imply that the oral accounts do not provide valuable insight into the realities of slave experience. See: Federal Writers' Project, *Slave Narratives: A Folk History of Slavery in the United States from Interviews with Former Slaves,* vols. 1–17 (Washington, D.C.: WPA, 1941); George Rawick, ed., *The American Slave: A Composite Autobiography,* vols. 1–19 (Westport, Conn.: Greenwood, 1972); and John W. Blassingame, ed., *Slave Testimony: Two Centuries of Letters, Speeches, Interviews, and Auto-biographies* (Baton Rouge: Louisiana State Univ. Press, 1977).

10. John Hawkins Simpson, *Horrors of the Virginian Slave Trade and of the Slave-Rearing Plantations: The True Story of Dinah, an Escaped Virginian Slave* (London: A.W. Bennett, 1863); Bethany Veney, *Aunt Betty's Story: The Narrative of Bethany Veney, a Slave Woman,* 2d ed. (Boston: A.P. Bicknell, 1890). Simpson writes his narrative of Dinah's suffering and sexual misuse in the third person from "the true story of the escaped slave" (p. 6n.). "M.W.G.," the unnamed editor of Bethany Veney's narrative, writes that Veney's experiences were transcribed in this first-person account, but that the former slave

woman's "language cannot be transcribed" and "the little particulars that give coloring and point, tone and expression, are largely lost" (preface).

11. Two novels by black writers of the nineteenth and early twentieth centuries, William Wells Brown's *Clotel* and Pauline Hopkins' *Contending Forces,* which might be expected to contain interesting materials about cross-racial female relationships in North and South, simply do not. Hopkins' novel is about black society of Boston and contains no cross-racial female relationships of substance. *Clotel* does involve a triangle between Clotel, the Virginia gentleman to whom she is "married" and whose child she bears, and his white bride; but the two women have no real relationship except through the weak Horatio, who discards black "wife" for white with little remorse. See William Wells Brown, *Clotel* (1853; rpt. New York: Arno, 1969); Pauline E. Hopkins, *Contending Forces: A Romance Illustrative of Negro Life North and South* (1900; rpt. New York: AMS, 1971).

Modern writers of fiction about the Old South who might be expected to join Faulkner, Cather, and Walker in probing the volatile nature of cross-racial female relationships in that milieu seem to have other concerns or focuses. Ernest Gaines's Jane Pittman has three unpleasant experiences with white women: one with a cruel mistress who beats her because she insists upon taking a new "free" name, and two with women who hate blacks whom she encounters as she begins her journey to Ohio. But these encounters are a brief and seemingly small part of the total experience of a heroic southern black woman whose long life spans the transition of Old to New South. See Ernest Gaines, *The Autobiography of Miss Jane Pittman* (New York: Dial, 1971).

Frank Yerby's *Captain Rebel* is about white romantic relationships, and his *A Darkness at Ingraham's Crest: A Tale of the Slaveholding South* depicts the conflict between a strong and proud African male, Wes Parks, and the white establishment. The primary cross-racial relationship is between Wes and Pamela Ingraham, the stereotypical white lady who lusts predictably after her black male slave. In Margaret Mitchell's *Gone with the Wind,* Scarlett O'Hara is, also predictably, devoted to her "Mammy," a "shining black, pure African, devoted to her last drop of blood to the O'Haras," who infantilizes and chastises her white female charge. Significantly, at the end of the novel, in the devastation and ruins of lost home and shattered culture, Scarlett yearns for "Mammy, the last link with the old days." Yet here as in *The Autobiography of Miss Jane Pittman,* the relationship between black and white women seems only peripheral to the fiction. Stark Young's *So Red the Rose* is, even more than *Gone with the Wind,* a white saga in which black life is unimportant to the fiction. Young's plantation mistress, Mrs. Bedford, in fact, calls all of her female house slaves by the same name, "Celie," to expedite the housework and to avoid the trouble of remembering several different names. See Frank Yerby, *Captain Rebel* (London: Heinemann, 1957); *A Darkness at Ingraham's Crest: A Tale of the Slaveholding South* (New York: Dial, 1979); Margaret Mitchell, *Gone with the Wind* (New York: Macmillan, 1936), pp. 23, 1037; and Stark Young, *So Red the Rose* (New York: Scribner's, 1934).

In the case of short fiction, Katherine Anne Porter's sketch "The Old Order" is a powerful if brief study of strong, positive cross-racial bonds between two women of the Old South, Sophia Jane and Nannie, grounded in a shared past and mutual nurturance through the pain and joy of years long gone. As in many of the short oral accounts of female slaves, however, "The Old Order" suggests and sketches, where more sustained autobiographical and fictional works delineate and dramatize. See Katherine Anne Porter, "The Old Order," in *The Old Order* (New York: Harcourt, Brace, & World, 1958), pp. 11–33.

12. Seymour Gross, "Introduction: Stereotype to Archetype: The Negro in American Literary Criticism," in *Images of the Negro in American Literature,* ed. Seymour Gross and John Hardy (Chicago: Univ. of Chicago Press, 1966), p. 1.

13. Harriet Beecher Stowe, *Uncle Tom's Cabin; or, Life among the Lowly,* ed. Kenneth S. Lynn (Cambridge: Belknap Press, Harvard Univ. Press, 1962); Mary H. Eastman, *Aunt Phillis's Cabin; or, Southern Life as It Is* (1852; rpt. New York: Negro Universities Press, 1960).

14. Kate Stone, *Brokenburn: The Journal of Kate Stone 1861–1868,* ed. John Q. Anderson (Baton Rouge: Louisiana State Univ. Press, 1972), p. 8.

15. Willa Cather, *Sapphira and the Slave Girl* (New York: Knopf, 1940).

16. Margaret Walker, *Jubilee* (Boston: Houghton Mifflin, 1966).

CHAPTER I

1. Richard Beale Davis, "Mrs. Stowe's Characters-In-Situations and a Southern Literary Tradition," in *Essays on American Literature in Honor of Jay B. Hubbell*, ed. Clarence Gohdes (Durham: Duke Univ. Press, 1967), p. 109. Like Eastman, the writers of many of these novels apparently read *Uncle Tom's Cabin* in serial form and wrote and published their fictional responses within one year.

2. Baldwin, "Everybody's Protest Novel," pp. 578–85.

3. See Charles Foster, *The Rungless Ladder: Harriet Beecher Stowe and New England Puritanism* (Durham: Duke Univ. Press, 1954); Helen Papashivly, *All the Happy Endings: A Study of the Domestic Novel in America, the Women Who Wrote It, the Women Who Read It, in the Nineteenth Century* (New York: Harper, 1956); Ernest Cassara, "The Rehabilitation of Uncle Tom: Significant Themes in Mrs. Stowe's Antislavery Novel," *CLA Journal* 57 (Dec. 1973): 230–40; Thomas Graham, "Harriet Beecher Stowe and the Question of Race," *New England Quarterly* 46 (Dec. 1973): 614–22; David Levin, "American Fiction as Historical Evidence: Reflections on *Uncle Tom's Cabin*," *Negro American Literature Forum* 5 (Winter 1972): 132–36, 156; and Cushing Strout, "*Uncle Tom's Cabin* and the Portent of Millennium," *Yale Review* 57 (Spring 1968): 375–85.

4. The emotional realities of the cross-racial relationships of white and black women during the mid-nineteenth century are more clearly reflected in their autobiographical writings, which will be examined in Chapter 2, but even there the writers' purposes in composing and publishing the diaries and slave narratives often modify such realities, or create new ones, and thereby produce works which, like most autobiographical writings, are more interesting as psychological studies than historical treatises.

5. Harriet Beecher Stowe, *The Key to "Uncle Tom's Cabin"* (Boston: John P. Jewett, 1853), p. iii.

6. For discussions of the plantation legend in fact and fiction, see Francis P. Gaines, *The Southern Plantation: A Study in the Development and the Accuracy of a Tradition* (New York: Columbia Univ. Press, 1925); William R. Taylor, *Cavalier and Yankee: The Old South and American National Character* (New York: George Braziller, 1961); and Sterling Brown, *The Negro in American Fiction* (1937; rpt. Port Wash-

ington, N.Y.: Kennikat, 1968). For a more recent analysis of the southern chivalric code, see Wyatt-Brown, *Southern Honor.*

7. David Levy, "Racial Stereotypes in Antislavery Fiction," *Phylon* 31 (Fall 1970): 265.

8. See Catherine Starke's discussion of the symbolism of the black mammy in *Black Portraiture in American Fiction: Stock Characters, Archetypes, and Individuals* (New York: Basic Books, 1971), p. 251. Starke's chap. 3 is particularly interesting in its discussion of archetypal patterns in black characterization. Other recent book-length treatments of stereotyping of black characters are: Gross and Hardy, eds., *Images of the Negro in American Literature;* George M. Fredrickson, *The Black Image in the White Mind: The Debate on Afro-American Character and Destiny, 1817–1914* (New York: Harper & Row, 1971); and Jean Yellin, *The Intricate Knot: Black Figures in American Literature, 1776–1863* (New York: New York Univ. Press, 1972). Most work in this area is built on Brown's *The Negro in American Fiction.*

9. Taylor, *Cavalier and Yankee,* pp. 162–63.

10. Starke, *Black Portraiture in American Fiction,* p. 30.

11. Barbara Welter, "The Cult of True Womanhood: 1820–1860," *American Quarterly* 18 (Summer 1966): 152.

12. For extended analyses of the female sphere in *Uncle Tom's Cabin,* see Alice C. Crozier, *The Novels of Harriet Beecher Stowe* (New York: Oxford Univ. Press, 1969); and Elizabeth Ammons, "Heroines in *Uncle Tom's Cabin,*" in *Critical Essays on Harriet Beecher Stowe,* ed. Elizabeth Ammons (Boston: G.K. Hall, 1980), pp. 152–68.

13. Levin, "American Fiction as Historical Evidence," p. 135.

14. Davis, "Mrs. Stowe's Characters-In-Situations," p. 109.

15. Foster, *The Rungless Ladder,* p. 40.

16. Both Crozier and Ammons discuss this opposition in the novel of male and female spheres.

17. Nina Baym, *Woman's Fiction: A Guide to Novels by and about Women in America, 1820–1870* (Ithaca: Cornell Univ. Press, 1978), p. 49.

18. Stowe, *Key,* pp. 8 and 12.

19. Stowe, *Uncle Tom's Cabin,* p. 13. Subsequent references will be designated parenthetically.

20. Stowe, *Key,* p. 133.

21. Levin, "American Fiction," p. 154.

22. George Fredrickson writes: "The tyranny of slaveholders over affectionate and forgiving blacks seemed to be matched only by the brutality of males who took advantage of feminine tenderness and devotion; and the romantic reformist concept of female 'superiority' that developed during this period was very similar to the notion of the moral and spiritual preeminence of the Negro" (*The Black Image*, p. 114).

23. John Adams' *Harriet Beecher Stowe* (New York: Twayne, 1963) is one of several literary biographies to propound this theory. See also Forrest Wilson, *Crusader in Crinoline: The Life of Harriet Beecher Stowe* (Philadelphia: Lippincott, 1941); Foster, *The Rungless Ladder;* Edward Wagenknecht, *Harriet Beecher Stowe: The Known and the Unknown* (New York: Oxford Univ. Press, 1965); and E. Bruce Kirkham, *The Building of "Uncle Tom's Cabin"* (Knoxville: Univ. of Tennessee Press, 1977).

24. Stowe's writing was a valuable source of extra income. *Uncle Tom's Cabin,* she hoped, would provide enough money for a silk dress. (Wilson, *Cavalier and Yankee,* p. 277).

25. See Ammons, "Heroines in *Uncle Tom's Cabin*," p. 163. Kathryn Kish Sklar first used the term *domestic feminism* to characterize Catharine Beecher in *Catharine Beecher: A Study in American Domesticity* (New York: Norton, 1973). In her article "Four Novels of Harriet Beecher Stowe: A Study in Nineteenth-Century Androgyny," Laurie Crumpacker discusses how domestic feminism fits with the notions of female identity reflected in Stowe's life and work. See *American Novelists Revisited: Essays in Feminist Criticism,* ed. Fritz Fleischmann (Boston: G. K. Hall, 1982), pp. 78–106.

26. Quoted in Samuel Sillen, *Women against Slavery* (New York: Masses & Mainstream, 1955), p. 39. See also Jean Lebedun, "Harriet Beecher Stowe's Interest in Sojourner Truth," *American Literature* 46 (Nov. 1974): 362–63.

27. Severn Duvall, "*Uncle Tom's Cabin:* The Sinister Side of the Patriarchy," in Gross and Hardy, eds., *Images of the Negro in American Literature,* pp. 175–79. Reprinted from *New England Quarterly* 36 (1963): 3–22.

Perhaps the most accurate measure of the feminist undercurrents in *Uncle Tom's Cabin* and of the impact of a woman's having extended the literary and cultural spheres prescribed for female fiction in order to castigate what was basically a patriarchal system may be found in some of the *argumentum ad feminam* responses to the book. The *Weekly Picayune* of New Orleans, 30 August 1852, labeled Stowe's authorship "a desecration of woman's nature . . . a sorry and a rare sight even in this age of feminine aspirations to rivalry with man in all his harshest of traits and all his most unamiable pursuits." From the *Southern Literary Messenger* of June 1853 came the vituperative attack characterizing Stowe as "an obscure Yankee schoolmistress, eaten up with fanaticism, festering with the malignant virus of abolitionism, self-sanctified by the virtues of a Pharisaic religion devoted to the assertion of women's rights, and an enthusiastic believer in many neoteric heresies."

Quoted in Arthur Maurice, "Famous Novels and Their Contemporary Critics: *Uncle Tom's Cabin*," *Bookman* 17 (Mar. 1903): 26, 23–24.

Most scholars attribute to William Gilmore Simms the anonymous "A Key to *Uncle Tom's Cabin*," *Southern Quarterly Review* 7 (July 1853): 214–54, in which Stowe's *Key*, as well as *Uncle Tom's Cabin*, are soundly criticized as being the work of a "woman-reasoner." See Severn Duvall, "W. G. Simms' Review of Mrs. Stowe," *American Literature* 30 (March 1958): 107–17, who argues that the review articulates Simms's theories of literature, employs antifeminism similar to his attack on Harriet Martineau, and echoes previous essays.

28. Keith Melder, *Beginnings of Sisterhood: The American Woman's Rights Movement, 1800–1850* (New York: Schocken, 1977), p. 76.

29. *Liberator,* 3 March 1832, p. 34; 2 Jan. 1837, p. 2.

30. Melder, *Beginnings,* pp. 60–61.

31. Ammons, "Heroines in *Uncle Tom's Cabin*," p. 156.

32. Charles Edward Stowe, *The Life of Harriet Beecher Stowe* (Boston: Houghton Mifflin, 1889), p. 198. Stowe's sympathy with black mothers who lost their children also may have been indirectly aroused by the popular poem "The African Mother at Her Daughter's Grave" by Lydia H. Sigourney, which appeared in the 1834 volume *Poems* (Philadelphia: Key & Biddle) and was reprinted many times.

33. Stowe, *Key,* p. 12.

34. Ibid., p. 34.

35. Duvall, "*Uncle Tom's Cabin*," pp. 176–77.

See, for instance, Mary Chesnut's famous remark: "Harriet

Beecher Stowe did not hit the sorest spot. She makes Legree a bachelor." *Mary Chesnut's Civil War*, ed. C. Vann Woodward (New Haven: Yale Univ. Press, 1981), p. 168.

36. The most complete list, which includes William Gilmore Simms's *Woodcraft* (which some scholars do not count as a direct fictional response to *Uncle Tom's Cabin*), may be found in Jean W. Ashton, *Harriet Beecher Stowe: A Reference Guide* (Boston: G.K. Hall, 1977), appendix 1, pp. 137–38. Other lists and studies of these novels are found in Jeannette Tandy, "Pro-Slavery Propaganda in American Fiction of the Fifties," *South Atlantic Quarterly* 21 (Jan. 1922): 41–50; (April 1922): 170–78; Margaret Browne, "Southern Reactions to *Uncle Tom's Cabin*" (M.A. thesis, Duke Univ., 1941); and Barrie Hayne, "Yankee in the Patriarchy: T.B. Thorpe's Reply to *Uncle Tom's Cabin*," *American Quarterly* 20 (1968): 180–95.

37. Eastman, *Aunt Phillis's Cabin*, p. 111. Subsequent references will be designated parenthetically. The notation is Eastman's.

38. Tandy, "Pro-Slavery Propaganda," (Jan. 1922), p. 44.

39. Adrienne Rich, "Disloyal to Civilization: Feminism, Racism, Gynephobia," in *On Lies, Secrets, and Silence: Selected Prose 1966–1978* (New York: Norton, 1979), p. 310.

CHAPTER II

1. See for example: Blassingame, *The Slave Community;* Cash, *The Mind of the South;* Clinton, *The Plantation Mistress;* Angela Davis, *Women, Race & Class* (New York: Random House, 1981); Gutman, *The Black Family in Slavery and Freedom*; Bell Hooks, *"Ain't I a Woman?": Black Women and Feminism* (Boston: South End, 1981); Scott, *The Southern Lady*; Stampp, *The Peculiar Institution*; C. Vann Woodward, *The Burden of Southern History* (Baton Rouge: Louisiana State Univ. Press, 1960).

2. Katherine Fishburn, *Women in Popular Culture: A Reference Guide* (Westport, Conn.: Greenwood, 1982), pp. 10–11.

3. Studies such as Harris's *From Mammies to Militants* examine relationships between black and white women in modern literature.

4. Roy Pascal, *Design and Truth in Autobiography* (Cambridge: Harvard Univ. Press, 1960), p. 185.

5. Scott, *The Southern Lady*, p. x.

6. Cash, *The Mind of the South*, p. 86.

7. Ibid., pp. 84–86. Exaltation and desexualization were not limited to southern women in nineteenth-century America. See Nancy Cott's study of New England women in her article "Passionlessness: An Interpretation of Victorian Sexual Ideology, 1790–1850," *Signs* 4 (Winter 1978): 219–36.

8. Scott, *The Southern Lady*, p. x.

9. Ibid., p. xi.

10. Davis, *Women, Race & Class*, p. 23.

11. Carl Jung, *The Basic Writings of C. G. Jung,* ed. Violet De-Laszlo (New York: Modern Library, 1959), p. 333.

12. Stephen Butterfield, *Black Autobiography in America* (Amherst: Univ. of Massachusetts Press, 1974), p. 3.

13. Frances Foster, *Witnessing Slavery: The Development of Antebellum Slave Narratives* (Westport, Conn.: Greenwood, 1979), p. 65.

14. Harriet Jacobs, *Incidents in the Life of a Slave Girl,* ed. L. Maria Child (1861; rpt. New York: Harcourt Brace Jovanovich, 1973), p. 31. Subsequent references will be designated parenthetically.

15. Foster, *Witnessing Slavery,* pp. 60–61.

16. W.E.B. DuBois, *The Souls of Black Folk* (Chicago: A.C. McClurg, 1903), p. 3.

17. Pascal, *Design and Truth in Autobiography,* p. 83.

18. Estelle Jelinek, ed., *Women's Autobiography* (Bloomington: Indiana Univ. Press, 1980), p. 15.

19. Foster, *Witnessing Slavery,* p. 3.

20. Marion Starling lists more than 6000. See "The Slave Narrative: Its Place in American Literary History" (Ph.D. diss., New York Univ., 1946).

21. For separate bibliographies of women's slave narratives, see: Erlene Stetson, "Studying Slavery," in *But Some of Us Are Brave,* ed. Gloria Hull, Patricia Bell Scott, and Barbara Smith (Old Westbury, N.Y.: Feminist Press, 1982), pp. 82–84 (contains several errors); Stetson, "Black Women In and Out of Print," in *Women in Print-I,* ed. Joan Hartman and Ellen Messer-Davidson (New York: MLA, 1982), p. 97 (a more selective, but also more accurate listing). Starling, "The Slave Narrative"; Foster, *Witnessing Slavery;* and Charles Nichols, *Many Thousand Gone: The Ex-Slaves' Account of Their Bondage and Freedom,* 2d ed. (Bloomington: Indiana Univ. Press, 1969) list female

and male narratives together. For collected excerpts of some women's narratives, see Bert Loewenberg and Ruth Bogin, *Black Women in Nineteenth-Century American Life: Their Thoughts, Their Words,
Their Feelings* (University Park: Pennsylvania State Univ. Press,
1976).

22. These are similar to Rawick's categories of slave narratives
before the Civil War. See *The American Slave*, p. xv.

23. *Aunt Sally; or, The Cross the Way of Freedom* (1858; rpt. Miami:
Mnemosyne, 1969), pp. 163–82.

24. Simpson, *Horrors of the Virginian Slave Trade*, pp. 51–52.

25. Larison, *Silvia Dubois (Now 117 Yers Old.)*, p. 63.

26. Sarah Bradford, *Harriet Tubman: The Moses of Her People*, 2d
ed. (1886; rpt. Secaucus, N.J.: Citadel Press, 1961), pp. 18–20.

27. Veney, *Aunt Betty's Story*, pp. 26–27.

28. Wilson, *Our Nig*, p. 105; Lee, *Religious Experience and Journal of
Mrs. Jarena Lee*, pp. 55–56; Foote, *A Brand Plucked from the Fire*, pp.
24–27.

29. This is not to say that the oral accounts do not provide valuable
insights into the realities of slave experiences and the remaking of
those experiences both in book-length narratives of the nineteenth
and twentieth centuries and in the valuable collection of oral history
compiled during the years 1936–1938 by the Works Projects Admin-
istration. See: Federal Writers' Project, *Slave Narratives;* Rawick, ed.,
The American Slave; and Blassingame, ed., *Slave Testimony.*

30. See, for example, Gutman, *The Black Family*; and Blassingame, *The Slave Community*.

31. Starling, "The Slave Narrative," p. 294.

32. Sidonie Smith, *Where I'm Bound: Patterns of Slavery and Freedom
in Black American Autobiography* (Westport, Conn.: Greenwood,
1974), p. 10.

33. Foster, *Witnessing Slavery*, p. 64.

34. Stetson, "Studying Slavery," in Hull et al., eds., *But Some of Us
Were Brave*, p. 79.

35. Hooks, *"Ain't I a Woman?"* p. 26. In her dissertation by the
same primary title as Hooks's book, Deborah White takes the opposite view from Hooks, and essentially from Davis, Stetson, Genovese, Gutman, and Blassingame (as well as from Jacobs and Keckley). White's thesis is that slave women were "in some respects"
actually " 'freer' than many other antebellum women." They gained

this "freedom" and "positive self-concept," White argues, from acquiring "skill in the art of self-protection," from holding "the most important position in the slave family" which White says was "matrifocal," and by working outside the home. Surprisingly, White further states that "slave women did not leave us a collection of records which detailed their condition," and her bibliography lists only one published book-length autobiography by a black woman (Jacobs) in contrast to many by white women and black men. See Deborah White, " 'Ain't I a Woman?' Female Slaves in the Antebellum South" (Ph.D. diss., Univ. of Illinois at Chicago Circle, 1979), pp. 3–6.

36. See Starling, "The Slave Narrative"; Foster, *Witnessing Slavery;* Nichols, *Many Thousand Gone*; Butterfield, *Black Autobiography*.

37. Foster makes these distinctions in *Witnessing Slavery,* p. 150.

38. Nichols, *Many Thousand Gone*, p. ix.

39. As Butterfield puts it, "The self belongs to the people and the people find a voice in the self." *Black Autobiography,* p. 3.

40. Pascal, *Design and Truth in Autobiography*, pp. 3–5.

41. Starling, "The Slave Narrative," p. 311.

42. Nichols, *Many Thousand Gone*, p. xi.

43. Child, introduction, *Incidents in the Life of a Slave Girl,* p. xi.

44. See, for example, *Narrative of Jane Brown and Her Two Children* (Hartford: Published for G.W. Offley, 1860).

45. Dorothy Porter, introduction to Elizabeth Keckley, *Behind the Scenes; or, Thirty Years a Slave, and Four Years in the White House* (New York: Arno, 1968), pp. i–ii. *Behind the Scenes* was initially recalled from the market at the request of Robert Lincoln, who rebuked Keckley for publishing his mother's letters. In 1935 an Associated Press story credited Jane Swisshelm, a Washington reporter, with authorship of the book and denied the existence of Elizabeth Keckley. John Washington, author of *They Knew Lincoln,* soundly refuted this report. The extent of Child's and Redpath's assistance is not known. Subsequent references to *Behind the Scenes* will be designated parenthetically.

46. Annie Burton, *Memories of Childhood's Slavery Days* (Boston: Ross, 1909), p. 3. Subsequent references will be designated parenthetically.

47. Walter Teller, introduction, *Incidents in the Life of a Slave Girl,* p. x.

48. Kate Drumgoold, *A Slave Girl's Story* (Brooklyn, N.Y.: Published by the Author, 1898), p. 24. Subsequent references will be designated parenthetically.

49. Clinton, *The Plantation Mistress,* p. 189.

50. Davis, *Women, Race and Class,* p. 23; Hooks, *"Ain't I a Woman?"* p. 27.

51. Clinton, *The Plantation Mistress,* p. 188.

52. Foster, *Witnessing Slavery,* p. 150; Suzanne Lebsock, *The Free Women of Petersburg: Status and Culture in a Southern Town, 1784–1860* (New York: Norton, 1983), p. 90.

53. Lucy Delaney, *From the Darkness Cometh the Light; or, Struggles for Freedom* (St. Louis: J.T. Smith, 1891), pp. 18–19. Subsequent references will be designated parenthetically.

54. Amanda Smith, *An Autobiography: The Story of the Lord's Dealings with Mrs. Amanda Smith the Colored Evangelist* (Chicago: Meyer & Brother, 1893), pp. 19–22. Subsequent references will be designated parenthetically.

55. Letitia Burwell, *A Girl's Life in Virginia before the War* (New York: Frederick A. Stokes, 1895), pp. 7, 44. Subsequent references will be designated parenthetically.

56. Sudie Duncan Sides, "Women and Slaves: An Interpretation Based on the Writings of Southern Women" (Ph.D. diss., Univ. of North Carolina at Chapel Hill, 1969), pp. 250–59.

57. Sallie A. Putnam, *Richmond during the War: Four Years of Personal Observation* (New York: G.W. Carleton, 1867), p. 88. Subsequent references will be designated parenthetically.

58. Eliza McHatton Ripley, *From Flag to Flag* (New York: D. Appleton, 1889), p. 64.

59. Eliza McHatton Ripley, *Social Life in Old New Orleans* (1912; rpt. New York: Arno, 1975), pp. 210–12.

60. Susan Bradford Eppes, *Through Some Eventful Years* (1926; rpt. Gainesville: Univ. of Florida Press, 1968), p. 18. Subsequent references will be designated parenthetically.

61. Sides, "Women and Slaves," p. 8.

62. Ibid., pp. 8–15.

63. Ibid., p. 30.

64. See Judith McGuire, *Diary of a Southern Refugee during the War* (1867; rpt. New York: Arno, 1972); Phoebe Yates Pember, *A Southern Woman's Story: Life in Confederate Richmond* (1879; rpt. Jackson,

Tenn.: McCowat-Mercer, 1959); Mary Webster Loughborough, *My Cave Life in Vicksburg with Letters of Trial and Travel* (New York: D. Appleton, 1864).

65. L. Minor Blackford, *Mine Eyes Have Seen the Glory* (Cambridge: Harvard Univ. Press, 1954), p. 3.

66. Catherine Ann Devereux Edmondston, *Journal of a Secesh Lady*, ed. Beth G. Crabtree and James W. Patton (Raleigh: North Carolina Division of Archives and History, 1979), p. 21. Subsequent references will be designated parenthetically.

67. Sarah Morgan Dawson, *A Confederate Girl's Diary*, (1913; rpt. Bloomington: Indiana Univ. Press, 1960), p. 277. Subsequent references will be designated parenthetically.

68. Eliza Frances Andrews, *The War-Time Journal of a Georgia Girl 1864–1865* (New York: D. Appleton, 1908), pp. 307, 316. Subsequent references will be designated parenthetically.

69. John F. Marszalek, ed., introduction, *The Diary of Miss Emma Holmes 1861–1866* (Baton Rouge: Louisiana State Univ. Press, 1979), p. xxi. Subsequent references to the diary will be designated parenthetically.

70. Mary Blackford, "Notes Illustrative of the Wrongs of Slavery," in L. Minor Blackford, *Mine Eyes Have Seen the Glory*, p. 44. Subsequent references will be designated parenthetically.

71. Stone, *Brokenburn*, p. 8. Subsequent references will be designated parenthetically.

72. Mary A.H. Gay, *Life in Dixie during the War*, 3d ed. (Atlanta: Charles P. Byrd, 1897), pp. 10–11. Subsequent references will be designated parenthetically.

73. Ralph Ellison, "Twentieth-Century Fiction and the Black Mask of Humanity," *Confluence* 2, no. 4 (1953): 3.

74. Susan Dabney Smedes, preface, *Memorials of a Southern Planter*, ed. Fletcher Green (Jackson: Univ. Press of Mississippi, 1981), p. lviii. Subsequent references will be designated parenthetically.

75. Sides, "Women and Slaves," p. 8.

76. Ibid.

77. Clinton, *The Plantation Mistress*, p. 202.

78. Ibid.

79. Louise Wigfall Wright, *A Southern Girl in '61: The War-Time Memories of a Confederate Senator's Daughter* (New York: Doubleday, Page, 1905), p. 16. Subsequent references will be designated parenthetically.

80. Ellen Call Long, *Florida Breezes; or, Florida, New and Old* (1883; rpt. Gainesville: Univ. of Florida Press, 1962), p. 106.

81. Constance Cary Harrison, *Recollections Grave and Gay* (New York: Charles Scribner's Sons, 1911), p. 42. Subsequent references will be designated parenthetically.

82. Sara Agnes Rice Pryor, *My Day: Reminiscences of a Long Life* (New York: Macmillan, 1909), pp. 60, 161, 268.

83. Cornelia McDonald, *A Diary with Reminiscences of the War and Refugee Life in the Shenandoah Valley 1860–1865,* annotated and supplemented by Hunter McDonald (Nashville: Cullom & Ghertner, 1935), p. 39. Subsequent references will be designated parenthetically.

84. Woodward writes that Chesnut disliked the term *Dixie* and never used it in her writing. See his introduction to *Mary Chesnut's Civil War*, p. xxviii. Subsequent references will be designated parenthetically.

85. Ben Ames Williams' edition was edited with the guiding principle of readability. He even changed Chesnut's words and phrases to achieve that goal.

86. Pascal, *Design and Truth in Autobiography*, p. 5.

87. Jung, *Basic Writings*, p. 334.

88. Clinton, *The Plantation Mistress*, p. 231.

CHAPTER III

1. Faulkner, *Absalom, Absalom!* p. 140. Subsequent references will be designated parenthetically.

2. Walter Slatoff, *Quest for Failure: A Study of William Faulkner* (Ithaca: Cornell Univ. Press, 1960), pp. 251, 264.

3. Joseph Fant III and Robert Ashley, ed., *Faulkner at West Point* (New York: Random House, 1964), p. 50.

4. Cleanth Brooks, *William Faulkner: The Yoknapatawpha Country* (New Haven: Yale Univ. Press, 1963), p. 319. Ellen Douglas's belief that Judith is "just naturally mean"—"Faulkner's Women," in *"A Cosmos of My Own": Faulkner and Yoknapatawpha, 1980,* ed. Doreen Fowler and Ann Abadie (Jackson: Univ. Press of Mississippi, 1981), p. 155—and Albert Guérard's statement that Faulkner saw in Judith "a marble coldness"—*The Triumph of the Novel: Dickens, Dostoevsky, and Faulkner* (New York: Oxford Univ. Press, 1976), p. 308—do not

take into account her *actions*. Like Clytie, Judith is ultimately unknowable, but her actions—nursing the sick and the wounded, erecting monuments to the dead, coping with her old drunkard father and his pregnant fifteen-year-old Milly—bespeak a willingness to struggle and endure, and to help others do the same. One of the most moving incidents in the book is Judith's sewing of Milly's maternity clothes. Despite her feelings about her father's impregnating a girl young enough to be his grandchild, she helps Milly as best she can with what she has.

5. Faulkner's ambivalence about blacks and the contradictory nature of his public statements about racial issues are well known. For recent published analyses of his fictional treatments of racial issues and black characters, see, for example: Thadious Davis, *Faulkner's "Negro": Art and the Southern Context* (Baton Rouge: Louisiana State Univ. Press, 1983); John Hagopian, "Black Insight in *Absalom, Absalom!*" *Faulkner Studies* 1 (1980): 29–37; Lee Jenkins, *Faulkner and Black-White Relations: A Psychoanalytic Approach* (New York: Columbia Univ. Press, 1981); George Kent, "The Black Woman in Faulkner's Works, with the Exclusion of Dilsey," *Phylon* 35 (Dec. 1974): 430–31, and 36 (March 1975): 55–67; Charles Nilon, "Blacks in Motion," in *"A Cosmos of My Own,"* pp. 227–51, first appearing in *Faulkner and the Negro* (New York: Citadel Press, 1965); Régine Robin, *"Absalom, Absalom!"* in *Le Blanc et le noir chez Melville et Faulkner,* ed. Viola Sachs (Mouton, France: Moutin & Cie, 1974); Heinrich Straumann, "Black and White in Faulkner's Fiction," *English Studies* 60 (Aug. 1979): 462–70; Eric Sundquist, *Faulkner: The House Divided* (Baltimore: Johns Hopkins Univ. Press, 1983); Walter Taylor, "Faulkner: Nineteenth-Century Notions of Racial Mixture and the Twentieth-Century Imagination," *South Carolina Review* 10 (Nov. 1977): 57–68; Darwin Turner, "Faulkner and Slavery," in *The South and Faulkner's Yoknapatawpha: The Actual and the Apocryphal,* ed. Evans Harrington and Ann Abadie (Jackson: Univ. Press of Mississippi, 1977), pp. 62–85; Margaret Walker, "Faulkner and Race," in *The Maker and the Myth: Faulkner and Yoknapatawpha,* ed. Evans Harrington and Ann Abadie (Jackson: Univ. Press of Mississippi, 1978), pp. 105–21; Robert Penn Warren, "Faulkner: The South, the Negro, and Time," in *Faulkner: A Collection of Critical Essays,* ed. Robert Penn Warren (Englewood Cliffs, N.J.: Prentice Hall, 1966), pp. 251–71. An earlier study of importance is Irving Howe,

"Faulkner and the Negroes," in *William Faulkner*, 3d ed. (Chicago: Univ. of Chicago Press, 1975), pp. 116–37.

For assessments of Faulkner's statements about racial issues, see Charles Peavy, *Go Slow Now: Faulkner and the Race Question* (Eugene: Univ. of Oregon Press, 1971). Donald Petesch discusses the relationship of the fiction to the statements in "Faulkner on Negroes: The Conflict between the Public Man and the Private Art," *Southern Humanities Review* 10 (1976): 55–64.

6. Frederick Gwynn and Joseph Blotner, ed., *Faulkner at the University* (Charlottesville: Univ. Press of Virginia, 1959), p. 9. Interestingly, Faulkner made this remark in answer to a question about the alleged viciousness of a female character in *Sanctuary*, Narcissa Benbow.

7. David Miller, "Faulkner's Women," *Modern Fiction Studies* 13 (Spring 1967): 3.

8. See Sally Page, *Faulkner's Women: Characterization and Meaning* (Deland, Fla.: Everett/Edwards, 1972), pp. xxii–xxiv, and Brooks's introduction to it, pp. xi–xx.

9. In recent years polar approaches to Faulkner's women have become less acceptable in assessing the complexity of the female psyche. Female revisionists have begun to make themselves heard in rejecting criticism which labels Faulkner's women as all one thing or all another. Those who view Faulkner as a misogynist see his women characters as lustful, devouring, destructive creatures—in Richardson's words, "a constant source of evil" that thwarts the active, positive male principle and reflects "the moral vacuum in society itself" (pp. 66–67). Most perceptive of these assessments is that of Ellen Douglas, who believes that Faulkner projected onto his female characters his own deep sense of failed culture and a "failed and sinful humanity." She expresses disappointment in Faulkner for not probing the constraints that have hindered southern women.

The other side of the coin is the Brooksian school, which asserts that Faulkner admired women who did what they were supposed to do: reproduce and nurture. This type of woman has, according to Brooks, "natural force of tremendous power," but like the earth she is a non-thinking vegetable power, somnolent in fertile immobility. One immediately thinks of Eula Varner or Lena Grove. None of the women in *Absalom* except the octoroon seems to fit into this category.

Approaches to Faulkner's women that insist upon polarity include assessments that female characters are creative or destructive (Page, *Faulkner's Women*); earth mothers or ghosts (Miller, "Faulkner's Women," pp. 2–17); "decent and virginal" or "sullied and sexual" (Judith Wittenberg, *Faulkner: The Transfiguration of Biography* [Lincoln: Univ. of Nebraska Press, 1979], p. 25); sexual or asexual (Irving Malin, *William Faulkner: An Interpretation* [Stanford: Stanford Univ. Press, 1957], p. 31); "feminine" or "defeminized" (Kae Irene Parks, "Faulkner's Women: Archetype and Metaphor" [Ph.D. diss., Univ. of Pennsylvania, 1980], pp. 3–6); "mindless daughters of the peasants" who are like "beasts in heat," or "sexually insatiable daughters of the aristocracy" (Leslie Fiedler, *Love and Death in the American Novel* [New York: Criterion Books, 1960], p. 310); "the earth mother," "the foster mother," or "the grandmother" (Kenneth Richardson, *Force and Faith in the Novels of William Faulkner* [The Hague, Paris: Mouton, 1967], p. 91).

Two summaries of critical inquiries into the nature of Faulkner's women are: Judith Wittenberg, "William Faulkner: A Feminist Consideration," in *American Novelists Revisited: Essays in Feminist Criticism*, ed. Fritz Fleischmann (Boston: G.K. Hall, 1982), pp. 325–39; and Carol Ann Twigg, "The Social Role of Faulkner's Women: A Materialist Interpretation" (Ph.D. diss., State Univ. of New York at Buffalo, 1978). Wittenberg and Twigg divide criticism into those who consider Faulkner a misogynist and those who believe him to be a gynecolatrist. Both views, they point out, dehumanize the characters. In the first school (I have added a few here) are Maxwell Geismar, "William Faulkner: The Negro and the Female," in *Writers in Crisis* (Boston: Houghton Mifflin, 1942); Fiedler, Howe, Guérard, Richardson, and Douglas. Citations may be found in Richardson, *Force and Faith*, pp. 66–67; and Douglas, "Faulkner's Women," pp. 164–66. As mentioned, Brooks and Page believe that Faulkner admired women as long as they stayed in traditionnal female roles. See Page, *Faulkner's Women*, and Brooks's introduction to it.

Two perceptive studies of the female characters in *Absalom* are: Elisabeth Muhlenfeld, "Shadows with Substance and Ghosts Exhumed: The Women in *Absalom, Absalom!*" *Mississippi Quarterly* 25 (Summer 1972): 289–304; and Elizabeth Sabiston, "Women, Blacks, and Thomas Sutpen's Mythopoeic Drive in *Absalom, Absalom!*" *Modernist Studies in Literature and Culture* 1, no. 3 (1974–75): 15–26.

Sabiston's essay is particularly helpful in connecting race and gender to the nature of Sutpen's design.

10. Brooks, introduction to Page, *Faulkner's Women*, p. xv; Page, ibid., pp. xxiii–xxiv. In such a polar construct, Faulkner's women, Brooks and Page agree, are either creative or destructive, depending upon how they respond to the natural life forces embodied in the female principle.

Thomas Lorch carries this model to the extreme in its application to *Absalom* by arguing that the novel "presents male aspiration and will and the passive, enduring, absorbent Female in more closely balanced conflict than we find in Faulkner's other novels." Thomas Sutpen is Faulkner's most powerful male figure, Lorch finds, but is finally destroyed by his own vessels, society and women, who "absorb and stifle his creative spark." Yet, writes Lorch, Faulkner "recognizes female nature as necessary and good, because it provides the living material for the male to shape and elevate." Man is "spirit," woman is "matter"; man is "soul," woman is "body": throughout Faulkner's works it is men who possess the creative "spark" to impose their wills on the "female inertia." See Thomas Lorch, "Thomas Sutpen and the Female Principle," *Mississippi Quarterly* 20 (Winter 1967): 38–42.

Elizabeth Sabiston responds: "An assumption of the virtue and rightness of Sutpen's creative vision subtends such an interpretation" (Sabiston, "Women," p. 22).

11. Page, *Faulkner's Women*, p. 104.

12. Brooks maintains that Faulkner's women do not do these things and his men do. See introduction to Page, *Faulkner's Women*, pp. xiv–xv.

13. John Irwin, *Doubling and Incest Repetition and Revenge: A Speculative Reading of Faulkner* (Baltimore: John Hopkins Univ. Press, 1975), pp. 27–33. Otto Rank conceives of the *Doppelgänger* in male terms in *The Double* (Chapel Hill: Univ. of North Carolina Press, 1971); and Irwin applies Rank's theory to Faulkner's works.

14. In its lyrical, ecstatic tribute to female sexuality, this passage is similar to descriptions of sexual awakening by such women writers as Kate Chopin (*The Awakening*) and Zora Neal Hurston (*Their Eyes Were Watching God*).

15. Melvin Backman, "The Pilgrimage of William Faulkner" (Ph.D. diss., Columbia Univ., 1960), p. 136.

16. Kent, "The Black Woman," *Phylon* 36 (March 1975): 63. Clytie's "fierce and faithful silence" is so powerful, Kent feels, because "she has already contemplated the limit of a reality—which seems disguised from other characters."

17. Melvin Seiden, "Faulkner's Ambiguous Negro," *Massachusetts Review* 4 (Summer 1963): 685.

18. Ellison, "Twentieth-Century Fiction and the Black Mask of Humanity," *Confluence* 2, no. 4 (1953): 8. Clytie serves, Ilse Lind writes, "primarily to illuminate—not her own psychology—but the psychological, social and moral aspects of the Negro-white conflict"; see "The Design and Meaning of *Absalom, Absalom!*" *PMLA* 70 (Dec. 1955): 888–89. Like Dilsey and Sam Fathers, Clytie is also, as Ward Miner suggests, "the carrier and even the teacher of the values needed by the South"; see "The Southern White–Negro Problem through the Lens of Faulkner's Fiction," *Journal of Human Relations* 14 (Fourth Quarter 1966): 516.

19. Jenkins, *Faulkner and Black-White Relations*, p. 60.

20. Robin, *"Absalom, Absalom!"* pp. 82–84.

21. Sundquist, *Faulkner: The House Divided*, p. 116.

22. Cleanth Brooks, "Faulkner's Vision of Good and Evil," *Massachusetts Review* 3 (Summer 1962): 696–97.

23. Cleanth Brooks, *William Faulkner: Toward Yoknapatawpha and Beyond* (New Haven: Yale Univ. Press, 1978), p. 358.

24. Davis, *Faulkner's "Negro,"* p. 199.

25. Ibid., p. 189.

26. Gerald Langford, *Faulkner's Revision of "Absalom, Absalom!"* (Austin: Univ. of Texas Press, 1971), pp. 152–55.

27. Understandably, Robin overlooks the significance of the name which Clytie uses: "La seule mention de son nom réveille en elle son héritage moral et social et lui injecte l'identité de la rose fanée, du champ infertile, tout en électrisant ses sens" (p. 85).

28. Davis, *Faulkner's "Negro,"* p. 207.

29. Robin, *"Absalom, Absalom!,"* p. 87.

30. Sundquist, *Faulkner: The House Divided*, p. 116. Margaret Walker also believes that Faulkner devoted much of his work to coming to terms with his own racism. See "Faulkner and Race," in *The Maker and the Myth*, p. 108.

31. Robin, *"Absalom, Absalom!,"* p. 105.

32. No autobiographical writings by southern women are listed

as part of Faulkner's library. See Joseph Blotner, *William Faulkner's Library: A Catalogue* (Charlottesville: Univ. Press of Virginia, 1964).

CHAPTER IV

1. Several critical treatments of *Sapphira*, such as that found in Patricia Fleming's dissertation, "The Integrated Self: Sexuality and the Double in Willa Cather's Fiction," Boston Univ., 1974, tend toward an overstatement that seems to belie the tone of the novel.

2. See Dorothy Van Ghent's statement: "Willa Cather's art is an art of the sensuous and concrete, a high art of feeling; the spirit of the 'idea' is always deadly to it." *Willa Cather* (Minneapolis: Univ. of Minnesota Press, 1964), p. 29.

3. John H. Randall III, *The Landscape and the Looking Glass: Willa Cather's Search for Value* (Boston: Houghton Mifflin, 1960), pp. 363–66. Phyllis Robinson agrees with this assessment and believes Cather, writing the book in her late sixties and in ill health, "to have been too weary to do more than suggest the implications of her grand design"; see *Willa: The Life of Willa Cather* (New York: Doubleday, 1983), p. 13.

4. Cather, *Sapphira and the Slave Girl*, p. 50. Subsequent references will be designated parenthetically.

5. Josephine Jessup, *The Faith of Our Feminists: A Study in the Novels of Edith Wharton, Ellen Glasgow, Willa Cather* (New York: Richard R. Smith, 1950), p. 74.

6. David Stouck, *Willa Cather's Imagination* (Lincoln: Univ. of Nebraska Press, 1975), pp. 231–32.

7. William Curtin, "Willa Cather: Individualism and Style," *Colby Library Quarterly* 8 (June 1968): 43.

8. Elizabeth Sergeant, *Willa Cather: A Memoir* (Philadelphia: Lippincott, 1953), p. 270.

9. James Woodress, *Willa Cather: Her Life and Art* (New York: Pegasus, 1970), p. 263.

10. Edward Bloom and Lillian Bloom, *Willa Cather's Gift of Sympathy* (Carbondale: Southern Illinois Univ. Press, 1962), p. 3.

11. Paul Wermuth, "Willa Cather's Virginia Novel," *Virginia Cavalcade* 7 (Spring 1958): 4.

12. Edith Lewis, *Willa Cather Living* (New York: Knopf, 1953), p. 182.

13. Bloom and Bloom, *Willa Cather's Gift of Sympathy*, p. 16.

14. Lewis, *Willa Cather Living*, pp. 12–13.

15. Mildred Bennett, *The World of Willa Cather* (Lincoln: Univ. of Nebraska Press, 1961), p. 7.

16. Woodress, *Willa Cather: Her Life and Art*, p. 22.

17. Sandra Seltzer, "The Family in the Novels of Willa Cather" (Ph.D. diss., St. John's Univ., 1982), p. 199.

18. Cather, "The Demands of Art," in *The Kingdom of Art,* ed. Bernice Slote (Lincoln: Univ. of Nebraska Press, 1966), pp. 408–9.

19. E.K. Brown, *Willa Cather: A Critical Biography,* completed by Leon Edel (New York: Knopf, 1953), p. 295.

20. Randall, *The Landscape and the Looking Glass,* p. 18.

21. Brown, *Willa Cather: A Critical Biography,* p. 314.

22. Sergeant, *Willa Cather: A Memoir,* p. 270.

23. Fleming, "The Integrated Self," p. 220.

24. Merrill Skaggs, "Willa Cather's Experimental Southern Novel," *Mississippi Quarterly* 35, no. 1 (Winter 1981–82):3–14.

25. Blanche Gelfant, "The Forgotten Reaping Hook: Sex in *My Ántonia,"* *American Literature* 43 (March 1971): 61.

26. Randall, *The Landscape and the Looking Glass,* pp. 94–95.

27. Cather, "The Demands of Art," in *The Kingdom of Art,* p. 409.

28. Brown, *Willa Cather: A Critical Biography,* p. 316.

29. Cather, "The Novel Démeublé," in *Not Under Forty* (New York: Knopf, 1936), p. 50.

30. Lewis, *Willa Cather Living,* p. 185.

CHAPTER V

1. Margaret Walker, *How I Wrote "Jubilee"* (Chicago: Third World Press, 1972), p. 28.

2. Margaret Walker, "The Humanistic Tradition of Afro-American Literature," *American Libraries* 1 (Oct. 1970): 853.

3. Ibid., pp. 853–54.

4. Ibid., p. 851.

5. Charles Rowell, "Poetry, History and Humanism: An Interview with Margaret Walker," *Black World* 25 (Dec. 1975): 12.

6. Walker, *How I Wrote "Jubilee"*, p. 12.

7. Ibid., pp. 16, 23.

8. This may account for the dearth of critical treatment of *Jubilee*. Of the few critical articles, the most comprehensive is Phyllis Klotman, " 'Oh Freedom': Women and History in Margaret Walker's *Jubilee*," *Black American Literature Forum* 11 (Winter 1977): 139–45. See also Joyce Pettis, "The Black Historical Novel as Best Seller," *Kentucky Folklore Record* 25, no. 3 (1979): 51–59; and Bertie Powell, "The Black Experience in Margaret Walker's *Jubilee* and Lorraine Hansberry's *The Drinking Gourd*," *CLA Journal* 21 (Dec. 1977): 304–11. Considerations of *Jubilee* and Walker as a novelist are notably absent in such studies or collections as Robert Hemenway, ed., *The Black Novelist* (Columbus, Ohio: Charles E. Merrill, 1970); Edward Margolies, *Native Sons: A Critical Study of Twentieth Century Black American Authors* (Philadelphia: Lippincott, 1968); and Roger Rosenblatt, *Black Fiction* (Cambridge: Harvard Univ. Press, 1974). Arthur P. Davis allocates some attention to the novel in *From the Dark Tower: Afro-American Writers 1900 to 1960* (Washington, D.C.: Howard Univ. Press, 1974), pp. 181–84; as does Barbara Christian, *Black Women Novelists* (Westport, Conn.: Greenwood, 1980), pp. 71–73. One of the most illuminating analyses of Walker's novel may be found in Blyden Jackson's entry on Walker in *Lives of Mississippi Authors 1817–1967*, ed. James B. Lloyd (Jackson: Univ. Press of Mississippi, 1981), pp. 444–46.

9. Davis, *From the Dark Tower*, p. 184.

10. Walker, "The Humanistic Tradition," p. 854.

11. Nikki Giovanni and Margaret Walker, *A Poetic Equation: Conversations Between Nikki Giovanni and Margaret Walker* (Washington, D.C.: Howard Univ. Press, 1974), p. 16.

12. Klotman, " 'Oh Freedom!' " p. 140.

13. Walker, "The Humanistic Tradition," p. 854.

14. Ibid.

15. Baldwin, "Everybody's Protest Novel," *Partisan Review* 16 (June 1949): 578–85.

16. Robert Lively, *Fiction Fights the Civil War* (Chapel Hill: Univ. of North Carolina Press, 1957), p. 55.

17. Giovanni and Walker, *A Poetic Equation*, p. 91.

18. Margaret Walker, "On Being Female, Black, and Free," in *The Woman Writer on Her Work*, ed. Janet Sternburg (New York: Norton, 1980), p. 96.

19. Ibid., p. 106.

20. Walker, *Jubilee*, p. 26. Subsequent references will be designated parenthetically.

21. Walker, *How I Wrote "Jubilee"*, p. 25.

22. Walker, "The Humanistic Tradition," p. 851.

23. Baldwin, "Everybody's Protest Novel," p. 585.

24. Lively, *Fiction Fights the Civil War*, p. 75.

CONCLUSION

1. Stampp, *The Peculiar Institution*, p. 3.

BIBLIOGRAPHY

BIBLIOGRAPHICAL NOTE

So that scholars may have readily accessible information in specialized areas, I have arranged the bibliography into several subsections under the main headings of Primary and Secondary Sources. Those subsections and the page numbers on which they begin are as follows:

Primary Sources:

Secondary sources:

If in very rare instances a work is applicable to more than one subsection, I have listed it under the subsection corresponding to the chapter in which it is cited most extensively.

PRIMARY SOURCES

Slave Narratives Written by Black Women of the
Southern and Border States

Burton, Annie L. *Memories of Childhood's Slavery Days*.
Boston: Ross, 1909.
Delaney, Lucy. *From the Darkness Cometh the Light; or, Struggles
for Freedom*. St. Louis: J.T. Smith, 1891.
Drumgoold, Kate. *A Slave Girl's Story*. Brooklyn, N.Y.: Pub-
lished by the author, 1898.
Jacobs, Harriet [Linda Brent]. *Incidents in the Life of a Slave
Girl*. Ed. Lydia Maria Child. 1861; rpt. New York: Har-
court Brace Jovanovich, 1973.
Keckley, Elizabeth. *Behind the Scenes; or, Thirty Years a Slave,
and Four Years in the White House*. 1868; rpt. New York:
Arno, 1968.
Smith, Amanda. *An Autobiography: The Story of the Lord's
Dealings with Mrs. Amanda Smith the Colored Evangelist*. Chi-
cago: Meyer & Brother, 1893.
Taylor, Susie King. *Reminiscences of My Life in Camp with the
33rd United States Colored Troops, late 1st S.C. Volunteers*.
1902; rpt. Salem, N.Y.: Ayer, 1968.

Journals and Memoirs Written by White Women
of the Old South

Andrews, Eliza Francis. *The War-Time Journal of a Georgia Girl
1864–1865*. New York: D. Appleton, 1908.
Andrews, Marietta. *Scraps of Paper*. New York: Dutton, 1929.
Avary, Myrta Lockett. *A Virginia Girl in the Civil War,
1861–1865*. New York: D. Appleton, 1903.
Beers, Fannie A. *Memories: A Record of Personal Experience and
Adventure during Four Years of War*. Philadelphia: J.B. Lippin-
cott, 1889.

Blackford, Mary Berkley Minor. "Notes Illustrative of the Wrongs of Slavery." In L. Minor Blackford, *Mine Eyes Have Seen the Glory*. Cambridge: Harvard Univ. Press, 1954.

Branch, Mary Polk. *Memoirs of a Southern Woman within the Lines*. Chicago: Joseph G. Branch, 1912.

Burwell, Letitia M. *A Girl's Life in Virginia before the War*. New York: Frederick A. Stokes, 1895.

Chesnut, Mary. *Mary Chesnut's Civil War*. Ed. C. Vann Woodward. New Haven: Yale Univ. Press, 1981.

Clay-Compton, Virginia. *A Belle of the Fifties*. Put into narrative form by Ada Sterling. New York: Doubleday, Page, 1905.

Clayton, Virginia. *White and Black under the Old Regime*. Milwaukee: Young Churchman, 1899.

Dawson, Sarah Morgan. *A Confederate Girl's Diary*. 1913; rpt. Bloomington: Indiana Univ. Press, 1960.

De Saussure, Nancy Bostick. *Old Plantation Days*. New York: Duffield, 1919.

Devereux, Margaret. *Plantation Sketches*. Cambridge: Riverside, 1906.

Edmondston, Catherine Ann Devereux. *Journal of a Secesh Lady*. Ed. Beth G. Crabtree and James W. Patton. Raleigh: North Carolina Division of Archives and History, 1979.

Eppes, Susan. *Through Some Eventful Years*. 1926; rpt. Gainesville: Univ. of Florida Press, 1968.

Felton, Rebecca Latimer. *Country Life in Georgia in the Days of My Youth*. Atlanta: Index Printing, 1919.

Gay, Mary A. H. *Life in Dixie during the War*. 3d ed. Atlanta: Charles P. Byrd, 1897.

Hague, Parthenia Antoinette. *A Blockaded Family: Life in Southern Alabama during the Civil War*. Boston: Houghton Mifflin, 1888.

Harrison, Constance Cary. *Recollections Grave and Gay*. New York: Scribner's, 1911.

Holmes, Emma. *The Diary of Miss Emma Holmes 1861–1866*. Ed. John F Marszalek. Baton Rouge: Louisiana State Univ. Press, 1979.

Kearney, Belle. *A Slaveholder's Daughter*. 1900; rpt. Westport, Conn.: Greenwood, 1981.

LeGrand, Julia. *The Journal of Julia LeGrand: New Orleans, 1862–1863*. Richmond: Everett Waddey, 1911.

Logan, Kate Virginia Cox. *My Confederate Girlhood*. Richmond: Garret and Massie, 1932.

Logan, Mary. *Reminiscences of the Civil War and Reconstruction*. Ed. George Worthington Adams. Carbondale: Southern Illinois Univ. Press, 1970.

Long, Ellen Call. *Florida Breezes; or, Florida, New and Old*. 1883; rpt. Gainesville: Univ. of Florida Press, 1962.

Loughborough, Mary Webster. *My Cave Life in Vicksburg with Letters of Trial and Travel*. New York: D. Appleton, 1864.

Lunt, Dolly Sumner. *A Woman's War Time Journal*. New York: Century, 1918.

McDonald, Cornelia. *A Diary with Reminiscences of the War and Refugee Life in the Shenandoah Valley 1860–1865*. Annotated and supplemented by Hunter McDonald. Nashville: Cullom & Ghertner, 1935.

McGuire, Judith W. *Diary of a Southern Refugee during the War*. 1867; rpt. New York: Arno, 1972.

Merrick, Caroline. *Old Times in Dixie Land: A Southern Matron's Memories*. New York: Grafton, 1901.

Pember, Phoebe Yates. *A Southern Woman's Story: Life in Confederate Richmond*. 1879; rpt. Jackson, Tenn.: McCowat-Mercer, 1959.

Pringle, Elizabeth Allson. *Chronicles of Chicora Wood*. New York: Scribner's, 1922.

———[Patience Pennington]. *A Woman Rice Planter*. Ed. Cornelius Cathey. Cambridge: Belknap Press, Harvard Univ. Press, 1961.

Pryor, Sara Agnes Rice. *My Day: Reminiscences of a Long Life*. New York: Macmillan, 1909.

———. *Reminiscences of Peace and War*. New York: Macmillan, 1905.

Putnam, Sallie A. *Richmond during the War: Four Years of Personal Observation*. New York: G. W. Carleton, 1867.

Ripley, Eliza McHatton. *From Flag to Flag*. New York: D. Appleton, 1889.

———. *Social Life in Old New Orleans*. 1912; rpt. New York: Arno, 1975.

Saxon, Elizabeth L. *A Southern Woman's Wartime Reminiscences.* Memphis: Pilcher Printing Co., 1905.

Smedes, Susan Dabney. *Memorials of a Southern Planter.* Ed. Fletcher M. Green. Jackson: Univ. Press of Mississippi, 1981.

Stone, Kate. *Brokenburn: The Journal of Kate Stone 1861–1868.* Ed. John Q. Anderson. Baton Rouge: Louisiana State Univ. Press, 1972.

Watters, Fanny C. *Plantation Memories of the Cape Fear River Country.* Asheville: Stephens, 1942.

Wright, Louise Wigfall. *A Southern Girl in '61: The War-Time Memories of a Confederate Senator's Daughter.* New York: Doubleday, Page, 1905.

Fiction

Brown, William Wells. *Clotel.* 1853; rpt. New York: Arno, 1969.

Cather, Willa. *Sapphira and the Slave Girl.* New York: Knopf, 1940.

Eastman, Mary H. *Aunt Phillis's Cabin; or, Southern Life as It Is.* 1852; rpt. New York: Negro Universities Press, 1960.

Faulkner, William. *Absalom, Absalom!* New York: Modern Library, 1966.

Gaines, Ernest. *The Autobiography of Miss Jane Pittman.* New York: Dial, 1971.

Hopkins, Pauline. *Contending Forces: A Romance Illustrative of Negro Life North and South.* 1900; rpt. New York: AMS. 1971.

Mitchell, Margaret. *Gone with the Wind.* New York: Macmillan, 1936.

Porter, Katherine Anne. *The Old Order.* New York: Harcourt, Brace & World, 1958.

Stowe, Harriet Beecher. *Uncle Tom's Cabin; or, Life among the Lowly.* Ed. Kenneth S. Lynn. Cambridge: Belknap Press, Harvard Univ. Press, 1962.

Walker, Margaret. *Jubilee.* Boston: Houghton Mifflin, 1966.

Yerby, Frank. *Captain Rebel.* London: Heinemann, 1957.

————. *A Darkness at Ingraham's Crest: A Tale of the Slaveholding South*. New York: Dial, 1979.

Young, Stark. *So Red the Rose*. New York: Scribner's, 1934.

Other Primary Sources

Aunt Sally; or, The Cross the Way of Freedom. 1858; rpt. Miami: Mnemosyne, 1969.

Blassingame, John W., ed. *Slave Testimony: Two Centuries of Letters, Speeches, Interviews, and Autobiographies*. Baton Rouge: Louisiana State Univ. Press, 1977.

Bontemps, Arna, ed. *Great Slave Narratives*. Boston: Beacon Press, 1969.

Botkin, B.A. *Lay My Burden Down: A Folk History of Slavery*. Chicago: Univ. of Chicago Press, 1945.

Bourne, George. *Slavery Illustrated in Its Effects upon Woman and Domestic Society*. 1837; rpt. Freeport, N.Y.: Books for Libraries Press, 1972.

Bradford, Sarah. *Harriet Tubman: The Moses of Her People*. 2d ed. 1886; rpt. Secaucus, N.J.: Citadel Press, 1961.

Carleton, George Washington. *The Suppressed Book about Slavery*. 1864; rpt. New York: Arno, 1968.

Child, Lydia Maria. *An Appeal in Favor of That Class of Americans Called Africans*. New York: John S. Taylor, 1836.

Elaw, Zilpha. *Memoirs of the Life, Religious Experience, Ministerial Travels and Labours, of Mrs. Zilpha Elaw*. London: Published by the Author and sold by T. Dudley, 1846.

Eppes, Susan Bradford. *The Negro of the Old South: A Bit of Period History*. Macon, Ga.; J.W. Burke, 1941.

Federal Writers' Project. *Slave Narratives: A Folk History of Slavery in the United States from Interviews with Former Slaves*. Vols. 1–17. Washington, D.C.: WPA, 1941.

Foote, Julia A.J. *A Brand Plucked from the Fire: An Autobiographical Sketch of Mrs. Julia Foote*. Printed for the Author by W.F. Schneider, 1879.

Fuller, Margaret. *Woman in the Nineteenth Century and Kindred Papers*. 1855; rpt. Boston: Roberts, 1874.

Griffith, Mattie. *Autobiography of a Female Slave*. New York: Redfield, 1857.

Grimké, Angelina Emily. *Appeal to the Christian Women of the South*. 1836; rpt. New York: Arno, 1969.

Kemble, Frances Anne. *Journal of a Residence on a Georgian Plantation in 1838–1839*. London: Longman, Green, Longman, Roberts & Green, 1863.

Killion, Ronald, and Charles Waller, eds. *Slavery Time: When I Was Chillun Down on Marster's Plantation*. Savannah, Ga.: Beehive, 1973.

Larison, C. W. *Silvia Dubois (Now 116 Yers Old.) A Biografy of The Slav who Whipt her Mistres and Gand her Fredom*. 1883; rpt. New York: Negro Universities Press, 1969.

Lee, Jarena. *Religious Experience and Journal of Jarena Lee*. 2d ed. Philadelphia: Published for the Author, 1849.

Lerner, Gerda, ed. *Black Women in White America*. New York: Vintage, 1972.

Loewenberg, Bert James, and Ruth Bogin, eds. *Black Women in Nineteenth-Century American Life: Their Thoughts, Their Words, Their Feelings*. University Park: Pennsylvania State Univ. Press, 1976.

Martineau, Harriet. *Retrospect of Western Travel*. 1838; rpt. New York: Johnson, 1968.

Memoirs of Elleanor Eldridge. 2d ed. Providence: B. T. Albro, 1842.

Miller, Randall M. *"Dear Master": Letters of a Slave Family*. Ithaca: Cornell Univ. Press, 1978.

Offley, G. W. "Sketch of Jane Brown and Her Two Children." In *A Narrative of the Life and Labors of Rev. G. W. Offley*. Hartford: G. W. Offley, 1860.

Pierson, Emily Catharine. *Jamie Parker, the Fugitive*. Hartford: Brockett, Fuller, 1851.

Pollard, Edward A. *Black Diamonds Gathered in the Darkey Homes of the South*. 1859; rpt. New York: Negro Universities Press, 1968.

Prince, Nance. *A Narrative of the Life and Travels of Mrs. Nancy Prince Written by Herself*. 2d ed. Boston: Published by the Author, 1853.

Rawick, George P., ed. *The American Slave: A Composite Autobiography*. Vols. 1–19. Westport, Conn.: Greenwood, 1972.

Simpson, John Hawkins. *Horrors of the Virginian Slave Trade and of the Slave-Rearing Plantations: The True Story of Dinah, an Escaped Virginian Slave.* London: A.W. Bennett, 1863.

Smith, Lillian. *Killers of the Dream.* 2d ed. New York: Anchor Books, 1963.

Truth, Sojourner. *Narrative of Sojourner Truth with a History of Her Labors and Correspondence Drawn from Her "Book of Life."* Ed. Frances Titus. 1878; rpt. New York: Arno, 1968.

Veney, Bethany. *Aunt Betty's Story: The Narrative of Bethany Veney, a Slave Woman.* 2d ed. Dorchester, Mass.: A.P. Bicknell, 1890.

Wilson, Harriet. *Our Nig; or, Sketches from the Life of a Free Black.* Ed. Henry Louis Gates, Jr. 1859; rpt. New York: Vintage Books, 1983.

Yetman, Norman R. *Voices from Slavery:* New York: Holt, Rinehart & Winston, 1970.

SECONDARY SOURCES

Uncle Tom's Cabin, Aunt Phillis's Cabin, and Related Fiction

Adams, F.C. *A Review from Home in Answer to the Reviewers and Repudiators of "Uncle Tom's Cabin" by Harriet Beecher Stowe.* 1853; rpt. Freeport, N.Y.: Books for Libraries Press, 1970.

Adams, John. *Harriet Beecher Stowe.* New York: Twayne, 1963.

———. "Heroines in *Uncle Tom's Cabin.*" *American Literature* 49 (May 1977): 116–79; rpt. Ammons, ed., *Critical Essays on Harriet Beecher Stowe.*

Ammons, Elizabeth, ed. *Critical Essays on Harriet Beecher Stowe.* Boston: G.K. Hall, 1980.

Ashton, Jean. *Harriet Beecher Stowe: A Reference Guide.* Boston: G.K. Hall, 1977.

Baldwin, James. "Everybody's Protest Novel." *Partisan Review* 16 (June 1949): 578–85; rpt. Ammons, ed., *Critical Essays on Harriet Beecher Stowe.*

Banning, Margaret. "*Uncle Tom's Cabin.*" *Georgia Review* 9 (1955): 461–65.

Baym, Nina. *Woman's Fiction: A Guide to Novels by and about Women in America, 1820–1870*. Ithaca: Cornell Univ. Press, 1978.

Brown, Dorothy. "Thesis and Theme in *Uncle Tom's Cabin.*" *English Journal* 58 (Dec. 1969): 1330–34, 1372.

Brown, Herbert Ross. *The Sentimental Novel in America, 1789–1860*. Durham: Duke Univ. Press, 1940.

Brown, Sterling. *The Negro in American Fiction*. 1937; rpt. Port Washington, N.Y.: Kennikat, 1968.

Browne, Margaret. "Southern Reactions to *Uncle Tom's Cabin.*" M.A. Thesis, Duke Univ., 1941.

Canaday, Nicholas, Jr. "The Antislavery Novel Prior to 1852 and Hildreth's *The Slave* (1836)." *CLA Journal* 57 (Dec. 1973): 175–91.

Cassara, Ernest. "The Rehabilitation of Uncle Tom: Significant Themes in Mrs. Stowe's Antislavery Novel." *CLA Journal* 57 (Dec. 1973): 230–40.

Crozier, Alice C. *The Novels of Harriet Beecher Stowe*. New York: Oxford Univ. Press, 1969.

Crumpacker, Laurie. "Four Novels of Harriet Beecher Stowe: A Study in Nineteenth-Century Androgyny." In *American Novelists Revisited: Essays in Feminist Criticism,* ed. Fritz Fleischmann. Boston: G.K. Hall, 1982.

Davis, Richard Beale. "Mrs. Stowe's Characters-In-Situations and a Southern Literary Tradition." In *Essays on American Literature in Honor of Jay B. Hubbell,* ed. Clarence Gohdes. Durham: Duke Univ. Press, 1967.

Duvall, Severn. "*Uncle Tom's Cabin*: The Sinister Side of the Patriarchy." *New England Quarterly* 36 (1963): 3–22; rpt. Gross and Hardy, eds., *Images of the Negro in America*.

————. "W.G. Simms' Review of Mrs. Stowe." *American Literature* 30 (March 1958): 107–17.

Earnest, Ernest. *The American Eve in Fact and Fiction, 1775–1914*. Urbana: Univ. of Illinois Press, 1974.

Fletcher, Marie. "The Southern Heroine in the Fiction of Representative Southern Women Writers, 1850–1960." Ph.D. diss., Louisiana State Univ., 1963.

Flexner, Eleanor. *Century of Struggle: The Woman's Rights Movement in the United States*. Cambridge: Belknap Press, Harvard Univ. Press, 1959.

Foster, Charles H. *The Rungless Ladder: Harriet Beecher Stowe and New England Puritanism*. Durham: Duke Univ. Press, 1954.

Fredrickson, George M. *The Black Image in the White Mind: The Debate on Afro-American Character and Destiny, 1817–1914*. New York: Harper & Row, 1971.

Furnas, J.C. *Goodbye to Uncle Tom*. London: Secker and Warburg, 1956.

Graham, Thomas. "Harriet Beecher Stowe and the Question of Race." *New England Quarterly* 46 (Dec. 1973): 614–22.

Gross, Seymour, and John Edward Hardy, eds. *Images of the Negro in American Literature*. Chicago: Univ. of Chacago Press, 1966.

Hayne, Barrie. "Yankee in the Patriarchy: T.B. Thorpe's Reply to *Uncle Tom's Cabin*." *American Quarterly* 20 (1968): 180–95.

Hildreth, Margaret. *Harriet Beecher Stowe: A Bibliography*. Hamden, Conn.: Archon Books, 1976.

Johnston, Johanna. *Runaway to Heaven: The Story of Harriet Beecher Stowe*. Garden City, N.Y.: Doubleday, 1963.

"A Key to *Uncle Tom's Cabin*." *Southern Quarterly Review* 7 (July 1853): 214–54.

Kirkham, E. Bruce. *The Building of "Uncle Tom's Cabin."* Knoxville: Univ. of Tennessee Press, 1977.

Kramer, Maurice I. "The Fable of Endurance: A Study of the American Novel between Hawthorne and Howells." Ph.D. diss., Harvard Univ., 1958.

Lebedun, Jean. "Harriet Beecher Stowe's Interest in Sojourner Truth." *American Literature* 46 (Nov. 1974): 359–63.

Lee, Wallace, et al. "Is *Uncle Tom's Cabin* Anti-Negro?" *Negro Digest* 4 (Jan. 1946): 68–72.

Levin, David. "American Fiction as Historical Evidence: Reflections on *Uncle Tom's Cabin*." *Negro American Literature Forum* 5 (Winter 1972): 132–36, 156.

Levy, David. "Racial Stereotypes in Antislavery Fiction." *Phylon* 31 (Fall 1970): 265–79.

Maurice, Arthur. "Famous Novels and Their Contemporary Critics: *Uncle Tom's Cabin*." *Bookman* 17 (Mar. 1903): 23–30.

McDowell, Tremaine. "The Negro in the Southern Novel Prior to 1850." *Journal of English and Germanic Philology* 25

(1926): 455–73; rpt. Gross and Hardy, eds. *Images of the Negro in America.*

Melder, Keith. *Beginnings of Sisterhood: The American Woman's Rights Movement, 1800–1850.* New York: Schocken Books, 1977.

Miller, Randall M. "Stowe's Black Sources in *Uncle Tom's Cabin.*" *American Notes & Queries* 14 (1975): 38–39.

Nelson, John H. *The Negro Character in American Literature.* College Park, Md.: McGrath, 1926.

Nichols, Charles. "The Origins of *Uncle Tom's Cabin.*" *Phylon* 19 (1958): 328–32.

Papashvily, Helen. *All the Happy Endings: A Study of the Domestic Novel in America, the Women Who Wrote It, the Women Who Read It, in the Nineteenth Century.* New York: Harper & Bros., 1956.

Parker, Gail, ed. *The Oven Birds: American Women on Womanhood 1820–1920.* Garden City, N.Y.: Anchor Books, 1972.

Sigourney, Lydia. *Poems.* Philadelphia: Key & Biddle, 1834.

Sklar, Kathryn Kish. *Catharine Beecher: A Study in American Domesticity.* New York: Norton, 1973.

Starke, Catherine. *Black Portraiture in American Fiction: Stock Characters, Archetypes, and Individuals.* New York: Basic Books, 1971.

Stowe, Charles Edward. *The Life of Harriet Beecher Stowe.* Boston: Houghton Mifflin, 1889.

Stowe, Harriet Beecher. *The Annotated "Uncle Tom's Cabin."* Ed. Philip Van Doren Stern. New York: Paul S. Eriksson, 1964.

———. *The Key to "Uncle Tom's Cabin."* Boston: John P. Jewett, 1853.

Strout, Cushing. "*Uncle Tom's Cabin* and the Portent of Millenium." *Yale Review* 57 (Spring 1968): 375–85.

Tandy, Jeannette Reid. "Pro-Slavery Propaganda in American Fiction of the Fifties." *South Atlantic Quarterly* 21 (Jan. 1922): 41–50 (Apr. 1922): 170–78.

Turner, Lorenzo Dow. *Anti-Slavery Sentiment in American Literature Prior to 1865.* 1929; rpt. Port Washington, N.Y.: Kennikat, 1966.

Veach, Carston. "Harriet Beecher Stowe: A Critical Study of Her Early Novels." Ph.D. diss., Univ. of Indiana, 1967.

Wagenknecht, Edward. *Cavalcade of the American Novel*. New York: Henry Holt, 1952.

_____. *Harriet Beecher Stowe: The Known and the Unknown*. New York: Oxford Univ. Press, 1965.

Ward, Hazel Mae. "The Black Woman as Character: Images in the American Novel 1852–1953." Ph.D Diss., Univ. of Texas at Austin, 1977.

Ward, John W. *Red, White & Blue: Men, Books and Ideas in American Culture*. New York: Oxford Univ. Press, 1969.

Weld, Theodore. *American Slavery as It Is: Testimony of a Thousand Witnesses*. 1839; rpt. New York: Arno, 1968.

Welter, Barbara. "The Cult of True Womanhood: 1820–1860." *American Quarterly* 18 (Summer 1966): 151–74.

Wilson, Edmund. *Patriotic Gore: Studies in the Literature of the American Civil War*. New York: Oxford Univ. Press, 1962.

Wilson, Forrest. *Crusader in Crinoline: The Life of Harriet Beecher Stowe*. Philadelphia: J.B. Lippincott, 1941.

Yellin, Jean F. *The Intricate Knot: Black Figures in American Literature, 1776–1863*. New York: New York Univ. Press, 1972.

Zanger, Jules. "The 'Tragic Octoroon' in Pre-Civil War Fiction." *American Quarterly* 18 (1966): 63–70.

Black and White Women of the Old South:
Their Lives and Writings

Andrews, Matthew Page. *The Women of the South in War Times*. Baltimore: Norman, Remington, 1923.

Bartlett, Irving, and C. Glenn Cambor. "The History and Psychodynamics of Southern Womanhood." *Women's Studies* 2 (1974): 9–24.

Bayliss, John F. *Black Slave Narratives*. New York: Macmillan, 1970.

Bell, Roseann, Bettye Parker, and Beverly Gwy-Sheftall. *Sturdy Black Bridges: Visions of Black Women in Literature*. Garden City, N.Y.: Anchor Books, 1979.

Blassingame, John W. *The Slave Community: Plantation Life in the Antebellum South*. New York: Oxford Univ. Press, 1972.

Boles, John B. *Black Southerners, 1619–1869*. Lexington: Univ. Press of Kentucky, 1983.

Bracey, John, August Meier, and Elliott Rudwick, eds. *Black Matriarchy: Myth or Reality?* Belmont, Calif.: Wadsworth, 1971.

Burger, Mary Williams. "Black Autobiography: A Literature of Celebration." Ph.D. Diss., Washington Univ. 1973.

Burnham, Dorothy. "Black Women as Producers and Reproducers for Profit." In *Woman's Nature: Rationalizations for Inequality,* ed. Marian Lowe and Ruth Hubbard. New York: Pergamon, 1983.

Butterfield, Stephen. *Black Autobiography in America*. Amherst: Univ. of Massachusetts Press, 1974.

Cash, W.J. *The Mind of the South*. New York: Knopf, 1941.

Clinton, Catherine. *The Plantation Mistress: Woman's World in the Old South*. New York: Pantheon, 1982.

Cott, Nancy. "Passionlessness: An Interpretation of Victorian Sexual Ideology, 1790–1850." *Signs* 4 (Winter 1978): 219–36.

Davis, Angela. *Women, Race & Class*. New York: Random House, 1981.

Davis, Lenwood G. *The Black Woman in American Society: A Selected Annotated Bibliography*. Boston: G.K. Hall, 1975.

DuBois, W.E.B. *The Souls of Black Folk*. Chicago: A.C. McClurg, 1903.

Fishburn, Katherine. *Women in Popular Culture: A Reference Guide*. Westport, Conn.: Greenwood, 1982.

Foster, Frances. *Witnessing Slavery: The Development of Ante-Bellum Slave Narratives*. Westport, Conn.: Greenwood, 1979.

Gaines, Francis P. *The Southern Plantation: A Study in the Development and the Accuracy of a Tradition*. New York: Columbia Univ. Press, 1925.

Genovese, Eugene D. *In Red and Black: Marxian Explorations in Southern and Afro-American History*. 1968; rpt. Knoxville: Univ. of Tennessee Press, 1984.

Grier, William, and Price Cobbs. *Black Rage*. New York: Basic Books, 1968.

Gutman, Herbert G. *The Black Family in Slavery and Freedom, 1750–1925*. New York: Pantheon Books, 1976.

Hagood, Margaret. *Mothers of the South*. Chapel Hill: Univ. of North Carolina Press, 1939.

Harris, Trudier. *From Mammies to Militants: Domestics in Black American Literature*. Philadelphia: Temple Univ. Press, 1982.

Hartman, Joan, and Ellen Messer-Davidson, eds. *Women in Print-I*. New York: MLA, 1982.

Hawks, Joanne V. and Sheila L. Skemp, eds. *Sex, Race, and the Role of Women in the South*. Jackson: Univ. Press of Mississippi, 1983.

Hernton, Calvin C. *Sex and Racism*. London: Andre Deutsch, 1969.

Hill, Herbert, ed. *Anger and Beyond: The Negro Writer in the United States*. New York: Harper & Row, 1966.

Hoffman, Nancy. "White Women, Black Women: Inventing an Adequate Pedagogy." *Women's Studies Newsletter* 5 (Spring 1977): 21–24.

Hooks, Bell. *"Ain't I A Woman?": Black Women and Feminism*. Boston: South End Press, 1981.

Hull, Gloria, Patricia Bell Scott, and Barbara Smith, eds. *But Some of Us Are Brave*. Old Westbury, N.Y.: Feminist Press, 1982.

Inge, M. Thomas, Maurice Duke, and Jackson R. Bryer. *Black American Writers*. 2 vols. New York: St. Martin's, 1978.

Jackson, Margaret Young. "An Investigation of Biographies and Autobiographies of American Slaves Published between 1840 and 1860." Ph.D. Diss., Cornell Univ., 1954.

Jelinek, Estelle, ed. *Women's Autobiography*. Bloomington: Indiana Univ. Press, 1980.

Johnson, Paul D. "'Goodbye to Sambo': The Contribution of Black Slave Narratives to the Abolition Movement." *Negro American Literature Forum* 6 (Fall 1972): 79–84.

Johnston, James H. *Miscegenation in the Ante-Bellum South*. 1939; rpt. New York: AMS Press, 1972.

Jones, Anne Goodwyn. *Tomorrow Is Another Day: The Woman Writer in the South, 1859–1936*. Baton Rouge: Louisiana State Univ. Press, 1981.

Jones, Katharine. *Heroines of Dixie*. Indianapolis: Bobbs-Merrill, 1955.

Jordan, Winthrop. *White over Black*. Chapel Hill: Univ. of North Carolina Press, 1968.

Jung, C.G. *Analytical Psychology: Its Theory and Practice*. New York: Pantheon Books, 1968.

———. *The Basic Writings of C.G. Jung*. Ed. Violet DeLaszlo. New York: Modern Library, 1959.

Klotman, Phyllis, et al. *The Black Family and the Black Woman: A Bibliography*. Bloomington: Indiana Univ. Library, 1972.

Lebsock, Suzanne. *The Free Women of Petersburg: Status and Culture in a Southern Town, 1784–1860*. New York: Norton, 1984.

Lester, Julius, ed. *To Be a Slave*. New York: Dial, 1968.

Loggins, Vernon. *The Negro Author: His Development in America to 1900*. 1931; rpt. Port Washington, N.Y.: Kennikat, 1964.

Lumpkin, Katharine. *The Emancipation of Angelina Grimké*. Chapel Hill: Univ. of North Carolina Press, 1974.

Lyons, Anne Ward. "Myth and Agony: The Southern Woman as Belle." Ph.D. Diss., Bowling Green State Univ., 1974.

Muhenfeld, Elisabeth. *Mary Boykin Chesnut: A Biography*. Baton Rouge: Louisiana State Univ. Press, 1981.

Myrdal, Gunnar. *An American Dilemma: The Negro Problem and Modern Democracy*. New York: Harper & Bros., 1944.

Nichols, Charles. *Many Thousand Gone: The Ex-Slaves' Account of Their Bondage and Freedom*. 2d ed. Bloomington: Indiana Univ. Press, 1969.

———. "Who Read the Slave Narratives?" *Phylon* 20 (Summer 1959): 149-62.

Olney, James, ed. *Autobiography: Essays Theoretical and Critical*. Princeton: Princeton Univ. Press, 1980.

———. *Metaphors of Self: The Meaning of Autobiography*. Princeton: Princeton Univ. Press, 1972.

Owens, Harry P., ed. *Perspectives and Irony in American Slavery*. Jackson: Univ. Press of Mississippi, 1976.

Pascal, Roy. *Design and Truth in Autobiography*. Cambridge: Harvard Univ. Press, 1960.

Payne, Ladell. *Black Novelists and the Southern Literary Tradition*. Athens: Univ. of Georgia Press, 1981.

Rank, Otto. *The Double*. Chapel Hill: Univ. of North Carolina Press, 1971.

Rich, Adrienne. *On Lies, Secrets, and Silence: Selected Prose 1966–1978*. New York: Norton, 1979.

Sayre, Robert. *The Examined Self.* Princeton: Princeton Univ. Press, 1968.

Scott, Anne Firor. *The Southern Lady: From Pedestal to Politics 1830–1930.* Chicago: Univ. of Chicago Press, 1970.

Showalter, Elaine. "Feminist Criticism in the Wilderness." *Critical Inquiry* 7 (Winter 1981): 179–205.

Sides, Sudie Duncan. "Women and Slaves: An Interpretation Based on the Writings of Southern Women." Ph.D. Diss., Univ. of North Carolina at Chapel Hill, 1969.

Sillen, Samuel. *Women against Slavery.* New York: Masses & Mainstream, 1955.

Simkins, Francis, and James Patton. *The Women of the Confederacy.* Richmond: Garrett and Massie, 1936.

Smith, Barbara. "Toward a Black Feminist Criticism." *Conditions* 1 (1977): 25–32.

Smith, Sidonie. *Where I'm Bound: Patterns of Slavery and Freedom in Black American Autobiography.* Westport, Conn.: Greenwood, 1974.

Sprull, Julia Cherry. *Women's Life and Work in the Southern Colonies.* Chapel Hill: Univ. of North Carolina Press, 1938.

Stampp, Kenneth M. *The Era of Reconstruction 1865–1877.* New York: Knopf, 1965.

_____. *The Peculiar Institution: Slavery in the Ante-Bellum South.* New York: Knopf, 1956.

Starling, Marion. "The Slave Narrative: Its Place in American Literary History." Ph.D. Diss., New York Univ., 1946.

Stetson, Erlene. "Studying Slavery: Some Literary and Pedagogical Considerations on the Black Female Slave." In Hull et al., eds., *But Some of Us Are Brave.*

Stone, Albert E., ed. *The American Autobiography: A Collection of Critical Essays.* Englewood Cliffs, N.J.: Prentice-Hall, 1981.

Taylor, William R. *Cavalier And Yankee: The Old South and American National Character.* New York: George Braziller, 1961.

Terborg-Penn, Rosalyn, and Sharon Harley, eds. *The Afro-American Woman: Struggles and Images.* Port Washington, N.Y.: National Univ. Publications, 1978.

Walker, Alice. "One Child of One's Own: A Meaningful

Digression within the Work(s)—An Excerpt." In Hull et al., eds., *But Some of Us Are Brave.*

Washington, Mary Helen. "New Lives and New Letters: Black Women Writers at the End of the Seventies." *College English* 43 (Jan. 1981): 1–11.

White, Deborah G. "'Ain't I A Woman?' Female Slaves in the Antebellum South." Ph.D. Diss., Univ. of Illinois at Chicago Circle, 1979.

Wiley, Bell Irvin. *Confederate Women*. Westport, Conn.: Greenwood, 1975.

Woodward, C. Vann. *The Burden of Southern History*. Baton Rouge: Louisiana State Univ. Press, 1960.

Wyatt-Brown, Bertram. *Southern Honor: Ethics and Behavior in the Old South*. New York: Oxford Univ. Press, 1982.

William Faulkner—*Absalom, Absalom!*

Adams, Richard P. *Faulkner: Myth and Motion:* Princeton: Princeton Univ. Press, 1968.

Atkins, Anselm. "The Matched Halves of *Absalom, Absalom!*" *Modern Fiction Studies* 15, no. 2 (Summer 1969): 264–65.

Backman, Melvin. "The Pilgrimage of William Faulkner." Ph.D. Diss., Columbia Univ., 1960.

Bassett, John. *William Faulkner: An Annotated Checklist of Criticism*. New York: David Lewis, 1972.

Beauchamp, Fay Elizabeth. "William Faulkner's Use of the Tragic Mulatto Myth." Ph.D. Diss., Univ. of Pennsylvania, 1974.

Beck, Warren. "Faulkner and the South." *Antioch Review* 1 (Spring 1941): 82–94.

Berzon, Judith. *Neither White Nor Black: The Mulatto Character in American Fiction*. New York: New York Univ. Press, 1978.

Blotner, Joseph. *Faulkner: A Biography*. 2 vols. New York: Random House, 1974.

_____, ed. *Selected Letters of William Faulkner.* New York: Random House, 1977.

_____. *William Faulkner's Library: A Catalogue*. Charlottesville: Univ. Press of Virginia, 1964.

Brooks, Cleanth. "Faulkner's Vision of Good and Evil." *Massachusetts Review* 3 (Summer 1962): 692–712.

———. *William Faulkner: The Yoknapatawpha Country.* New Haven: Yale Univ. Press, 1963.

———. *William Faulkner: Toward Yoknapatawpha and Beyond.* New Haven: Yale Univ. Press, 1978.

Brylowski, Walter. *Faulkner's Olympian Laugh.* Detroit: Wayne State Univ. Press, 1968.

Burns, Mattie Ann. "The Development of Women Characters in the Works of William Faulkner." Ph.D. Diss., Auburn Univ., 1974.

Cooley, John R. *Savages and Naturals: Black Portraits by White Writers in Modern American Literature.* Newark: Univ. of Delaware Press, 1982.

Davis, Thadious M. *Faulkner's "Negro": Art and the Southern Context.* Baton Rouge: Louisiana State Univ. Press, 1983.

———. "The Yoking of 'Abstract Contradictions': Clytie's Meaning in *Absalom Absalom!*" *Studies in American Fiction* 7 (1979): 209–19.

Doster, William Clark. "William Faulkner and the Negro." Ph.D. Diss., Univ. of Florida, 1955.

Douglas, Ellen. "Faulkner's Women." In *"A Cosmos of My Own": Faulkner and Yoknapatawpha, 1980,* ed. Doreen Fowler and Ann Abadie. Jackson: Univ. Press of Mississippi, 1981.

Edmonds, Irene. "Faulkner and the Black Shadow." In *Southern Renascence,* ed. Louis D. Rubin, Jr., and Robert D. Jacobs. Baltimore: Johns Hopkins Univ. Press, 1953.

Ellison, Ralph. "Twentieth-Century Fiction and the Black Mask of Humanity." *Confluence* 2, no. 4 (1953): 3–21.

Faulkner at West Point. Ed. Joseph Fant III and Robert Ashley. New York: Random House, 1964.

Faulkner in the University. Ed. Frederick Gwynn and Joseph Blotner. Charlottesville: Univ. Press of Virginia, 1959.

Fiedler, Leslie. *Love and Death in the American Novel.* New York: Criterion Books, 1960.

Foran, Donald James. "William Faulkner's *Absalom, Absalom!* An Exercise in Affirmation." Ph.D. Diss., Univ. of Southern California, 1973.

Fowler, Doreen, and Ann Abadie, eds. *"A Cosmos of My Own:" Faulkner and Yoknapatawpha, 1980.* Jackson: Univ. Press of Mississippi, 1981.

Geismar, Maxwell. "William Faulkner: The Negro and the Female." In *Writers in Crisis: The American Novel between Two Wars.* Boston: Houghton Mifflin, 1942.

Gissendanner, John. "The 'Nether Channel': A Study of Faulkner's Black Characters." Ph.D. Diss., Univ. of California, San Diego, 1982.

Glicksberg, Charles. "William Faulkner and the Negro Problem." *Phylon* 10, no. 2 (1949): 153–60.

Goldman, Arnold, ed. *Twentieth Century Interpretations of "Absalom, Absalom!"* Englewood Cliffs, N.J.: Prentice-Hall, 1971.

Goodenberger, Mary Ellen. "William Faulkner's Compleat Woman." Ph.D. Diss., Univ. of Nebraska, Lincoln, 1976.

Gresham, Jewell Handy. "The Fatal Illusion: Self, Sex, Race, and Religion in William Faulkner's World." Ph.D. Diss., Columbia Univ., 1970.

Guérard, Albert. *The Triumph of the Novel: Dickens, Dostoevsky, and Faulkner.* New York: Oxford Univ. Press, 1976.

Hagopian, John V. "Black Insight in *Absalom, Absalom!*" *Faulkner Studies* 1 (1980): 29–37.

Harrington, Evans, and Ann Abadie, eds. *The Maker and the Myth: Faulkner and Yoknapatawpha.* Jackson: Univ. Press of Mississippi, 1978.

———. *The South and Faulkner's Yoknapatawpha: The Actual and the Apocryphal.* Jackson: Univ. Press of Mississippi, 1977.

Hoffman, Frederick J. *William Faulkner.* 2d ed. New York: Twayne, 1966.

———, and Olga Vickery, eds. *William Faulkner: Three Decades of Criticism.* New York: Harcourt, Brace & World, 1960.

Howe, Irving. *William Faulkner.* 3d ed. Chicago: Univ. of Chicago Press, 1975.

Hunt, John W. *William Faulkner: Art in Theological Tension.* Syracuse: Syracuse Univ. Press, 1965.

Irwin, John. *Doubling and Incest Repetition and Revenge: A Speculative Reading of Faulkner.* Baltimore: Johns Hopkins Univ. Press, 1975.

Jackson, Naomi. "Faulkner's Woman: 'Demon-Nun and Angel-Witch.'" *Ball State Univ. Forum* 8 (Winter 1967): 12–20.

Jehlen, Myra. *Class and Character in Faulkner's South.* New York: Columbia Univ. Press, 1976.

Jenkins, Lee. *Faulkner and Black-White Relations: A Psychoanalytic Approach.* New York: Columbia Univ. Press, 1981.

———. "Faulkner, the Mythic Mind, and the Blacks." *Literature and Psychology* 27, no. 2 (1977): 74–91.

Johnson, Beulah. "The Treatment of Negro Woman as a Major Character in American Novels, 1900–1950." Ph.D. Diss., New York Univ., 1955.

Kent, George. "The Black Woman in Faulkner's Works, with the Exclusion of Dilsey." *Phylon* 35 (Dec. 1974): 430–41; 36 (March 1975): 55–67.

Kerr, Elizabeth. "William Faulkner and the Southern Concept of Woman." *Mississippi Quarterly* 15 (Winter 1962): 1–16.

———. *Yoknapatawpha: Faulkner's "Little Postage Stamp of Native Soil."* New York: Fordham Univ. Press, 1969.

Langford, Gerald. *Faulkner's Revision of "Absalom, Absalom!"* Austin: Univ. of Texas Press, 1971.

Lensing, George. "The Metaphor of Family in *Absalom, Absalom!*" *Southern Review* 11 (Winter 1975): 99–117.

Levin, David *"Absalom, Absalom!* The Problem of Re-creating History." In *In Defense of Historical Literature.* New York: Hill and Wang, 1967.

Levins, Lynn Gartrell. *Faulkner's Heroic Design: The Yoknapatawpha Novels.* Athens: Univ. of Georgia Press, 1976.

Lind, Ilse Dusoir. "The Design and Meaning of *Absalom, Absalom!*" *PMLA* 70 (Dec. 1955): 887–912.

———. "Faulkner's Women." In Harrington and Abadie, eds., *The Maker and the Myth.*

Lorch, Thomas M. "Thomas Sutpen and the Female Principle." *Mississippi Quarterly* 20 (Winter 1967): 38–42.

Malin, Irving. *William Faulkner: An Interpretation.* Stanford, Calif.: Stanford Univ. Press, 1957.

McHaney, Thomas. *William Faulkner: A Reference Guide.* Boston: G.K. Hall, 1976.

Miller, David M. "Faulkner's Women." *Modern Fiction Studies* 13 (Spring 1967): 3–17.

Millgate, Michael. *The Achievement of William Faulkner.* New York: Random House, 1966.

Milloy, Sandra Delores. "The Development of the Black Character in the Fiction of William Faulkner." Ph.D. Diss., Univ. of Michigan, 1979.

Miner, Ward L. "The Southern White–Negro Problem through the Lens of Faulkner's Fiction." *Journal of Human Relations* 14 (Fourth Quarter 1966): 507–17.

———. *The World of William Faulkner.* New York: Cooper Square, 1963.

Muhlenfeld, Elisabeth. "Shadows with Substance and Ghosts Exhumed: The Women in *Absalom, Absalom!*" *Mississippi Quarterly* 25 (Summer 1972): 289–304.

Nilon, Charles. "Blacks in Motion." In Fowler and Abadie, eds., *"A Cosmos of My Own."*

———. *Faulkner and the Negro.* New York: The Citadel Press, 1965.

O'Brien, Matthew. "A Note on Faulkner's Civil War Women." *Notes on Mississippi Writers* 1 (Fall 1968): 56–63.

Page, Sally R. *Faulkner's Women: Characterization and Meaning.* Deland, Fla.: Everett/Edwards, 1972.

Parks, Kae Irene. "Faulkner's Women: Archetype and Metaphor." Ph.D. Diss., Univ. of Pennsylvania, 1980.

Peavy, Charles D. *Go Slow Now: Faulkner and the Race Question.* Eugene: Univ. of Oregon Press, 1971.

Peters, Erskine Alvin. "The Yoknapatawpha World and Black Being." Ph.D. Diss., Princeton Univ. 1976.

Petesch, Donald. "Faulkner on Negroes: The Conflict between the Public Man and the Private Art." *Southern Humanities Review* 10 (1976): 55–64.

Pikoulis, John. *The Art of William Faulkner.* Totowa, N.J.: Barnes & Noble, 1982.

Pilkington, John. *The Heart of Yoknapatawpha.* Jackson: Univ. Press of Mississippi, 1981.

Richardson, Kenneth E. *Force and Faith in the Novels of William Faulkner.* The Hague: Mouton, 1967.

Robin, Régine. *"Absalom, Absalom!"* In *Le Blanc et le noir chez Melville et Faulkner,* ed. Viola Sachs. Mouton: Mouton & Cie, 1974.

Rollyson, Carl E. "The Re-creation of the Past in *Absalom, Absalom!*" *Mississippi Quarterly* 29 (Summer 1976): 361–74.

Sabiston, Elizabeth. "Women, Blacks, and Thomas Sutpen's Mythopoeic Drive in *Absalom, Absalom!*" *Modernist Studies in Literature and Culture* 1, no. 3 (1974–75): 15–26.

Schmidtberger, Loren. "*Absalom, Absalom!* What Clytie Knew." *Mississippi Quarterly* 35 (Summer 1982): 255–63.

Seiden, Melvin. "Faulkner's Ambiguous Negro." *Massachusetts Review* 4 (Summer 1963): 675–90.

Siegel, Roslyn. "Faulkner's Black Characters: A Comparative Study." Ph.D. Diss., City Univ. of New York, 1974.

Slatoff, Walter J. *Quest for Failure: A Study of William Faulkner.* Ithaca: Cornell Univ. Press, 1960.

Steinberg, Aaron. "Faulkner and the Negro." Ph.D. Diss. New York Univ. 1963.

Strandberg, Victor. *A Faulkner Overview: Six Perspectives.* Port Washington, N.Y.: Kennikat Press, 1981.

Straumann, Heinrich. "Black and White in Faulkner's Fiction." *English Studies* 60 (Aug. 1979): 462–70.

Sundquist, Eric J. *Faulkner: The House Divided.* Baltimore: Johns Hopkins Univ. Press, 1983.

Swiggart, Peter. *The Art of Faulkner's Novels.* Austin: Univ. of Texas Press, 1962.

Taylor, Walter. "Faulkner: Nineteenth-Century Notions of Racial Mixture and the Twentieth-Century Imagination." *South Carolina Review* 10 (Nov. 1977): 57–68.

———. *Faulkner's Search for a South.* Urbana: Univ. of Illinois Press, 1983.

Tischler, Nancy M. *Black Masks: Negro Characters in Modern Southern Fiction.* University Park: Pennsylvania State Univ. Press, 1969.

Turner, Darwin. "Faulkner and Slavery." In Harrington and Abadie, eds. *The South and Faulkner's Yoknapatawpha.*

Twigg, Carol Ann. "The Social Role of Faulkner's Women: A Materialist Interpretation." Ph.D. Diss. State Univ. of New York at Buffalo, 1978.

Vickery, Olga. *The Novels of William Faulkner.* Baton Rouge: Louisiana State Univ. Press, 1959.

Volpe, Edmond. *A Reader's Guide to William Faulkner.* New York: Farrar, Straus and Giroux, 1964.

Wagner, Linda. "Faulkner and (Southern) Women." In Harrington and Abadie, eds., *The South and Faulkner's Yoknapatawpha.*

Walker, Margaret. "Faulkner and Race." In Harrington and Abadie, eds., *The Maker and the Myth.*

Warren, Robert Penn, ed. *Faulkner: A Collection of Critical Essays.* Englewood Cliffs, N.J.: Prentice-Hall, 1966.

Waters, Maureen Anne. "The Role of Women in Faulkner's Yoknapatawpha." Ph.D. Diss. Columbia Univ. 1975.

Weatherby, H.L. "Sutpen's Garden." *Georgia Review* 21 (Fall 1967): 354–69.

Williams, David. *Faulkner's Women: The Myth and the Muse.* Montreal: McGill-Queen's Univ. Press, 1977.

Wittenberg, Judith. *Faulkner: The Transfiguration of Biography.* Lincoln: Univ. of Nebraska Press, 1979.

_____. "William Faulkner: A Feminist Consideration." In *American Novelists Revisited: Essays in Feminist Criticism,* ed. Fritz Fleischmann. Boston: G.K. Hall, 1982.

York, Samuel. "Faulkner's Woman: The Peril of Mankind." *Arizona Quarterly* 17 (Summer 1961): 119–29.

Zink, Karl E. "Faulkner's Garden: Women and the Immemorial Earth." *Modern Fiction Studies* 2 (Autumn 1956): 139–49.

Willa Cather—*Sapphira and the Slave Girl*

Arnold Marilyn. "Cather's Last Stand." *Research Studies* 43 (1975): 245–52.

Barba, Sharon. "Willa Cather: A Feminist Study." Ph.D. Diss., Univ. of New Mexico, 1973.

Bennett, Mildred. "Willa Cather's Bodies for Ghosts." *Western American Literature* 17 (May 1982): 39–51.

_____. *The World of Willa Cather.* Bison ed. Lincoln: Univ. of Nebraska Press, 1961.

Bloom, Edward A., and Lillian D. Bloom. *Willa Cather's Gift of Sympathy.* Carbondale: Southern Illinois Univ. Press, 1962.

Bonham, Barbara. *Willa Cather.* New York: Chilton, 1970.

Brown, E.K. *Willa Cather: A Critical Biography.* Completed by Leon Edel. New York: Knopf, 1953.

Cather, Willa. *The Kingdom of Art*. Ed. Bernice Slote. Lincoln: Univ. of Nebraska Press, 1966.

————. *Not Under Forty*. New York: Knopf, 1936.

————. *Willa Cather on Writing*. New York: Knopf, 1949.

————. *The World and the Parish*. 2 vols. Ed. William Curtin. Lincoln: Univ. of Nebraska, 1970.

Cooper, Clara Bomanji. "Willa Cather: The Nature of Evil and Its Purgation." Ph.D. Diss., Florida State Univ., 1969.

Curtin, William. "Willa Cather: Individualism and Style." *Colby Library Quarterly* 8 (June 1968): 37–70.

Daiches, David. *Willa Cather: A Critical Introduction*. Ithaca: Cornell Univ. Press, 1951.

Ditsky, John. "Nature and Character in the Novels of Willa Cather." *Colby Library Quarterly* 10 (Sept. 1974): 391–412.

Edel, Leon. "Willa Cather." *Literary Lectures Presented at the Library of Congress*. Washington D.C.: Library of Congress, 1973.

Fleming, Patricia Jean. "The Integrated Self: Sexuality and the Double in Willa Cather's Fiction." Ph.D. Diss., Boston Univ., 1974.

Gale, Robert L. "Willa Cather and the Past." *Studi Americani* 4 (1958): 209–22.

Geismar, Maxwell. "Willa Cather: Lady in the Wilderness." In *Willa Cather and Her Critics*, ed. James Schroeter. Ithaca: Cornell Univ. Press, 1967.

Gelfant, Blanche. "The Forgotten Reaping Hook: Sex in *My Ántonia*." *American Literature* 43 (March 1971): 60–82.

Gerber, Philip. *Willa Cather*. Boston: Twayne, 1975.

Giannone, Richard. "Willa Cather and the Unfinished Drama of Deliverance." *Prairie Schooner* 52 (Spring 1978): 25–46.

Handy, Yvonne. *L'Oeuvre de Willa Cather*. Rennes: Imprimeries Oberthur, 1940.

Jessup, Josephine. *The Faith of Our Feminists: A Study in the Novels of Edith Wharton, Ellen Glasgow, Willa Cather*. New York: Richard R. Smith, 1950.

Jobes, Lavon. "Willa Cather's Last Novel." *University Review* 34 (1967): 77–80.

Kazin, Alfred. *On Native Grounds*. New York: Harcourt, Brace & World, 1942.

Lewis, Edith. *Willa Cather Living*. New York: Knopf, 1953.

Lilienfeld, Jane. "Reentering Paradise: Cather, Colette, Woolf and Their Mothers." In *The Lost Tradition: Mothers and Daughters in Literature*, ed. Cathy Davidson and E.M. Broner. New York: Ungar, 1980.

McFarland, Dorothy Tuck. *Willa Cather*. New York: Frederick Ungar, 1972.

Miracles of Perception: The Art of Willa Cather. Foreword by Joan Crane. Charlottesville: Alderman Library, Univ. of Virginia, 1980.

Murphy, John J. "Willa Cather: The Widening Gyre." In *Five Essays on Willa Cather*, ed. John J. Murphy. North Andover, Mass.: Merrimack College, 1974.

O'Brien, Sharon. "Mothers, Daughters, and the 'Art Necessity' Willa Cather and the Creative Process." In *American Novelists Revisited: Essays in Feminist Criticism*, ed. Fritz Fleischman. Boston: G.K. Hall, 1982.

Pers, Mona. *Willa Cather's Children*. Stockholm: Almquist & Wiksell, 1975.

Randall, John H., III. *The Landscape and the Looking Glass: Willa Cather's Search for Value*. Boston: Houghton Mifflin, 1960.

Rapin, René. *Willa Cather*. New York: Robert M. McBride, 1930.

Robinson, Phyllis C. *Willa: The Life of Willa Cather*. New York: Doubleday, 1983.

Rosowski, Susan. "The Pattern of Willa Cather's Novels." *Western American Literature* 15 (Winter 1981): 243–63.

_____. "Willa Cather's Women." *Studies in American Fiction* 9 (Autumn 1981): 261–75.

Schroeter, James, ed. *Willa Cather and Her Critics*. Ithaca, N.Y.: Cornell Univ. Press, 1967.

Seltzer, Sandra. "The Family in the Novels of Willa Cather." Ph.D. Diss., St. John's Univ., 1982.

Sergeant, Elizabeth. *Willa Cather: A Memoir*. Philadelphia: Lippincott, 1953.

Skaggs, Merrill Maguire. "Willa Cather's Experimental Southern Novel." *Mississippi Quarterly* 35, no. 1 (Winter 1981–82): 3–14.

Slote, Bernice. "Willa Cather." In *Sixteen Modern American Writers*, ed. Jackson Bryer. New York: Norton, 1973.

——. "Willa Cather and the Sense of History." In *Women, Women Writers, and the West*, ed. L.L. Lee and Merrill Lewis. Troy, N.Y.: Whitston, 1980.

——, and Virginia Faulkner, ed. *The Art of Willa Cather*. Lincoln: Univ. of Nebraska Press, 1974.

Stouck, David. *Willa Cather's Imagination*. Lincoln: Univ. of Nebraska Press, 1975.

——. "Willa Cather's Last Four Books." *Novel* 7 (Fall 1973): 41–53.

Throne, Marilyn. "The Two Selves: Duality in Willa Cather's Protagonists and Themes." Ph.D. Diss., Ohio State Univ. and Miami Univ., 1969.

Van Ghent, Dorothy. *Willa Cather*. Minneapolis: Univ. of Minnesota Press, 1964.

Wermuth, Paul C. "Willa Cather's Virginia Novel." *Virginia Cavalcade* 7 (Spring 1958): 4–7.

Woodress, James. *Willa Cather: Her Life and Art*. New York: Pegasus, 1970.

——. "Willa Cather and History." *Arizona Quarterly* 34 (Autumn 1978): 239–54.

Margaret Walker—*Jubilee*

Bennett, Stephen, and William Nichols. "Violence in Afro-American Fiction: An Hypothesis." *Modern Fiction Studies* 17, no. 2 (1971): 221–28.

Blackburn, Regina. "In Search of the Black Female Self: African-American Women's Autobiographies and Ethnicity." In *Women's Autobiography*, ed. Estelle Jelinek. Bloomington: Indiana Univ. Press, 1980.

Bone, Robert. *The Negro Novel in America*. New Haven: Yale Univ. Press, 1965.

Christian, Barbara. *Black Women Novelists*. Westport, Conn.: Greenwood, 1980.

Davis, Arthur P. *From the Dark Tower: Afro-American Writers 1900 to 1960*. Washington D.C.: Howard Univ. Press, 1974.

Ford, Nick Aaron. *The Contemporary Negro Novel: A Study in*

Race Relations. 1936; rpt. College Park, Md.: McGrath, 1968.

Gayle, Addison. *The Black Aesthetic.* Garden City, N.Y.: Doubleday, 1971.

———, ed. *Black Expression: Essays by and about Black Americans in the Creative Arts.* New York: Weybright and Talley, 1969.

———. *The Way of the New World.* Garden City, N.Y.: Anchor/ Doubleday, 1975.

Gibson, Donald. "Afro-American: Contemporary Fiction: Contemporary Research and Criticism, 1965–1978." *American Quarterly* 30, no. 3 (1978): 395–409.

———. "Individualism and Community in Black History and Fiction." *Black American Literature Forum* 11 (Winter 1977): 123–29.

Giddings, Paula. "'A Shoulder Hunched Against A Sharp Concern': Some Themes in the Poetry of Margaret Walker." *Black World* 21, no. 2 (Dec. 1971): 20–25.

Giovanni, Nikki, and Margaret Walker. *A Poetic Equation: Conversations between Nikki Giovanni and Margaret Walker.* Washington, D.C.: Howard Univ. Press, 1974.

Gloster, Hugh. *Negro Voices in American Literature.* 1948; rpt. New York: Russell & Russell, 1965.

Hemenway, Robert, ed. *The Black Novelist.* Columbus, Ohio: Charles E. Merrill, 1970.

Henderson, Harry B. *Versions of the Past: The Historical Imagination in American Fiction.* New York: Oxford Univ. Press, 1974.

Hill, Herbert, ed. *Anger and Beyond: The Negro Writer in the United States.* New York: Harper & Row, 1966.

Jackson, Blyden. "Margaret Walker." In *Lives of Mississippi Authors 1817–1967,* ed. James B. Lloyd. Jackson: Univ. Press of Mississippi, 1981.

Klotman, Phillis. *Another Man Gone.* Port Washington, N.Y.: Kennikat, 1977.

———. "'Oh Freedom'—Women and History in Margaret Walker's *Jubilee."* *Black American Literature Forum* 11 (Winter 1977): 139–45.

Leisy, Ernest E. *The American Historical Novel.* Norman: Univ. of Oklahoma Press, 1950.

Littlejohn, David. *Black on White: A Critical Survey of Writing by American Negroes.* New York: Grossman, 1966.

Lively, Robert A. *Fiction Fights the Civil War.* Chapel Hill: Univ. of North Carolina Press, 1957.

Margolies, Edward. *Native Sons: A Critical Study of Twentieth Century Black American Authors.* Philadelphia: Lippincott, 1968.

Martin, Odette. "Curriculum and Response: A Study of the Images of the Black Woman in Black Fiction." Ph.D. Diss., Univ. of Chicago, 1980.

Miller, R. Baxter. "The 'Etched Flame' of Margaret Walker: Biblical and Literary Re-Creation in Southern History." *Tennessee Studies in Literature* 26 (1981): 157–72.

O'Brien, John, ed. *Interviews with Black Writers.* New York: Liveright, 1973.

Pettis, Joyce. "The Black Historical Novel as Best Seller." *Kentucky Folklore Record* 25, no. 3 (1979): 51–59.

Popkin, Michael. *Modern Black Writers: A Library of Literary Criticism.* New York: Ungar, 1978.

Powell, Bertie. "The Black Experience in Margaret Walker's *Jubilee* and Lorraine Hansberry's *The Drinking Gourd.*" *CLA Journal* 21 (Dec. 1977): 304–11.

Pullin, Faith. "Landscapes of Reality: The Fiction of Contemporary Afro-American Woman." In *Black Fiction: New Studies in the Afro-American Novel Since 1945,* ed. A. Robert Lee. Plymouth, Eng.: Vision, 1980.

Rosenblatt, Roger. *Black Fiction.* Cambridge: Harvard Univ. Press, 1974.

Rowell, Charles. "Poetry, History and Humanism: An Interview with Margaret Walker." *Black World* 25 (Dec. 1975): 4–17.

Schultz, Elizabeth. "The Insistence upon Community in the Contemporary Afro-Amerian Novel." *College English* 41 (1979): 170–84.

Torrence, Juanita. "A Literary Equation: A Comparison of Representative Works of Margaret Walker and Nikki Giovanni." Ph.D. Diss., Texas Woman's Univ., 1979.

Varga-Coley, Barbara Jean. "The Novels of Black American Women." Ph.D. Diss., State Univ. of New York at Stony Brook, 1981.

Walker, Margaret. *How I Wrote "Jubilee."* Chicago; Third World Press, 1972.

———. "The Humanistic Tradition of Afro-American Literature." *American Libraries* 1 (Oct. 1970): 849–54.

———. "On Being Female, Black and Free." In *The Woman Writes on Her Work,* ed. Janet Sternburg. New York: Norton: 1980.

———. "Religion, Poetry and History: Foundations for a New Educational System." In *The Black Seventies,* ed. Floyd Barbour. Boston: Porter Sargent, 1970.

INDEX

229

Index